Introduction

You are reading one of the best accessories that you could purchase for your car. Whether you are a keen do-it-yourself enthusiast or just eager to cut the cost of motoring, this repair manual will guide you through all the stages of various mechanical repairs - from a simple oil and filter change; fitting new brake shoes; checking the hydraulics; tuning the engine; dealing with the electrics; or even removing and overhauling the engine - all the knowledge and information you are likely to need are here!

The easy-reference contents page and individual chapter headings will guide you to the appropriate section dealing with the part of your car to be checked or repaired. The clear line-drawings will show you what fits where giving you all the confidence to tackle a job for the first time. Each chapter contains easy-to-follow repair sequences with a comprehensive Technical Data section included at the end. If problems occur that can't be solved easily then turn to the special Trouble-shooting chart to be found at the end of the appropriate section.

A large proportion of this manual is devoted to routine and preventative maintenance with a complete chapter covering the servicing of your car - indeed, a money saver in itself!

Tools are of obvious importance to the do-it-yourself car owner and, like this repair manual, can be termed as a good investment. Purchase wisely, not over-spending but just purchasing good quality tools needed for a certain job and building up your equipment as you go. Tools required for general servicing aren't that many but it will be the wise do-it-yourself motorist who invests in a good jack and axle stands or wheel ramps. Some of the operations shown in this book require special tools and, in many cases, they can be hired locally. If specialist knowledge is required then we state as much. If it is possible to manage without special aids then we tell you how. Sometimes a little ingenuity can save a lot of time and money.

Now you can be the expert and the cost of this repair manual will be easily recovered the first time that you use it.

Jack Hay

Editor

Quick Reference Data

GENERAL DIMENSIONS

	Saloon	Estate Car
Overall length	167.7 in (4260 mm)	171.7 in (4361 mm)
Overall width	67.1 in (1704 mm)	67.1 in (1704 mm)
Overall height (unladen)	53.9 in (1369 mm)	54.2 in (1377 mm)
Turning circle, between kerbs	32.6 ft (10.0 m)	32.6 ft (10.0 m)

Nominal kerb weight:

	Saloon	Estate Car
1300:		
2-door	2183 lb (990 kg)	—
4-door	2227 lb (1010 kg)	2370 lb (1075 kg)
1600:		
2-door	2216 lb (1005 kg)	—
4-door	2260 lb (1025 kg)	2403 lb (1090 kg)
2000:		
2-door	2304 lb (1045 kg)	—
4-door	2348 lb (1065 kg)	2480 lb (1125 kg)

NOTE: Where automatic transmission is fitted, add 22 lb (10 kg) to the above figures for 1600 models, and 11 lb (5 kg) for 1300 models

	Saloon	Estate Car
Maximum roof rack loading	165 lb (75 kg)	220 lb (100 kg)

CAPACITIES

Engine oil sump (inc filter):
- 1300/1600 OHV .... 6.16 pints (3.5 litres)
- 1600/2000 OHC .... 6.6 pints (3.75 litres)

Manual gearbox:
- 1300/1600 models .... 1.76 pints (1.0 litre)
- 2000 models .... 2.91 pints (1.66 litres)

Automatic transmission (inc converter and oil cooler) .... 11.25 pints (6.4 litres)

Rear axle:
- 1300/1600 models .... 1.76 pints (1.0 litre)
- 2000 models .... 1.94 pints (1.1 litres)

Fuel tank .... 11.9 gallons (54 litres)

TYRE PRESSURES

Cold; in lb/sq. in (kg/cm^2)

	Normal Laden		Fully Laden	
	Front	Rear	Front	Rear
Saloon:				
6.00 x 13 4 PR	23 (1.6)	24 (1.7)	26 (1.8)	30 (2.1)
6.95 x 13 4 PR	23 (1.6)	23 (1.6)	26 (1.8)	28 (2.0)
165 x 13	26 (1.8)	26 (1.8)	28 (2.0)	36 (2.5)
185/70 x 13	23 (1.6)	23 (1.6)	26 (1.8)	30 (2.1)
Estate:				
6.95 x 13 4 PR	23 (1.6)	24 (1.7)	26 (1.8)	34 (2.4)
165 x 13	26 (1.8)	26 (1.8)	28 (2.0)	40 (2.8)
185/70 x 13	23 (1.6)	24 (1.7)	26 (1.8)	33 (2.3)

NOTE: For Engine Tune-Up Specifications, see end of TUNE-UP sections

Pass the MoT

Once a year, the MoT test falls due for vehicles, three years old or more. (UK only). The test fee paid to the garage covers the cost of carrying out the inspection whether the vehicle passes the test or fails, so it makes sense to ensure that you get the maximum value out of the inspection by carrying out your own pre-test check beforehand.

In this way, you can possibly save yourself the cost of a failure certificate by putting right any likely reasons for failure. Bear in mind that an 'official' tester will more than likely follow a different criterion when examining the same component as the DIY owner, but, by just being aware of what checks the tester will make could avoid a needless failure certificate. Even a simple item like a brake light or one of the screen washers not working could 'fail' the test.

All the items that will some under the testers scrutiny are included in this repair manual in one way or another although it is obviously not compiled specifically for passing the test. However, if you work your way through the check list below, and turn to the appropriate page number referred to, you will have the information required either to check or to service the relevant components.

LIGHTING EQUIPMENT, STOP LIGHTS, REFLECTORS, INDICATORS . . . . Page 145
All external lights must be in working order - including the headlamp main and dipped beams - and visible from a reasonable distance. Light lenses must not be damaged or missing. The indicators must flash at the correct rate - between one and two flashes per second - and the panel warning lights must also be functioning. Headlamps must be correctly aligned.

STEERING . . . . Page 123
Check for excessive play in all the steering components from the road wheels to the steering wheel. Check the tightness of all nuts and clamp bolts. Check for any unusual stiffness in the steering operation. Examine the steering rack gaiters for security and for any splits or tears.

FRONT WHEEL BEARINGS . . . . Page 118
Raise and support the front of the vehicle and check for bearing roughness by rotating the front wheels. A worn bearing will either be heard or felt at the tyre as the wheel turns. Check for excessive or insufficient bearing clearance.

SUSPENSION. . . . . Pages 113/118
The vehicle will have to be raised and supported to check the suspension. Using a suitable long lever or screwdriver to give leverage, check for excessive play in all the suspension joints. Note that some of the rear joints are of the 'voided' type where vertical movement is normal. Check the condition of all shock absorber units - looking for fluid leakage and the security of the upper and lower mountings. Check the operation of the shock absorbers with the vehicle on the road.

BRAKES. . . . . Page 129
Check the operation of the brakes and the handbrake. Check for brakes pulling to one side and ascertain the cause. Check the condition of the flexible brake hoses looking for signs of cracking and for corrosion on the rigid metal pipes - especially around the rear axle. Check that the brake servo - if fitted, is working properly. Remember that the testing station now uses a 'roller brake tester' to check the efficiency of each wheel.

WHEELS AND TYRES . . . . Page 18
Check the condition of the tyres - the tread depth, the side walls, both inner as well as outer, and that they are inflated to the correct pressure (The latter may affect the brake test). Check the tyre 'mix' - radial tyres to the rear and cross-plies on the front wheels. Check the condition of the wheel rims for damage or distortion.

SEAT BELTS . . . . Page 19
Check the seat belts for security and the fabric for chafing or obvious damage.

GENERAL - WIPERS, WASHERS, HORN, EXHAUST. . . . . Pages 19/145
Both the windscreen wipers and washers should be working efficiently. The horn should also operate clearly. Check that the exhaust system does not leak or make an excessive amount of noise. The best way to check for a leaking exhaust is to place a gloved hand over the end of the tailpipe with the engine idling and listen for the 'hiss' of any leakage.

CORROSION . . . . Page 19
Check the body panels for any damage or corrosion on the vehicle likely to render it unsafe.

NOTE: The above check list is only a guide so that the keen DIY owner can check his or her Cortina before submitting it for the MoT test. Although it is based on the official MoT check list at the time of publication, it is only a guide and should be treated as such.

Contents

Routine Maintenance

ENGINE OIL & FILTER . . . . [1]

Oil Leaks

Check all joints on the engine which can be seen from above for oil leaks.

Check the underside of the engine for leaks at the following places: oil drain plug, sump joint, oil filter, engine to transmission flange, front oil seal at crankshaft pulley, and generally around the front end of the engine.

If any evidence of oil leakage is found, the source should be sought and, if serious, remedial action taken immediately.

Oil Level

It is essential that the engine oil is maintained at the correct level. The oil level should be checked at least once a week and always before a long run (Figs. A:1 and A:2).

If the engine has just been run, wait a few minutes after switching off to allow the oil to drain back into the sump. The car must be on level ground when checking the oil.

The oil level should be maintained at the 'MAX' mark on the dipstick, and must never be allowed to fall below the 'MIN' mark.

If the level is low, add oil of the appropriate grade through the filler aperture in the rocker cover after removing the filler cap. See Service Data at the end of this Section for list of specified lubricants.

The approximate quantity of oil required to raise the level from the 'MIN' to the 'MAX' mark on the dipstick is 1.75 pts (1.0 litre).

Do NOT over-fill as this may result in oil leaks and increased oil consumption.

NOTE: If oil is required more often than normal suspect engine wear or an oil leak. Check first around the engine for oil leaks and then the exhaust for excessive 'smoking'.

Oil Change

The engine oil must be changed at least every 6,000 miles or twice a year and the oil filter changed at the same time.

If the vehicle is used under severe operating conditions the oil should be changed more frequently, but in this case it will suffice to change the filter every second oil change.

The most severe type of operation, and that which gives rise to sludge formation, is light engine loading, slow speeds and short journeys. High speeds over long journeys are generally kinder to the engine. Modern engine oils contain additives which go a long way towards preventing sludge formation, but even these have certain limitations.

The dipstick can provide some guide as to the conditions of the engine oil. An additive (detergent) type of oil keeps the carbon particles in suspension, and even a small amount of carbon causes the oil to darken rapidly. However, if the dipstick is found to be heavily coated with sludge, then obviously the oil should be changed. The presence of beads of moisture on the valve rockers, as seen through the oil filler neck, indicates adverse running conditions. When such is the case, more frequent draining and renewal of the oil is highly desirable.

Drain the oil when the engine is still warm by unscrewing the drain plug from the sump. Clean the drain plug and refit it with a new sealing washer. Tighten the plug firmly, but do not use excessive force.

If the oil filter is being changed, renew it as detailed later. Refill the engine with the appropriate quantity of oil, dependent on whether or not the oil filter has been renewed. Run the engine for a few minutes then check the oil level and top up if necessary.

Oil Filter

The oil filter should be changed at the same time as

Service Schedule

- Check engine oil level
- Check coolant level
- Check windscreen washer level
- Check battery electrolyte level
- Check tyre pressures, including spare
- Check operation of all lights

EVERY 6,000 MILES (10,000 KM) OR 6 MONTHS – STANDARD SERVICE

- Check condition and security of seats and seat belt
- Check operation of all lights and controls
- Check condition of windscreen wiper blades
- Check adjustment of windscreen washer jets (also rear screen washer jet, where applicable)
- Lubircate all locks and hinges, door check straps and bonnet safety catch
- Check level in windscreen washer reservoir(s)
- Check coolant level in radiator
- Check fluid level in brake master cylinder reservoir
- Check level and specific gravity of battery electrolyte
- Clean and grease battery terminals
- Check automatic transmission fluid level
- Check, and if necessary adjust, valve clearances
- Clean spark plugs and adjust gaps, or renew
- Examine/renew distributor points. Adjust points gap or dwell angle
- Lubricate distributor. Clean coil, distributor cap and HT leads
- Check ignition timing. Check operation of distributor advance/retard mechanism
- Clean sediment from fuel filter (in-line) and fuel pump
- Lubricate throttle linkage. Check adjustment of cable
- Check carburettor idle and mixture settings
- Check generator belt tension and condition
- Check tightness of generator mounting bolts
- Check all radiator and heater hoses for condition
- Change engine oil and filter
- Check engine generally for oil, water and fuel leaks
- Check clutch adjustment
- Check oil level in manual transmission. Check transmission for oil leaks
- Check oil level in rear axle. Check axle for oil leaks
- Check exhaust system for leakage and security
- Inspect rear brake shoes for wear and drums for condition. Check operation of self-adjust mechanism
- Lubricate handbrake linkage. Check adjustment
- Inspect front brake pads for wear
- Check visually all brake pipes, hoses and unions for leaks or damage
- Check steering unit for oil leaks and gaiter condition
- Check steering and front suspension linkage for wear
- Check condition of ball joint covers
- Check shock absorbers for leaks
- Check tyres for damage and wear
- Have headlamp alignment checked
- Have front wheel alignment (toe-setting) checked

EVERY 18,000 MILES (30,000 KM) OR 18 MONTHS – EXTENDED SERVICE
As for Standard Service above, plus the following additional items:

- Clean crankcase emission valve and oil filler cap
- Renew air cleaner element
- Change brake fluid completely

EVERY 36,000 MILES (60,000 KM) OR 3 YEARS – MAJOR SERVICE
As for Extended Service above, plus the following additional items:

- Clean and repack front wheel bearings. Adjust end-float
- Lubricate front suspension ball joints
- Renew all brake cylinder seals. Examine all flexible hoses and renew if necessary

OTHER ITEMS

Every 2 years the cooling system should be drained, flushed and refilled with fresh anti-freeze mixture

MIDWAY SERVICE

If the vehicle is used under severe operating conditions, covers a very low annual mileage or its use includes a high proportion of short journeys, the following service is recommended between scheduled services.

- Check engine oil level (or change engine oil and filter, if required)
- Check coolant level
- Check windscreen washer reservoir
- Check brake fluid level
- Check battery electrolyte level
- Check tyre pressure and condition, including spare
- Check clutch pedal free-play
- Check distributor points gap (or dwell angle) and ignition timing
- Check carburettor idle and mixture settings with engine warm
- Inspect brake system for leaks and hoses for chafing
- Check for evidence of oil, water, fuel or exhaust leaks
- Check operation of all lights, controls and instruments
- Carry out road test and check general condition of car

the engine oil if the oil is renewed every 6,000 miles, or at every alternate oil change if the oil is changed more frequently.

The oil filter element is of the throw-away cartridge type, and is screwed into a mounting pad on the left-hand side of the cylinder block. It should be possible to unscrew the filter by hand, but if not a special strap wrench will be required to release it (Figs. A:3 and A:4).

An alternative method of releasing a tight filter is to drive a screwdriver blade through the filter and use this to obtain extra leverage. This is, however, a rather messy business as oil will then spill out through the holes.

A drip tray should be placed under the filter prior to removal as a quantity of oil will be released when it is unscrewed. Discard the oil filter cartridge.

Clean the mounting face on the engine. Check that the rubber sealing ring on the new cartridge is correctly located, then wet it with clean engine oil. Screw the cartridge onto the threaded adaptor by hand until the seal just contacts the mounting face, then tighten a further three-quarters of a turn - BUT NO MORE.

After refilling the engine with fresh oil, start the engine and check the filter for any signs of leakage - stop the engine IMMEDIATELY if any signs are present as this indicates that the filter is not sealing correctly.

CRANKCASE VENTILATION SYSTEM . . . . [3]

The crankcase ventilation system should be serviced at least every 18,000 miles to ensure correct functioning of the system, as otherwise a pressure build-up in the crankcase can occur, causing subsequent oil leaks in the engine with an increase in oil consumption.

The system air intake filter is incorporated in the oil filler cap at the rocker cover, and the cap should be removed and washed in petrol or preferably paraffin. Probe the breather holes in the underside of the cap to ensure they are clear. Shake the cap dry before refitting it. Do NOT dry the filter element with compressed air as this may damage the element. If the element is badly clogged or excessively dirty, the cap should be renewed.

Remove the system regulator valve from the oil separator on the side of the cylinder block (Fig. A:5). The valve is a push-fit into the rubber grommet in the separator. Clean the valve with solvent, as for the cap above, and dry with compressed air. If the valve is defective or excessively dirty, it should be renewed.

Clean the system hoses with solvent, and the connecting nozzle on the inlet manifold by probing the nipple with a piece of wire.

A malfunction of the ventilation system may be indicated by rough engine idle. Do not attempt to compensate for this condition by making carburettor adjustments or disconnecting the emission system, as removal of the system from the engine will adversely affect the fuel economy and engine ventilation, with resultant shortening of engine life.

To determine whether the rough idle condition is caused by a mal-function in the system, exchange the regulator valve for a known good one and compare the idle

condition. If the condition persists, the valve is not at fault. Check the rest of the system for restrictions and clean as described above. If the malfunction still persists, further engine component diagnosis should be carried out.

GENERATOR . . . . [4]

Drive Belt Tension

Correct tensioning of the generator and water pump drive belt is important to ensure efficient operation of the cooling and charging systems. Excessive tightness will cause rapid wear of the belt, and place undue strain on the pump and generator bearings.

When correctly tensioned, a total deflection of 0.5 in should be possible under moderate finger pressure at the midway point on the longest belt run between the two pulleys (Fig. A:6).

If adjustment is required, slacken the bolt securing the adjusting link to the generator, and the two bolts securing the generator to its mounting bracket (Fig. A:7). Move the generator towards or away from the engine as necessary until the correct tension is obtained - avoid over-tightening. Apply any leverage necessary to the generator drive end bracket only, using a soft metal or wooden lever. Retighten the generator mounting bolts, then re-check the belt tension.

Belt Replacement

The condition of the drive belt(s) should be checked periodically. If nicked, cut, excessively worn, or otherwise damaged, the belt should be replaced.

If the belt is noisy in operation, check for misalignment of the pulleys.

To replace the belt, proceed as for adjusting, but press the generator fully towards the engine and detach the belt(s) from the pulleys.

Fit the new belt ensuring that it is not twisted, and adjust the tension as described above. Do NOT attempt to lever a new belt onto the pulleys as this can easily cause damage to the belt or pulleys.

The tension of a new belt should be rechecked after approximately 100 miles use.

BATTERY . . . . [5]

Electrolyte Level

The level of the battery electrolyte in each cell should be checked periodically, and distilled water added if the level is below the separators, or the bottom of the filling tube on trough-fill type batteries. Do not over-fill the battery.

In some cases the battery case is translucent to allow the level to be checked without the need for lifting the vent cover.

It is good practice to run the car immediately after topping-up the battery, especially in cold weather, to ensure thorough mixing of the acid and water and so prevent

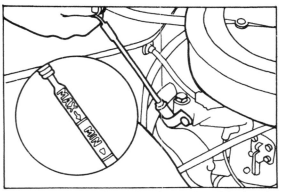

Fig. A:1 Engine dipstick is located at right-hand rear on OHV models

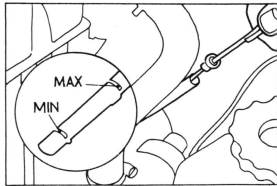

Fig. A:2 Dipstick tube is at rear left-hand corner of engine on OHC engines

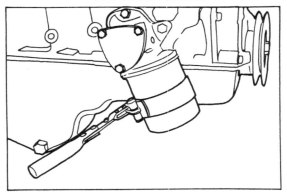

Fig. A:3 Remove oil filter cartridge, using special filter wrench, on 1.3 litre engine

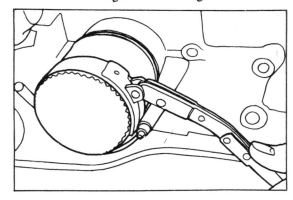

Fig. A:4 Unscrewing filter cartridge on OHC engine

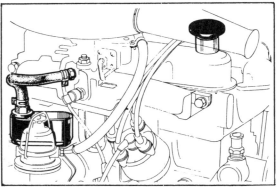

Fig. A:5 Crankcase emission system components (OHV engine)

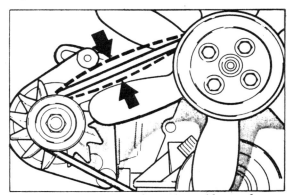

Fig. A:6 Check fan belt tension mid-way along longest belt run between pulleys

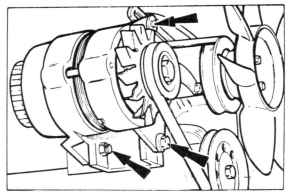

Fig. A:7 To adjust the belt tension, slacken alternator adjusting/mounting bolts as shown

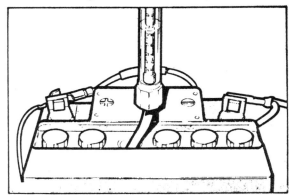

Fig. A:8 Test specific gravity of each cell in turn with a suitable hydrometer

freezing.

If the battery is found to need frequent topping-up steps should be taken to discover the reason. For example, the battery may be receiving an excessive charge from the alternator, in which case the charging system charge rate should be checked.

If one cell in particular needs topping-up more than the others, check the condition of the battery case. If there are signs of acid leakage, the source should be traced and corrective action taken.

NOTE: The electrolyte level should not be topped-up within half an hour of the battery having been charged from an external source, lest it floods.

State of Charge

The state of charge of the battery can be determined by checking the specific gravity of the electrolyte in each cell with a hydrometer and measuring the voltage under load across the battery terminals with a heavy discharge tester. It is unlikely that the normal owner-driver will possess the latter piece of equipment, but a suitable hydrometer to test the specific gravity can be obtained quite cheaply from a motor accessory shop (Fig. A:8).

A specific gravity reading of at least 1.275 should be obtained if the battery is fully charged, or 1.120 if discharged. It is more important that the readings in each cell be equal, as a low s.g. in one cell indicates an internal fault and this will affect its ability to hold its charge.

Connections

The battery terminals and leads should be kept clean to ensure good connections. Remove the battery if necessary to clean the terminals, but always detach the earth lead first.

If the battery posts or cable terminals are corroded, they can normally be removed by pouring boiling water over them, then brushing them with a wire brush.

When reconnecting the cables, apply a thin film of petroleum jelly or grease to both the terminals and posts. Tighten the terminals securely.

The battery earth strap and the engine earth strap should also be checked for proper connection and condition.

COOLING SYSTEM . . . . [6]

General Check

All hoses and connections in the cooling and heating system should be checked carefully for leaks. Diagrams of the hose runs on both the OHV and the OHC engines are included in the COOLING SYSTEM section and reference should be made for details.

Check particularly the joints at the water pump, cylinder head gasket, inlet manifold gasket, cylinder block core plugs, drain plugs, radiator and all hoses and connections.

Examine the hoses for perishing, swelling, or other damaged. Inspect the radiator fins to ensure they are not damaged, or clogged with dirt.

Fan Belt

Check the tension and condition of the fan belt as detailed above under 'GENERATOR'.

Coolant Level

The coolant level in the radiator should be checked at least weekly, and topped up as necessary. Check the level when the engine is cool. If the system is at normal operating temperature, allow it to cool first. Muffle the cap with a thick cloth to protect the hands against scalding and turn the cap slowly anti-clockwise to the first stop to release the pressure in the system through the over-flow tube before completely removing the cap (Fig. A:9).

The coolant level should be about 1 inch (25 mm) below the bottom of the radiator filler neck. If the level in the system has fallen appreciably, suspect a leak in the system; check the hoses and hose connections first.

NOTE: When the system contains anti-freeze, ensure that the strength of the mixture is maintained when topping up.

Anti-freeze

Because of the properties of anti-freeze in raising the boiling point of the coolant, as well as lowering the freezing point, it is recommended that an "All-Season' type anti-freeze be used permanently in the cooling system to afford maximum protection against both freezing and over-heating. The presence of a corrosion inhibitor in most anti-freezes will also help to prevent corrosion and the formation of scale in the system.

During the winter months an anti-freeze mixture MUST be used in the system to protect against frost damage. The concentration of the solution will depend on the degree of protection required, and dilution should be carried out in accordance with the manufacturer's instructions. As a guideline a 45% solution of anti-freeze by volume will remain fluid down to -32°C (-26°F).

Before filling the system with anti-freeze solution, inspect all hoses, hose connections and cooling system joints. Tighten or renew where necessary. After adding the anti-freeze, run the engine up to normal operating temperature and check for leaks. A label should be attached to the radiator to record the date of filling.

The anti-freeze concentration in the system should be checked periodically and in any case before the beginning of the winter season. The specific gravity of the mixture can be checked using a suitable hydrometer. The specific gravity of a 45% concentration solution should be 1.065 providing no other additive is in the cooling system.

Flushing

The cooling system should be completely drained, flushed and refilled with a fresh mixture of anti-freeze and water at least every two years or as recommended by the anti-freeze manufacturer. Full details of the flushing operation are included in the COOLING SYSTEM section

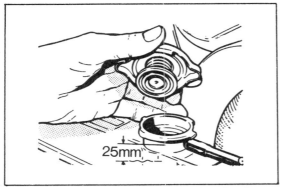

Fig. A:9 Checking radiator coolant level

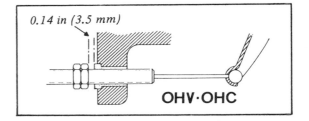

0.14 in (3.5 mm)

OHV·OHC

Fig. A:10 Clutch cable adjustment

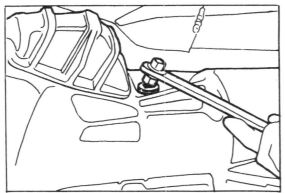

Fig. A:11 Checking oil level in manual gearbox

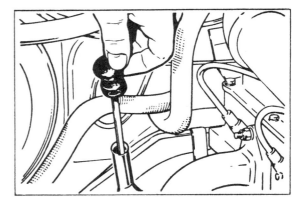

Fig. A:12 Auto transmission dipstick is located at right-hand rear of engine compartment

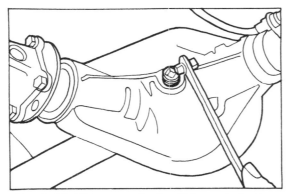

Fig. A:13 Oil in rear axle should be up to bottom edge of filler hole

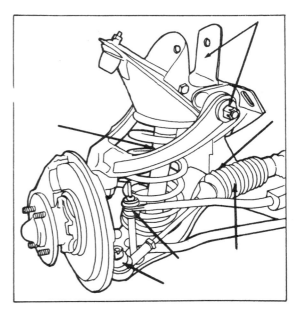

Fig. A:14 Checking points on front suspension. Check swivel ball joints and wheel bearing end-float also.

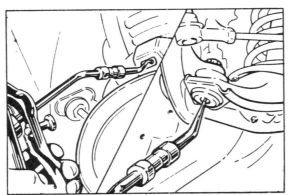

Fig. A:15 Lubricate front suspension ball joints using a grease gun with suitable adaptor nozzle

later in the manual, and reference should be made for details.

CLUTCH..........................[7]

When correctly adjusted, a free-play of 0.14 in (3.5 mm) should exist between the outer cable adjuster nut and the abutment flange on the clutch housing. This free-play is intended as an allowance for operating temperature expansion and so that there will be adequate provision for clutch wear between services.

To check the clearance raise and support the front of the car, then pull the clutch outer cable away from the housing abutment flange and measure the clearance at the flange with a feeler gauge (Fig. A:10).

If adjustment is needed, then fully depress the clutch pedal twice and then allow it to return to its stop. Slacken the cable locknut and screw the adjuster nut along the cable sleeve until the correct clearance is obtained. Recheck the clearance again after tightening the locknut.

MANUAL TRANSMISSION.............[8]

Oil Level

The oil level in the gearbox should be checked after the vehicle has been standing on level ground for some time, as foaming of the oil during use will cause the level to rise and give an incorrect indication of the lubricant content.

The oil level is checked at the filler hole in the left-hand side of the gearbox casing, and a special key (obtainable from most accessory shops) will be required to remove the filler plug which has a square recessed-head.

The gearbox oil level is correct when it reaches the lower edge of the filler opening. If necessary, top up with SAE 80 EP Gear Oil (Fig. A:11).

Lack of oil in the transmission can only result from leakage, and this should be investigated if the level is found to be excessively low.

AUTOMATIC TRANSMISSION..........[9]

Fluid Level

The transmission fluid level is best checked immediately after a short run (2-4 miles/3 - 5 km) when the fluid will have reached its normal operating temperature.

With the vehicle standing on level ground and the handbrake applied, start the engine and run it at idle. Move the manual selector lever through all positions at least three times, then move it into 'P' and allow the engine to idle for a further 1 to 2 minutes.

The fluid level dipstick is located in the transmission filler tube on the right-hand side of the engine at the rear (Fig. A:12).

With the engine still idling, withdraw the dipstick and wipe it clean on a non-fluffy rag or piece of paper. Re-insert the dipstick fully into the filler tube then withdraw it again immediately. Check the fluid level indicated on the dipstick - it should be between the two marks.

If low, add fluid through the dipstick tube to bring it up to the correct level. The difference between the 'Low' and 'Full' marks on the dipstick is 1 pint (0.6 litres). Use only Automatic Transmission Fluid to specification SQM2C-9007-AA or M2C-33F for topping up.

Do NOT overfill the transmission, as this will cause the fluid to become aerated.

Should it be necessary to check the fluid level when the gearbox is cold, carry out the procedure as above, when the level should be approximately 0.4 in (10 mm) below the 'Full' mark otherwise it will be too high at normal operating temperature when the fluid has expanded. Recheck the level when the gearbox is at normal running temperature.

Cooling Vents

The underside of the transmission unit, especially the cooling vents, must be kept free from mud, etc., otherwise overheating may result. The cooling vents are recognised as rectangular cut-outs in the converter housing with a mesh cover.

REAR AXLE ....[10]

Oil Level

The oil level in the rear axle differential unit should be checked with the car standing on level ground to ensure an accurate reading.

The oil level plug is located in the left-hand side of the unit housing directly in front of the drive shaft and, as for the gearbox, a special key will be required to unscrew the plug (Fig. A:13).

The oil level is correct when it is up to the bottom edge of the filler opening. Top up if necessary with SAE 90 Hypoid Gear Oil.

SUSPENSION.......................[11]

General Check

Check the shock absorbers for evidence of fluid leakage on the unit body below the piston rod. Check the basic operation of the shock absorber, i.e. whether its operation is stiff, notchy or spongy.

Check the condition of the front suspension steering swivel ball joints. This is best done with the road wheel jacked clear of the ground with the jack positioned under the lower suspension arm. Also check the bushes at the inner ends of the upper and lower suspension arms and the stabiliser bar mounting rubbers (Fig. A:14).

Any worn or suspect parts should be renewed as soon as possible.

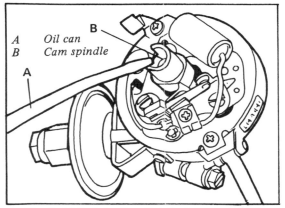

A Oil can
B Cam spindle

Fig. A:16 Lubricating distributor cam spindle

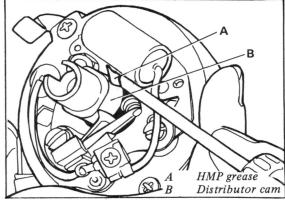

A HMP grease
B Distributor cam

Fig. A:17 Lubricating distributor cam

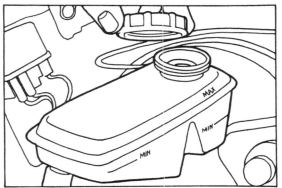

Fig. A:18 Check that the brake reservoir fluid level is maintained at the MAX level mark

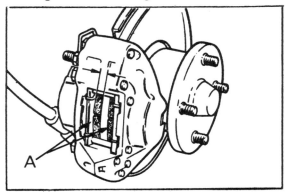

Fig. A:19 Brake pads should be renewed when pad thickness is down to 0.125 in (3 mm)

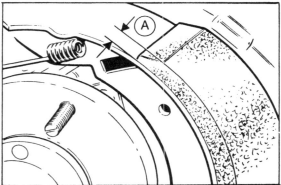

Fig. A:20 Rear brake shoes should always have at least 1/16 in depth of lining material

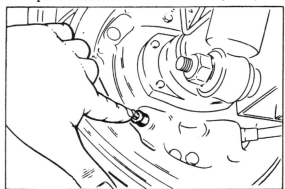

Fig. A:21 Check handbrake adjustment by depressing plunger at brake backplate

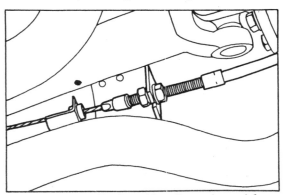

Fig. A:22 Handbrake cable adjuster is on right-hand abutment bracket on floorpan

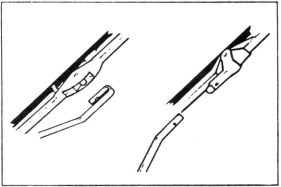

Fig. A:23 Wiper blade fitting may be one of two types - hooked type (left) or push-on type

Front Wheel Alignment

A quick and easy check of the front wheel alignment can be made by inspecting the tread wear pattern on the front tyres. If uneven tyre wear is evident, a fuller check of the toe setting should be made. This should be carried out by an Authorised Dealer or Tyre Centre who will have the specialised equipment necessary for this operation.

Front Suspension Ball Joints

The front suspension ball joints should be lubricated every 36,000 miles.

The front of the car must be jacked up and the front wheels removed to allow access.

Each grease point is protected by a blanking plug which must first be removed. Using a grease gun fitted with a suitable adaptor, fill each joint with suitable multi-purpose grease (Fig. A:15). Refit the blanking plugs when lubrication is complete.

Front Wheel Bearings

The front wheel bearings should be cleaned and re-packed, and the end-float reset every 36,000 miles. Full details of the relevant procedures are included in the 'FRONT SUSPENSION' section under the heading 'FRONT HUBS'.

STEERING . . . . [12]

Check the track rod end ball joints for wear and their boots for tears or other damage.

Inspect the steering unit gaiters for tears, splits or signs of perishing. If damaged in any way, the gaiters must be renewed as otherwise dirt and water will enter the steering unit with dire (and expensive) consequences.

Check the steering unit mountings for security.

DISTRIBUTOR. . . . . [13]

Lubrication

Lubrication of the distributor should be carried out at the same time as the engine oil change.

Unclip and remove the distributor cap and pull off the rotor arm from central spindle.

Apply one or two drops of clean engine oil to the felt wick in the end of the cam spindle (Fig. A:16).

Lightly smear the breaker cam with petroleum jelly or high melting point grease (to Ford Spec. ESF-M1C66-A). Use a screwdriver or similar instrument to distribute the lubricant uniformly around the cam surface (Fig. A:17). When the cam is rotated a small fillet of lubricant should be built up on the back of the points rubbing block.

Avoid over-lubricating. Carefully wipe away any surplus lubricant and check that the contact breaker points are perfectly clean and dry. Refit the rotor arm and distri-

butor cap. See TUNE-UP for details on contact breaker inspection and replacement.

BRAKES. . . . . [14]

Fluid Level

The brake fluid level in the master cylinder reservoir should be maintained between the 'Max' and 'Min' marks on the side (Fig. A:18).

If topping up is necessary, clean the area around the filler cap before removing it. Use only Disc Brake Fluid to specification ESEA-M6C-1001-A to top it up.

Ensure that the dividing baffle between the two sections of the reservoir is always covered.

Check that the vent hole in the filler cap is clear before fitting the cap.

It should be noted that brake fluid will damage paintwork if allowed to come into contact with it. Any spilt fluid must be wiped (or washed off with cold water) from the affected area immediately.

The fluid level in the reservoir will drop slightly over a period of time as the disc caliper pistons move outwards to compensate for pad lining wear - this is normal. However, if the fluid level falls excessively, or requires frequent topping up, this indicates a leak in the hydraulic system and steps should be taken immediately to establish and deal with the cause.

The brake fluid should be changed completely every 18,000 miles or 18 months, whichever is the sooner.

Brake Lines, Hoses and Cylinder Seals

Periodically, all hydraulic pipes, hoses and unions should be checked visually for chafing, leaks and corrosion. Any component which is damaged or suspect should be renewed immediately.

As preventive maintenance, at 36,000 miles, all fluid seals in the braking system should be renewed, and all flexible hoses examined thoroughly and renewed if necessary.

The procedures for renewing the seals in the various hydraulic components of the braking system are fully described under the appropriate headings in the BRAKES section.

Brake Adjustment

Both the disc front and drum rear brakes are self-adjusting and consequently do not require periodic adjustment.

The operation of the self-adjusting mechanism in the rear brakes should be checked when the brake shoes are being examined to ensure that the mechanism is operating correctly.

Handbrake adjustment will not normally be required as this should be taken up automatically by the rear shoe adjuster mechanism.

If the brake adjustment appears to come up when the pedal is pumped several times, indicated by the pedal becoming 'harder', this suggests that there is air in the hy-

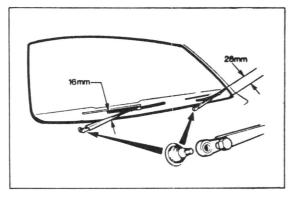

Fig. A:24 When refitting wiper arms, they should be positioned as shown

Fig. A:25 Prise out plastic hinge plug and apply a few drips of light oil to lubricate hinge

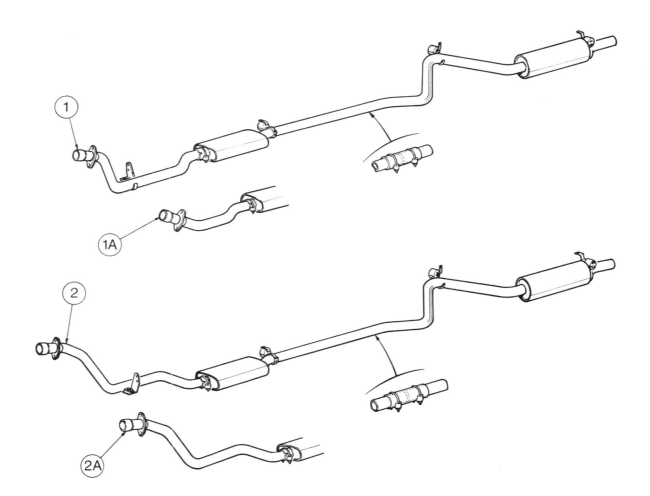

1. *Basic exhaust system for OHV models*
1a. *Front pipe section for 1600cc OHV GT models*
2. *Basic exhaust system for OHC models*
2a. *Front pipe section for OHC GT models*

Fig. A:26 The Cortina exhaust system arrangement

draulic system and the brakes should be bled as detailed in the BRAKES section to eliminate this condition.

Front Brake Pads

The front wheels must be removed to allow inspection of the disc brake pads.

Check the pad wear by measuring the thickness of the pad material 'A', as shown in Fig. A:19. When this dimension is reduced to approximately 1/8 in (3 mm), and never less than 1/16 in (1.5 mm), the pads must be renewed.

Brake pads should always be renewed in sets of four to maintain braking balance.

If the pads are not being renewed, ensure that sufficient lining material remains to allow the car to run until the next service check.

The procedure for replacing the brake pads is fully detailed in the BRAKES section of the manual.

Rear Brake Shoes

The rear wheels and brake drums must be removed to allow inspection of the brake linings. Ensure that the handbrake is fully released before attempting to withdraw the brake drums.

Clean out the brake drums, shoes and backplates using a soft brush. Take care not to inhale the asbestos dust from the linings as this can be injurious to health.

Inspect the shoe linings for wear (Fig. A:20). If the lining material has worn down to the minimum permissible thickness of 1/16 in (1.5 mm) on bonded-type shoes, or within 0.040 in (1 mm) of the rivet heads on riveted type shoes, or will have done so before the next check is called for, the brake shoes should be renewed.

Brake shoes should be replaced in sets of four. On no account replace only one pair of shoes.

Also inspect the surface of the brake linings for oil, grease or brake fluid contamination. If present, then linings should be renewed once the cause has been established and dealt with. This should be attended to immediately.

Inspect the wheel cylinders for signs of fluid leakage. If present, the cylinder should be replaced or the seals renewed.

Details of brake shoe replacement are included in the BRAKES section of this manual.

Handbrake

The handbrake should be checked to ensure it is operating correctly. Check that the cable follows its correct run and is correctly located in its guides.

Lubricate the cable sparingly with grease at the equaliser bracket and where the cable enters the outer sleeves. Lubricate all pivot points and check that they are operating freely.

As stated above, the handbrake should not normally require adjustment as any free-play should be taken up automatically by the rear shoe adjuster mechanism. However, if movement at the handbrake lever is excessive the cable can be adjusted as follows:

With the handbrake lever in the 'OFF' position, check that the relay levers within the brake assemblies are in contact with their stops by depressing the plungers at each brake backplate (Fig. A:21). No perceptible movement of the plungers should be felt.

Adjustment is effected at the right-hand abutment bracket on the transmission tunnel (Fig. A:22). Adjust the cable using the adjusting nuts until all slack is eliminated from the cable.

Check the adjustment by depressing the plungers at each backplate. A plunger movement of 0.020 to 0.040 in (0.5 - 1.0 mm) should exist at each brake. The cable can be moved by hand from side to side to even up the clearance if biased one way due to friction in the system.

If the clearance is unequal at the two plungers, ensure that the total plunger movement at both sides when added together is between 0.040 and 0.080 in (1.0 - 2.0 mm). This permits a zero condition on one side only.

WHEELS & TYRES . . . . [15]

Tyre Condition

The condition of the tyres should be checked periodically as a safety measure.

Measure the depth of tread of each tyre, preferably with a proper tread depth gauge. Tyres should be replaced, at the latest, when the tread depth has reached 1 mm all round and on full tread width, as this is the absolute limit for safe driving. However, it is highly recommended that tyres be replaced before this as they will be more suseptible to punctures and have greatly reduced grip, especially in the wet.

Check the tyre casing visually for cuts in the casing fabric, exposure of ply or cords, or the presence of lumps or bulges. If any of these conditions are present, the tyre should be discarded.

Abnormal tyre wear may be caused by improper inflation pressures, wheel imbalance, suspension misalignment, or mechanical irregularities. When rapid or uneven tyre wear becomes apparent, the cause should be established and dealt with.

Fins or feathers on the tread surface are an indication of severe wheel misalignment. This conditon takes the form of a sharp 'fin' on the edge of each pattern rib, and the position of this indicates the direction of misalignment. Fins on the outboard edges are caused by excessive toe-out, whereas fins on the inboard edges of the pattern ribs are caused by excessive toe-in.

Finning on the near-side front tyre only may be due to severe road camber conditions and cannot be eliminated by mechanical adjustment. In this event, frequent interchanging of the affected wheel to even out tyre wear is the only solution.

Some mechanical defects which could be a cause of abnormal tread wear are: loose or worn wheel bearings, uneven braking due to dragging brakes, seized wheel cylinders or distorted brake discs, excessive looseness or damage in the suspension, loose steering connections, bent steering arms, or defective shock absorbers.

LIGHTS, CONTROLS & INSTRUMENTS . . [16]

The operation of all lights should be checked periodically and any defective bulbs replaced as necessary.

The operation of all controls, including the steering lock, horn, wipers, heated rear window, etc., should be checked periodically.

The function of the instruments is best carried out under road test conditions.

WIPERS & WASHERS . . . . [17]

Wiper Blades

The wiping speeds, intermittent wipe action (if fitted) and park position of the wiper blades as well as the condition of the blades and rubbers should be checked periodically.

Blades which are contaminated with insect or oil deposits should be removed and cleaned with a hard brush and detergent solution.

Worn blades will cause streaks and unsatisfactory cleaning of the glass. The wiping edge of the blades must not be perished or torn. Wear of the blades will increase under conditions of dust, air pollution and when used on a frozen or dry screen.

New blades should be fitted at least once a year according to condition.

The wiper blades fitting may be one of two types; either a hooked fitting or a straight push-fit (Fig. A:23).

With the hooked fitting type blade, the blade is removed by first lifting the blade away from the windscreen then turning it through 90° so that it is in a 'Tee' position with the wiper arm. Depress the locking spring tab on the outer arm of the hook and slide the blade down the arm to clear the hook. Refit the new blade in the reverse order of removing.

The straight push-fit type blade is secured in position by two locating dimples on the arm. To remove the blade, depress the spring lever on the underside of the blade to disengage the lower locating dimple. Tilt the blade assembly outwards away from the arm to disengage the upper locating peg and pull the blade up and off the arm. Push the new blade onto the arm until the locating peg and dimple engage in their locations.

In either case, check the operation of the wipers after fitting new blades. The parked position of the blades should be as shown in (Fig. A:24).

Washers

The level in the reservoir(s) should be checked regularly and topped up as required.

The addition of a proprietary brand of windscreen washer additive is recommended to ensure quick and efficient cleaning of the windscreen. In winter, the addition of up to 25% methylated spirits will prevent the washer fluid from freezing.

LOCKS, HINGES, ETC. . . . . [18]

All hinges, locks and door check straps should be lubricated periodically to prevent them seizing.

To lubricate the door hinges, remove the plastic plug covering the top end of the pin and apply a few drips of oil through the hole in the hinge (Fig. A:25). Refit the plastic plug.

Lightly oil the bonnet safety catch, and on estate car variants the tailgate catch.

The lock cylinders in the doors and boot lid, or tailgate should be lubricated by dipping the key in graphite powder then inserting it into the lock and turning it a few times.

EXHAUST SYSTEM . . . . [19]

The exhaust system should be checked for leaks by blocking the tail pipe with the palm of the hand, with the engine idling. The exhaust system mountings should show no signs of breaking or fraying and should be completely free from strain. The pipes and silencers should also be in sound condition but will inevitably show some corrosion but not weakened to the extent that a tap from the ball end of a light hammer does any damage. Before this stage is reached, new parts should be fitted. (Fig. A:26).

SEAT BELTS . . . . [20]

Although seat belts are fitted to a car this doesn't necessarily mean that they are working efficiently or, indeed, that they are capable of doing their job when they are actually needed. This is why the condition of the seat belt is now included in the annual MoT test. There are some simple checks to be made on a regular basis to see that they are in working order. They are as follows:
1. Pull each seat belt against its anchorage to see that it is properly secured to the vehicle structure.
2. Examine carefully the condition of the webbing looking for cuts or obvious signs of deterioration.
3. Fasten each seat belt locking mechanism and then try to pull the locked sections apart. Operate the mechanism, whilst pulling on the belt to determine that the mechanism releases when required.
4. Check the condition of the attachment fittings and adjusting fitting on each belt for distortion or fracture.
5. As far as practicable check the condition of the vehicle structure around the seat belt anchorages - this will be best carried out from below the vehicle.
6. If the seat belt is of the retracting type, pull a section of the webbing from the reel unit and then release it to see that the webbing automatically winds back. Bear in mind that some inertia reel belts require some manual assistance before retraction takes place.

BODY CORROSION . . . . [21]

We all recognise rust when it starts to appear around certain parts of our cars anatomy. Then, before we are aware, it's too late and metal has been replaced by a very poor substitute. The result is costly, can be dangerous and will not win the car any beauty awards!

The only way to beat rust is to prevent it in the first place or at the very least slow it down. To do this, first of all we must realise how rust is formed.

Think of a piece of metal with a bead of water sitting on top. The metal below the water is starved of air and is called anodic. The metal outside this area is known as cathodic. An electrolytic action is formed between these two conditions and it is this process that causes corrosion. There are acceleration factors involved such as dirt, grit or salt. These can be contained in the water and will increase the conductivity. So basically rust is formed by an electro-chemical reaction. Bear in mind that rain needn't necessarily be the water factor involved in the process - condensation plays its role too.

Obviously it doesn't take much logic to understand how rust can be prevented in the first place. The metal work of the car has to be protected from moisture and air. This protection is partly taken care of by the car manufacturer when the car is put together - paint on the outside and special inhibitors used on the inside. However, the rust protection is only as good as the application of these materials and one spot missed means that rust will accelerate all the more in this particular spot.

The importance of regular washing and touching up paintwork play their part in rust protection. For example, regular hosing down of the underneath of the car can help prevent any build up of mud forming in certain areas. Mud can act like a damp sponge during wet weather so that you have a constant moisture problem even during dry spells. You'll find that common rust problems on particular models usually originate from mud-traps.

You can always go one step further and improve on the manufacturers rust protection by tackling your own rustproofing. This involves applying light viscosity water-dispacing material inside all the box sections and/or applying underbody sealant.

There are various kits on the market designed specifically for the keen DIY motorist and even if you don't treat all the box sections it is worthwhile devoting some time to protecting the rust prone areas of your car.

An important part of protection is treating the car with an underbody sealant. Here preparation is of the utmost importance because if the sealant doesn't attach firmly to the car body then the air gap between seal and metal can help accelerate corrosion rather than prevent it.

First of all the car will have to be thoroughly cleaned underneath. A high pressure hose is obviously helpful in removing dirt but better still is to have the car steam cleaned first. Applying an underbody sealant is a dirty job and you should be well prepared with old clothes, gloves and a hat. If you are venturing underneath the car and it has to be jacked up then make certain that it is well supported on axle stands.

After thoroughly cleaning the underside you should go over stubborn dirt or caked mud with a good fine wire brush. The important thing is that the surface to be treated is absolutely clear of any foreign matter. For good application of underbody sealant use a cheap paint brush. It is important that the sealant used will remain flexible and will not chip or flake at a later date. Obviously care will have to be taken not to cover moving parts such as the drive shafts, handbrake linkages, etc. If necessary then mask these areas first.

The first part of this section on corrosion concentrates on the matter of protection, which is fine before corrosion takes place. But what happens if corrosion has already taken a hold?

It can be a costly business when corrosion dictates the vehicle being taken off the road through an MoT failure. As already explained in 'Passing the MoT' page at the beginning of this Repair Manual, an MoT tester will check for damage or corrosion in or on a vehicle that is likely to render it unsafe.

On the Cortina, the tester will pay special attention to the inner and outer side sills, the floor pan especially around the rear suspension attachment points, and the rear part of the inner front wing panel where it joins the front bulkhead.

Also, he'll check the seat belt mounting areas.

Having checked and identified the important areas, the MoT tester will check the extent or level of suspect corrosion. He should do this by pressing hard against the area and testing the amount of 'give' which results. Often he will also tap the component lightly (it should not be necessary to subject the area to heavy blows), listening for differences in sound which will result from unaffected metal compared with corroded metal.

Service Data

CAPACITIES

Sump: Oil change inc. filter
1300 OHV	.6.2 pts (3.5 litres)
1600 OHV	.6.2 pts (3.5 litres)
1600 OHC	.6.2 pts (3.5 litres)
2000 OHC	.6.2 pts (3.5 litres)

Gearbox
Type A - OHV engines	1.6 pts (0.9 litre)
Type B - OHC engines	.2.4 pts (1.35 litres)
Automatic transmission	.11.26 pts (6.4 litres)

Rear axle
    all except 2000 . . . . 1.76 pts (1.0 litre)
    2000 cc model . . . . .1.9 pts (1.1 litres)
Cooling system inc. heater:
    1300 OHV . . . . .10.3 pts (5.8 litres)
    1600 OHV . . . . .11.3 pts (6.3 litres)
    1600 OHC . . . . .11.4 pts (6.5 litres)
    2000 OHC . . . . .12.4 pts (7.1 litres)
Fuel tank . . . . 12 gallons (54 litres)
Washer bottle . . . . 2.5 pints (1.4 litres)

SPECIFIED LUBRICANTS

Engine oil . . . . .HD Motor oil
Manual transmission. . . . . .EP Gear Oil SAE 80 (SQ-M2C-9008-A)
Automatic transmission . . . . Automatic Transmission Fluid, Type
M2C-33-F (SQ-M2C-9007-AA)
Rear axle . . . . Hypoid Gear Oil SAE 90 (SQ-M2C-9002-AA)
Steering gear:
    Manual . . . . Hypoid Gear Oil SAE 90 (S-M2C-4053-AS
or E-M2C-29)
    Power assisted. . . . . .Oil SAE 40 (SS-M2C-9001-AA)
Power steering system . . . . .Automatic Transmission Fluid,
Type M3C-33-F (SQ-M2C-9007-AA)
Grease points . . . . .Lithium Base Grease (EM1C-3 with 1%
molybdenum disulphide)
Braking system . . . . .Disc Brake Fluid (ESEA-M6C-1001-A)
Cooling system . . . . Anti-freeze, 45% solution (SM-97B-1002-A)

TYRE PRESSURES Cold: Given in lb/sq in (kg/cm^2)

Model	Tyre Size	Normal Laden Pressures		Fully Laden Pressures	
		Front	Rear	Front	Rear
1300 Saloon	5.60-13 . . .	23 (1.6) . . .	24 (1.7) . . .	27 (1.9) . . .	30 (2.1)
1300 Estate	6.00-13 . . .	21 (1.5) . . .	23 (1.6) . . .	27 (1.9) . . .	36 (2.5)
1600 Saloon	165SR-13 . . .	23 (1.6) . . .	23 (1.6) . . .	26 (1.8) . . .	28 (2.0)
1600 Estate	165SR-13 . . .	23 (1.6) . . .	23 (1.6) . . .	26 (1.8) . . .	36 (2.5)
2000 Saloon	165SR-13 . . .	26 (1.8) . . .	26 (1.8) . . .	28 (2.0) . . .	36 (2.5)
	185HR-13 . . .	23 (1.6) . . .	23 (1.6) . . .	26 (1.8) . . .	30 (2.1)
2000 Estate	165SR-13 . . .	26 (1.8) . . .	26 (1.8) . . .	28 (2.0) . . .	40 (2.8)
	185HR-13 . . .	23 (1.6) . . .	24 (1.7) . . .	26 (1.8) . . .	33 (2.3)

Tune-up

INTRODUCTION . . . .[1]

Difficult starting, poor performance and excessive fuel consumption are some of the problems associated with an engine which is badly worn or out of tune. This is why, at every major service, the engine components should be checked and adjusted in accordance with the SERVICE SCHEDULE given on page 9.

Engine Tune-up has deliberately been presented as a separate section independent of the ROUTINE MAINTENANCE previously so that if trouble occurs between services the engine can be tackled on its own.

Often it is the condition or adjustment of only one component which is at fault and consequently it will not be necessary to carry out a complete engine tune-up. Unfortunately it is usually only by gradual elimination that the fault can be traced and rectified. To assist in pinpointing the source of any trouble a comprehensive 'Trouble-Shooting' chart is included at the end of this section.

The following checks and adjustments have been arranged in logical sequence and it is advised that they be followed in the order given when carrying out a complete engine tune-up. However, if attention to only one particular item is required - the spark plugs or contact breaker points for instance - then simply refer to the appropriate heading. This way either individual components or a complete engine tune can be tackled.

COMPRESSION TEST . . . .[2]

Valuable time can be wasted trying to tune an engine which is badly worn. This is particularly applicable in the case of an engine which has covered considerable mileage. It is therefore always worthwhile checking the cylinder compression pressures first to determine the general state of the unit.

A compression tester will be required for this operation, and one of these can be purchased quite cheaply from most motor accessory shops, or even hired.

The specified compression pressures are detailed in the respective ENGINE Technical Data section, but it should be noted that the engine must be at normal operating temperature to get reliable readings.

1. First run the engine up to normal operating temperature.
2. Remove all the spark plugs. When disconnecting the leads grasp the moulded cap and pull it off the plug. Do not pull on the lead itself otherwise the core inside the lead may be damaged.
3. Push or screw the connector of the compression tester into the No. 1 plug hole and, with the throttle held in the wide open position, crank the engine over with the starter. If the compression tester has to be held in position by hand hold it firmly ensuring that there is no leakage of compression.
4. As the engine turns, the gauge reading will increase in steps until the maximum pressure is reached. Note this reading carefully. The number of compression strokes, indicated by the 'pulses' on the gauge, required to reach the maximum pressure should also be noted.
5. Repeat this procedure for the other cylinders, noting in each case the reading obtained and the number of 'pulses'.
6. Compare the readings with the specified figure. If all the readings are high and within about 10% of each other this indicates that the engine is in good order, provided that the readings are close to the specified figure.
7. If one or more readings are low, the test should be repeated after injecting a small quantity of engine oil into the cylinder through the plug hole to form a seal between the piston and the cylinder wall. If a marked increase in pressure is then obtained, this shows that the leakage is mainly via the piston rings.
8. If no increase in compression is obtained, the fault must be due to leakage past the valves or gasket. However, it should be noted that if a cylinder has a badly scored bore, or damaged piston, the oil will fail to seal the leak and no improvement in compression will be obtained.
9. In any case, low readings will necessitate further investigation to determine the cause, and remedial action taken to correct it.

VALVE CLEARANCES . . . .[3]

The valve clearances should be checked and adjusted if necessary as detailed in the respective ENGINE section.

1. NORMAL — Core nose will be lightly coated with grey-brown deposits. Replace after 10,000 miles.

2. HEAVY DEPOSITS — Condition could be due to worn valve guides. Plug can be used again after servicing.

3. CARBON FOULING — Caused by rich mixture through faulty carburettor, choke or a clogged air cleaner.

4. OIL FOULING — Caused by worn valve guides, bores or piston rings. Hotter plug may cure.

5. OVERHEATING — Reasons could be over-advanced ignition timing, a worn distributor or weak fuel mixture.

6. PRE-IGNITION — This problem is caused through serious overheating. This could result in engine damage.

Fig. B:1 Typical spark plug conditions and the reasons why

Fig. B:2 Adjusting the value rocker clearances - OHV type engine shown

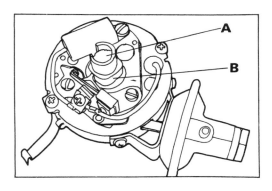

Fig. B:3 Apply two drops of engine oil to wick (A) and small blob of HMP grease to cam (B)

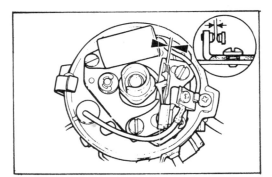

Fig. B:4 Check the contact points gap with heel of moving contact on top of lobe

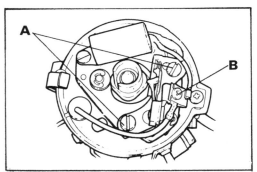

Fig. B:5 To replace contacts, detach LT/condenser wires (B) and undo screws (A)

SPARK PLUGS. . . . . [4]

Inspection

The spark plugs should be removed and examined periodically. When disconnecting the HT leads from the plugs, grasp the moulded cap and pull it off the plug. Do not pull on the plug lead itself otherwise the core inside the lead may be damaged.

Blow or brush any dirt away from around the plug base before removing the plug from the cylinder head.

Inspect the condition of the insulator tip and plug electrode as this can give a good indication as to the general state of the engine.

Typical examples of spark plug conditions are shown in Fig. B:1, and should be interpreted as follows:

Normal (Fig. B:1.1)

Ideally the plugs should look like the condition shown in this photograph. The colour of the electrodes should appear greyish-brown or tan-coloured. White to yellow deposits usually mean that the car has been used for long periods at high, constant speeds. Provided that the sparking plugs have not covered a large mileage they can be cleaned, re-set and refitted.

Heavy Deposits (Fig. B:1.2)

The sparking plug in this condition will probably look worse than it is. Heavy deposits could mean worn valve guides. When deposits have been cleaned off the sparking plug should be okay to use again providing it is not worn.

Carbon Fouled (Fig. B:1.3)

This is identified by dry, fluffy deposits which result from incomplete combustion. Too rich an air/fuel mixture or faulty action of the automatic choke can cause incomplete burning. The mixture being too rich can often be traced to a dirty or blocked air cleaner.

Defective contact breaker points or high tension cables can reduce voltage supplied to the sparking plug and cause misfiring. If fouling is evident in only one or two cylinders, sticking valves may be the problem. Excessive idling, slow speeds or stop/start driving can also keep plug temperatures so low that normal combustion deposits are not burned off.

Oil Fouled (Fig. B:1.4)

These are identified by black wet sludge deposits and is traceable to oil entering the combustion chamber either past the pistons and bores or through the valve guides. Hotter sparking plugs may cure the problem temporarily, but in severe cases an engine overhaul is called for.

Overheated (Fig. B:1.5)

Sparking plugs are usually identified by a white or blistered insulator nose and badly eroded electrodes. The engine overheating, or improper ignition timing could be responsible for this problem. If only a couple of sparking plugs are affected the cause may be uneven distribution of the coolant. Abnormal fast driving for sustained periods can also cause higher temperatures in the combustion chambers and, in these circumstances, colder sparking plugs should be used.

Adjusting

Spark plugs which are in good condition and with low mileage can be cleaned, preferably with a proper sandblast cleaner, but a stiff wire brush will also do. Clean the electrode surfaces and file them flat with a points file.

Check the electrode gap with a gap setting gauge or feeler gauges. The gap should be:-
OHV engines . . . . 0.030 in (0.75 mm)
OHC engines. . . . . 0.025 in (0.65 mm)

If necessary, adjust the gap by bending the outer electrode - NEVER attempt to bend the central electrode, otherwise the ceramic insulator may be cracked or broken.

When fitting new spark plugs, the electrode gaps should be checked before installing them in the engine. Ensure the replacement plugs are of the correct grade - see Service Data for specified types.

Great care should be taken to avoid overtightening the plug in the cylinder head. The OHV engines use gasket seated plugs and these should be tightened a maximum of 1/4 turn (90°) past finger tight. The OHC engines have taper-seat plugs and these must not be tightened more than 1/16th of a turn after finger tightening, otherwsie the interlocking action of the conical faces can make removal very difficult - if not impossible.

DISTRIBUTOR. . . . . [5]

Lubrication

The distributor should be lubricated at the specified intervals and when renewing the contact breaker points.

Apply one or two drops of oil only to the wick in the end of the distributor cam spindle (Fig. B:3).

Smear the contact surface of the distributor cam lightly with suitable high melting point grease or petroleum jelly.

Do not over-lubricate any part of the distributor. Take great care to avoid getting grease or oil onto the contact points as this will cause burning with consequent bad starting.

Contact Breaker Points

Remove the distributor cap and rotor arm and examine the distributor points. Points which are worn or badly burned should be renewed. Points which have become dirty or contaminated with oil or grease should be cleaned with meths and a stiff brush.

In most cases it will be more expedient to fit new contact breaker points rather than attempt to clean up the existing ones.

To renew the points, first disconnect the condenser

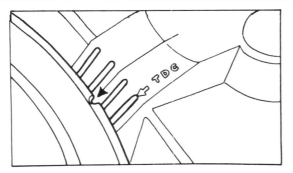

Fig. B:6 Ignition timing scale on the OHV engine.
Static setting 6 deg BTDC

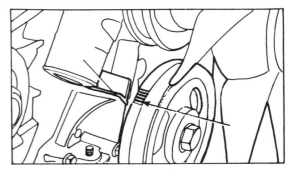

Fig. B:7 Ignition timing scale - OHC engine. For
correct setting, see Technical Data section

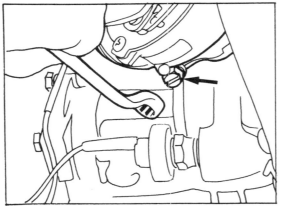

Fig. B:8 The location of the distributor clamp
bolt - OHV engine type shown

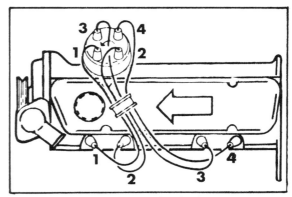

Fig. B:9 The distributor plug lead arrangement
and ignition firing order - OHV engine

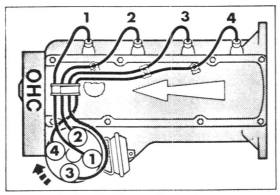

Fig. B:10 The distributor plug lead arrangement
and ignition firing order - OHC engine

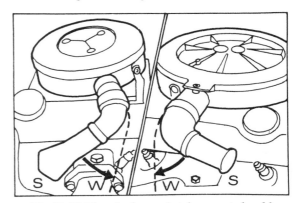

Fig. B:11 The air cleaner intake spout should
always be turned according to season

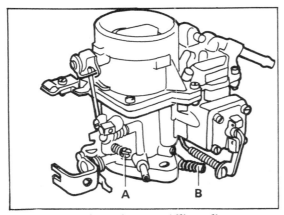

Fig. B:12 The carburettor idling adjustment
screws on Motorcraft carburettor

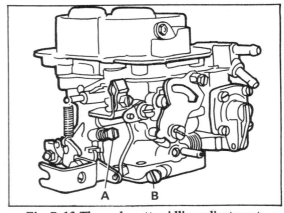

Fig. B:13 The carburettor idling adjustment
screws on Weber type carburettors

lead and LT lead from the terminal block on the contact set (Fig. B:5). Remove the two screws securing the contact set to the base plate and lift it out of the distributor. Take great care to ensure the securing screws are not dropped down inside the distributor body as, if this happens, the distributor must be removed to retrieve the screw.

Before installing the new contact set, clean out the inside of the distributor thoroughly. Wipe clean the contact surface of the breaker cam. Also wipe clean the contact faces of the points on the new set as these are normally coated with preservative. Methylated spirit is ideal for this purpose.

Position the new contact set on the base plate and secure with the locking screws. Tighten the screws only lightly at this stage. Reconnect the LT and condenser leads.

Lubricate the distributor cam and cam spindle as described above.

Check that the contact face of the fixed and moving contacts are parallel to each other, aligning them correctly if necessary.

Turn the engine over by hand until the rubbing block on the breaker arm is resting on the top of the cam lobe. Adjust the position of the fixed contact by moving the contact breaker bracket until the specified gap is obtained between the contact points. The feeler gauge should be a neat sliding fit between the contacts. (Fig. B:4).

When fitting new points it is advisable to set the gap slightly wider to allow for initial bedding in of the rubbing block.

When the gap is correct, tighten the locking screws. Turn the engine over until the rubbing block is on the opposite cam (180°) and re-check the clearance.

After fitting new points or adjusting the points gap, the dwell angle and ignition timing should be checked as described below.

Dwell Angle

For maximum efficiency and economy the contact breaker points setting should be checked with a dwell meter. Its use is particularly important in the case of used points where metal transfer has taken place between the points making accurate checking difficult using feeler gauges.

Relatively inexpensive units are available from most good accessory shops, and in some cases can even be hired.

The dwell angle of the ignition points is the angle of point closure. The wider the points gap the smaller will be the dwell angle, and vice-versa.

The specified limits for checking the dwell angle are:-
OHV engines . . . . .38 - 40°
OHC 1600 engines. . . . . .48 - 52°
OHC 2000 engines. . . . . .38 - 40°

If the reading is outside these limits, it should be reset as near as possible to the mean figure.

With new points it is good practice to set the dwell angle to the lower limit as the angle will increase (gap close) as the points rubbing block beds-in.

Connect the dwell meter in accordance with the manufacturer's instructions. Start the engine and run it at idle, then read off the dwell angle indicated on the meter. If the reading is outside the checking limits above, remove the distributor cap and rotor arm and adjust the contact breaker points to obtain the correct setting, while cranking the engine over on the starter.

As a check on the distributor condition, make a second reading with the engine speed increased to about 2,000 rpm. The needle of the dwell meter should then not deviate from the previous figure by more than 1^O. A larger deviation indicates that the distributor shaft is worn.

When the dwell angle has been adjusted, the ignition timing must be reset as detailed below.

Distributor Cap & Rotor Arm

Thoroughly clean the distributor cap, inside and out, with a clean cloth, paying particular attention to the spaces between the metal electrodes inside the cap. Check that the electrodes are not excessively eroded, and that there are no signs of tracking. Tracking is visible as hairlines on the surface of the cap and is caused by the HT voltage shorting between the electrodes or the central brush and an electrode. Once tracking is present it cannot be eliminated and the cap must be discarded. Also check that the small carbon brush in the centre of the cap is undamaged.

Similarly, clean the rotor arm and inspect for damage or excessive erosion of the electrode. Also check that the rotor is a neat sliding fit on the distributor spindle without excessive side-play.

Clean the outside surface of the central tower on the ignition coil and check for signs of damage or tracking.

Wipe all grease and dirt from the HT leads and check the leads for signs of cracking, chafing, etc. Ensure that all connections at the spark plugs, ignition coil and distributor cap are secure, and the moisture seals at each end of the HT leads are firmly in place.

IGNITION TIMING . . . . [6]

The contact breaker points gap or dwell angle must be correctly set before attempting to check or adjust the ignition timing. Conversely, the ignition setting should be checked after cleaning, renewing or resetting the contact breaker points.

Static Check

During this procedure the engine can be turned over using a suitable socket or ring spanner on the crankshaft pulley centre-bolt. Crankshaft rotation is clockwise, viewed from the front.

Locate the timing scale or notch on the crankshaft pulley and thoroughly clean both the scale and timing pointer on the cylinder block so that the marks can be observed. It will facilitate the timing operation if the notch or pointer and the appropriate mark on the timing scale are emphasised with white paint (Figs. B:6 and B:7).

Remove the distributor cap and connect a 12 volt test lamp between the distributor LT terminal and a good earth.

Rotate the crankshaft in its normal direction of rotation until the rotor arm is pointing approximately midway between the No. 1 and previous segment in the distributor. Note the direction of rotor arm rotation.

With the ignition switch on, continue rotating the crankshaft slowly until the test lamp just lights, indicating the points have opened. This gives the firing point for No. 1 cylinder. If the ignition setting is correct, the notch or pointer will now be aligned with the appropriate mark on the timing scale as shown in the diagram(Fig. B:6 and B:7).

The setting can be checked by gently pressing the rotor arm in the opposite direction to its normal rotation, when the test lamp should go out until the arm is released again.

If the timing is incorrect, it should be adjusted as described below.

Adjustment (Fig. B:8)

Turn the crankshaft until the notch or pointer is aligned with the specified mark on the timing scale. Slacken the distributor clamp bolt and rotate the distributor body past the point where the test lamp illuminates, then carefully rotate it back until the lamp just goes out. Tighten the clamp bolt without disturbing the body setting. Finally, recheck the setting as described above.

Dynamic Check

If possible, the ignition timing should be checked at idle speed using a stroboscopic timing light, as this will ensure optimum engine performance. In this case the equipment manufacturer's instructions should be followed.

The distributor vacuum pipe should be disconnected and plugged. With the engine running at normal idling speed, the ignition setting should be the same as that given for the static timing.

If adjustment is required, slacken the distributor clamp bolt and rotate the distributor body anti-clockwise to advance the setting or clockwise to retard it.

FUEL PUMP . . . . [7]

Filter Screen

A nylon mesh filter screen is incorporated in the fuel pump cover and this should be cleaned periodically to prevent the build-up of dirt and sediment.

As with any other part of the fuel system, it is recommended that the battery be disconnected before starting work on the fuel pump.

The pump top cover is secured by a single screw. Remove the screw and detach the cover. The filter screen is retained in the cover by the cover sealing ring and can be removed after prising out the seal (Fig. B:00).

Wash the cover and filter screen in petrol. Also clean any sediment from the chamber in the pump.

Inspect the sealing ring and renew if perished, worn, or otherwise damaged.

Carefully refit the filter in the pump cover and secure in position with the sealing ring. Ensure that the ring fits

correctly into the cover location. Assemble the cover to the pump and secure with the centre-screw. Some models have a notch in the cover and this must locate correctly in the groove in the pump housing.

When assembly is complete, start the engine and check for petrol leakage at the pump cover.

AIR CLEANER. . . . . [8]

Filter Element (Fig. B:11)

It is important that the air cleaner be serviced regularly as a dirty element will restrict the air flow to the carburettor intake, causing an over-richening of the fuel mixture, with subsequent increase in fuel consumption and loss of power.

The paper filter element in the air cleaner should normally be renewed every 18,000 miles (30.000 km) or every 2 years. However, in very dusty conditions the element should be cleaned or renewed more frequently.

On 1300 and 1600 OHV models the air cleaner lid is secured only by two self-tapping screws, and once removed the lid can be unclipped and the element lifted out.

On 1600 and 2000 OHC models the complete air cleaner assembly must first be removed from the engine. The cleaner is secured to the carburettor by four screws. Undo and remove the screws and carefully prise the two mounting stays clear of the carburettor to release the assembly. Once removed from the car, remove the further five screws securing the lid, unclip the lid and lift out the filter element.

CARBURETTOR . . . . [9]

As a requirement of the ECE and EEC vehicle 'Build' regulations "tamperproof" carburettors have been fitted progressively from mid-May 1975. The purpose of this requirement is to prevent unqualified persons from making adjustments which could increase emissions above a predetermined level, either through lack of understanding or unsuitable measuring equipment.

Two types of carburettor are used: both OHV and 1600 OHC models are equipped with a FoMoCo or Motorcraft single-barrel down-draught carburettor. On later 1300 cc OHV and 1600 cc OHC models a Motorcraft 'increased severity' carburettor is fitted which incorporates a 'by-pass' idle system. It is visually similar to the earlier carburettors but can be identified by comparing the number of screws retaining the upper body. The new unit has seven screws, the earlier model six. Servicing procedure is identical to the earlier type carburettor.

1600 GT and 2000 OHC vehicles have a Weber dual-barrel down-draught carburettor. On later 1600 and 2000 cc OHC models a Weber 'by-pass' carburettor is fitted, features of which are two independent idling systems. These systems are referred to as 'by-pass' idle and 'basic' idle. It is not necessary to service the 'basic' system at regular intervals - only when overhaul of the carburettor has been completed, or if correct idle cannot be achieved using the 'by-pass' adjuster.

The new carburettor can be easily identified by a plastic cap which is fitted to the 'basic' idle screw.

Also fitted to the later models is a fuel return flow line incorporated into the Weber carburettor and linked to the fuel tank. Identification is by cast housing on top of the carburettor at the supply pipe. Flow is indicated by two arrows and one outlet is blanked off.

Idle Adjustment - Motorcraft/Weber Carburettor (Early Types)(Figs. B:12 and B:13)

The carburettor slow running adjustment should preferably be set with the aid of a vacuum gauge or an E.G.A. (exhaust gas analyser), but can be set without these instruments. However, in each case, the crankcase ventilation system regulator valve must be connected to the inlet manifold while carrying out the adjustment.

With the engine at normal operating temperature, adjust the throttle stop screw to obtain satisfactory idling speed. Unscrew the volume control screw until the engine begins to "hunt" (i.e. run irregularly or lumpily), then screw it in again until the engine runs evenly. Re-adjust the throttle stop screw to obtain suitable engine idle speed. Repeat the operation if necessary, until a satisfactory idle is obtained.

Idle Adjustment - Motorcraft/Weber Carburettor (Later Type)

As stated previously, the only adjustment permissible is the correction of the idle speed setting.

This should be carried out with the engine at normal operating temperature. Stabilise the engine by running it at fast idle (approx. 3.000 rev/min) for about half a minute to clear the intake manifold of excess fuel.

On models with automatic transmission, select the 'P' or 'N' range and fully apply the handbrake when carrying out the idle adjustment.

Wait for the engine speed to stabilise, then adjust the idle speed screw (Motorcraft carb.) or the By-pass idle speed screw (Weber carb.) to achieve the correct idle speed of 825 ± 25 rev/min.

The locations of the carburettor adjusting screws are shown in the FUEL section.

Tune-up Data

OHV ENGINE 1300, 1600 cc (1.3 LITRE)

Compression pressure	131 to 159 lb/sq in (9 to 11 kg/cm^2)
Valve clearances:	
Inlet	0.008 in (0.20 mm)
Exhaust	0.022 in (0.55 mm)
Spark plugs:	
Type	Motorcraft AGR 22 standard, AGR 32 economy
Electrode gap	0.030 in (0.75 mm)
Firing order	1 - 2 - 4 - 3
Contact breaker gap	0.025 - 0.028 in (0.6 - 0.7 mm)
Dwell angle	38° to 40°
Ignition timing, static	6° BTDC
Idling speed	800 ± 25 rev/min
Emission at idle - 75 on, 1.3 litre economy model	1.5% vol CO

OHC ENGINE 1600, 2000 cc (1.6 & 2.0 LITRE)

Compression pressure	157 to 184 lb/sq in (11 to 13 kg/cm^2)
Valve clearances:	
Inlet	0.008 in (0.20 mm)
Exhaust	0.010 in (0.25 mm)
Spark plugs:	
Type	Motorcraft BF 32
Electrode gap	0.025 in (0.65 mm)
Firing order	1 - 3 - 4 - 2
Contact breaker gap:	
Motorcraft distributor	0.025 - 0.028 in (0.6 - 0.7 mm)
Dwell angle	
1.6 litre engines	48 to 52°
2.0 litre engines	38 to 40°
Ignition timing, Static:	
1600, 1.6 litre	6° BTDC
2000, 2.0 litre	4° BTDC
Later emission models - 75 on	8° BTDC
Idling speed	
OHC engines	825 ± 25 rev/min
Emission at idle: - 75 on	
1.6 litre	0.5% vol CO
2.0 litre	1.5% vol CO

NON-START
Trouble Shooter

FAULT	CAUSE	CURE
Starter will not turn engine (headlights dim)	1. Battery low 2. Faulty battery 3. Corroded battery cables or loose connections 4. Starter jammed 5. Seized engine	1. Charge battery and check charging system. 2. Fit new battery. 3. Clean battery connections or replace battery leads. Tighten battery and starter-motor connections. 4. Free starter. 5. Remove spark-plugs to confirm.
Starter will not turn engine (headlights bright)	1. Faulty starter solenoid 2. Faulty starter engagement (starter-motor whine) 3. Faulty starter 4. Faulty ignition switch	1. Replace solenoid. 2. Clean or replace starter bendix. 3. Repair or replace starter motor. 4. Fit new switch.
Engine turns slowly but will not start	1. Battery low 2. Faulty battery 3. Corroded battery leads or loose connections 4. Faulty starter	1. Charge battery and check charging system. 2. Replace battery. 3. Clean battery connections or replace battery leads. Tighten connections. 4. Repair or replace starter motor.
Engine turns but will not fire	1. Ignition fault 2. No spark at plug lead 3. Spark at plug lead 4. Fuel reaching carburettor 5. No fuel to carburettor 6. Check fuel pump	1. Check for spark at plug lead. 2. Check coil output to confirm high or low-tension fault. If spark from coil, check HT leads, distributor cap and rotor arm, particularly for cracks, tracking or dampness. If no spark from coil, check ignition-coil connections and contact-breaker points for short circuits or disconnection. 3. Remove air cleaner from carburettor and check choke operation. Loosen petrol-pipe union at carburettor. Turn engine by starter for a mechanical pump, or switch on ignition for electric pump. Check if petrol is being delivered. 4. Look into carburettor mouth. Operate throttle and observe whether damp or dry. If dry, clean jets and needle valve. If damp, remove spark-plugs, dry, clean and check gaps. 5. Remove petrol-tank cap and check for fuel. 7. Remove pump-top cover, clean pump filter and make sure the cover, when refitted, is airtight. Check flexible pipe to pump for air leaks.
Engine backfires	1. Ignition timing faulty 2. Damp distributor cap and leads	1. Check and reset ignition timing. 2. Dry thoroughly and check firing order.

Engine – ohv

OVERHAUL PROCEDURES . . . . [1]

Little overhaul or repair work can be carried out on the cylinder block assembly while the engine is installed in the car as the sump cannot be removed without first lifting out the engine. The oil pump, however, is located on the side of the cylinder block on this engine and can be removed for inspection and overhaul with the engine still in the car.

The crankshaft front and rear oil seals can be replaced with the engine still installed, but in the case of the rear oil seal the abutment flange on the oil seal carrier must first be cut-away with a special tool to allow the old oil seal to be withdrawn, and thus is not really a practical proposition.

The removal and installation of the engine ancillary components, i.e. water pump, distributor, alternator, etc., are not included in this section as these are covered in the relevant sections later in the manual.

Many operations require the use of special tools which it is unlikely that the normal owner-driver will posses. Wherever possible, a practical alternative using easily obtainable items is given, but unfortunately this does not always apply. In such cases it will be necessary to contract the work out to a local Machine Shop or Specialist Engineering Firm who will have the facilities and knowledge to carry out the job satisfactorily.

VALVE CLEARANCES . . . . [2]

The rocker cover must first be removed. Lift off the air cleaner after prising the three mounting stays clear of the cleaner body. Disconnect the HT leads from the spark plugs; pull off by grasping the moulded cap, not by pulling on the lead itself. Remove the 4 screws securing the rocker cover and lift it off together with its gasket.

It will facilitate turning over the engine if the spark plugs are removed at this point (see Tune-Up).

Crank the engine until the notch on the crankshaft pulley is aligned with TDC mark on the timing scale on the front cover. It will facilitate matters if the notch on the pulley is suitably marked with white paint to make it more easily seen. Throughout the adjustment procedure the engine must only be cranked in its normal direction of rotation (clockwise).

By turning the crankshaft to and fro a little and, at the same time, observing the rocker assembly, it can be determined whether the valves for No. 1 and No. 4 cylinder are rocking. The two rocker arms will be moving in opposite directions, the exhaust just closing and the inlet just starting to open. If the valves of No. 4 cylinder are rocking, the valve clearances at No. 1 cylinder should be:
1300/1600 OHV (cold).
Inlet 0.008 in (0.20 mm) Exhaust 0.020 in (0.55 mm)
1600 OHV - GT (cold).
Inlet 0.010 in (0.025 mm) Exhaust 0.022 in (0.55 mm).

The setting is correct when the appropriate thickness of feeler gauge is a neat sliding fit between the end of the valve stem and the pad on the rocker arm.

The valve arrangement, from the front, is: Ex - In - In - Ex - Ex - In - In - Ex.

If adjustment is necessary, rotate the adjusting nut on the push rod end of the rocker arm until the correct gap is obtained (Fig. C:1). These adjusting nuts are self-locking and only a suitable size of ring spanner ro socket in good condition should be used to turn them. Do NOT use an open-ended spanner.

When adjustment at No. 1 (or No. 4) cylinder is complete, turn the crankshaft through half a turn and check the clearances at No.2 or No. 3 cylinder, which ever is appropriate, in the same manner. Continue turning the crankshaft half a turn at a time and checking the appropriate valve clearances until all four cylinder have been done. The sequence is as follows:

Cylinder No. 4 rocking - Adjust cylinder No. 1
Cylinder No. 3 rocking - Adjust cylinder No. 2
Cylinder No. 1 rocking - Adjust cylinder No. 4
Cylinder No. 2 rocking - Adjust cylinder No. 3

When adjustment is complete, refit the rocker cover, using a new gasket if necessary. Ensure that the tabs on the outside of the gasket are correctly located in the notches in the cover. Refit the spark plugs, if removed, and reconnect the spark plugs leads. Finally, refit the air

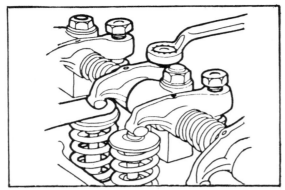

Fig. C:1 Adjust valve clearance by turning rocker adjusting screw with ring spanner

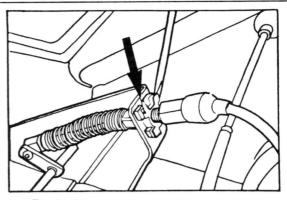

Fig. C:2 Disconnect throttle cable at throttle linkage and remove from abutment bracket

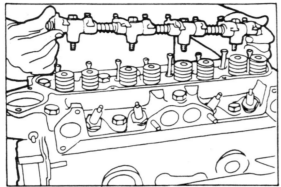

Fig. C:3 Rocker shaft assembly can be lifted off after unscrewing four rocker pedestal bolts

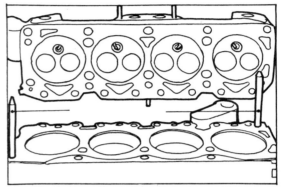

Fig. C:4 Installation of cylinder head will be simplified if two locating studs are fitted as shown

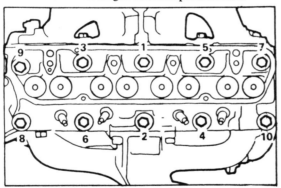

Fig. C:5 Tighten cylinder head bolts in sequence shown. Bolts are tightened in four stages

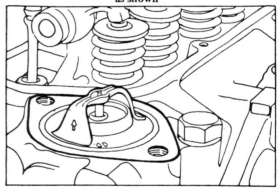

Fig. C:6 Ensure thermostat is located in cylinder head before refitting water outlet housing

Fig. C:7 Cover collet grooves in end of valve stem with adhesive foil or tape to avoid damaging seal during installation

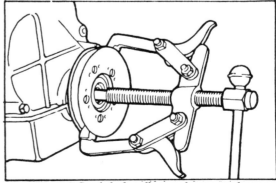

Fig. C:8 Crankshaft pulley can be removed using a suitable two-legged puller, as shown, or carefully levered off

cleaner assembly.

CYLINDER HEAD . . . . [3]

Removal

1. Disconnect the battery earth strap.
2. Drain the cooling system by disconnecting the bottom hose at the radiator. Also disconnect the top hose at the water outlet on the cylinder head.
3. Remove the air cleaner after prising the three mounting stays clear of the cleaner body.
4. Disconnect the choke cable at the carburettor. Disconnect the throttle cable from the throttle linkage and the abutment bracket on the engine (Fig. C:2). If difficulty is encountered in detaching the cable, refer to 'THROTTLE CABLE - Replacement' in the **Fuel System** section for details.
5. Disconnect the fuel chamber vent hose and the fuel supply hose at the carburettor. If the original crimped-type hose clamp is used in the latter case, this must be cut off and a new screwed type clamp used on reassembly.
6. Disconnect the distributor vacuum hose at the carburettor, the brake servo vacuum hose at the inlet manifold connection, and the engine breather hose at the oil separator.
7. Disconnect the heater hose at the inlet manifold water connection.
8. Detach the dipstick extension tube bracket from the inlet manifold.
9. Disconnect the wiring from the temperature sender unit on the cylinder head, and the HT leads from the spark plugs and ignition coil. Remove the distributor cap and rotor arm.
10. Remove the two nuts securing the exhaust pipe to the exhaust manifold.
11. Detach the water outlet housing from the front of the cylinder head and lift out the thermostat. (Fig. C:6).
12. Remove the spark plugs.
13. Remove the rocker cover and gasket.
14. Release the rocker shaft retaining bolts evenly and lift off the rocker assembly (Fig. C:3).
15. Lift out the push rods. Retain them in their correct order to ensure they are not interchanged during reassembly.
16. Release the cylinder head bolts evenly, in the reverse sequence to that shown in Fig. C:5, and lift off the cylinder head and gasket. Discard the head gasket.

Installation

Installation is a reversal of the removal procedure, with special attention to the following points:
a) Ensure that all joint surfaces, especially the mating surfaces of the cylinder head and block, are perfectly clean and free from old gasket material.
b) If the cylinder head was removed to replace a leaking or blown head gasket, check the mating faces on both the head and block for distortion before reassembly.
c) Use new gaskets where appropriate. A cylinder head

gasket set should be obtained, as this will contain all the necessary gaskets.
d) The use of two guide studs, made up and screwed into the cylinder head bolt holes, as shown in Fig. C:4, will facilitate correct alignment of the cylinder head and gasket during installation. Once the head is installed, the studs are then replaced by the proper cylinder head bolts.
e) Do not use sealing compound of any type on the cylinder head gasket.
f) The cylinder head bolts are of different lengths, two being shorter than the others, according to the varying height of the cylinder head. Ensure that the bolts are fitted in their correct respective positions.
g) Tighten the cylinder head bolts evenly, following the sequence of tightening shown in Fig. C:5. Note that the final tightening must be carried out after running the engine for 15 minutes . See **Tightening Torques**.
h) Ensure that the push rods are installed in their original positions. Dip the ends of the rods in clean engine oil prior to installing them.
i) When fitting the rocker shaft assembly, ensure that the rocker arm adjusting screws locate correctly in the cupped end of their respective push rods. If any work has been carried out on the valves (e.g. recutting the valve seats) the rocker arm adjusting screws should be released slightly before installing the rocker shaft assembly. Tighten the shaft pedestal bolts evenly to 28 lb ft (4.0 kgm).
j) Check the valve clearances, as detailed previously, and adjust if necessary.
k) When installation is complete, refill the cooling system, then run the engine and check for oil, water or exhaust leaks.
l) After the engine has been run at fast idle for 10 - 15 minutes, retighten the cylinder head bolts to the specified torque.
m) Finally, with the engine at normal operating temperature, check the ignition timing and engine idle setting, as detailed in the TUNE-UP section at the beginning of the manual.

Dismantling

1. Detach the inlet manifold, complete with the carburettor, from the cylinder head. Similarly, detach the exhaust manifold.
2. Remove all carbon deposits from the combustion chambers, valve heads and valve ports using a suitable scraper, such as a screwdriver, and a wire brush. Take care to avoid damaging the machined surface of the cylinder head.
3. Similarly, clean all deposits from the cylinder block face and piston crowns, but leave a ring of carbon around the outside of each piston and the top of each bore. Ensure that carbon particles are not allowed to enter the oil or water ways in the block. This can be prevented by plugging the passages with small pieces of cloth while the carbon is being removed.
4. At each valve in turn, compress the valve spring, using a suitable spring compressor tool, and extract the two split tapered collets from around the valve stem. Take great care to ensure the valve stem is not damaged by the spring retainer when pressing it down. Release the spring

Fig. C:9 Withdraw oil seal from front cover, using Special Tools Puller 15-048 and Adaptor 15-048-01

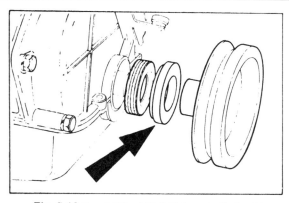

Fig. C:10 Special Tool 21-046 (arrowed) should be used to install new seal in cover

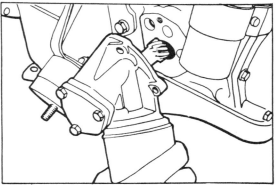

Fig. C:11 Oil pump is easily detached from cylinder block after removing three retaining bolts

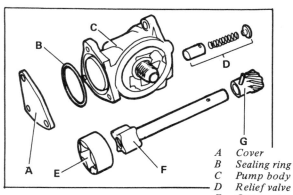

Fig. C:12 Details of oil pump assembly

A Cover
B Sealing ring
C Pump body
D Relief valve
E Outer rotor
F Inner rotor
G Drive gear

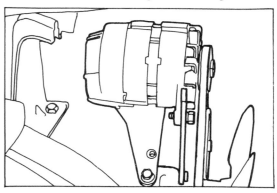

Fig. C:13 Remove alternator, together with its mounting bracket, from cylinder block

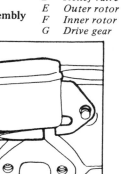

Fig. C:14 Remove oil separator by levering it up out of block with screwdriver

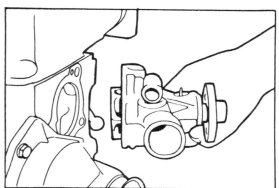

Fig. C:15 Water pump can be removed from block after unscrewing three retaining bolts

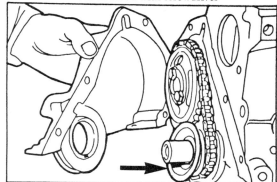

Fig. C:16 Removing timing cover and oil slinger. Note that oil slinger is fitted with concave side outwards

compressor tool and remove the spring retainer and valve spring. Remove the oil seal fitted to the valve stem and withdraw the valve from the cylinder head. Suitably mark the valve and associated components to identify their position in the cylinder head.

5. To dismantle the rocker assembly, remove the split pin from one end of the rocker shaft, and detach the flat washer, crimped spring washer and second flat washer which bear against the end rocker arm. The rocker arms, rocker shaft support pillars and springs can then be removed from the shaft. Note their respective positions for reassembly. If required, the plugs can be removed from each end of the shaft to facilitate cleaning, by piercing a hole in the plug and levering the plug out of the end of the rocker shaft.

Inspection & Overhaul

Clean the valves and seats, then examine them for signs of pitting, burning or other damage.

Examine the valve stems for abnormal wear and check the valve stem to guide clearance in its respective guide in the head. Replace any worn valves.

Push Rods

Clean the rods in solvent. Check the ends of the rods for nicks, grooves, roughness or excessive wear. Check each rod for straightness. Replace as necessary. Do NOT attempt to straighten a bent push rod.

The push rods can be checked visually for straightness while installed in the engine, by rotating them with the valve closed.

Rocker Gear

Inspect the shaft and rocker arm bores for nicks, scratches, scores or scuffs. Inspect the pad at the valve end of each rocker arm for indication of scuffing or abnormal wear. If the pad is grooved, replace the arm. Do NOT attempt to true the surface by grinding.

Check the fit of each rocker arm on the shaft. If the arm is a loose or sloppy fit, or if appreciable side-play is present, the shaft and/or arm should be replaced.

Check that all oil passages are clear. Replace any damaged adjusting screws.

Reassembly

Reassemble the cylinder head in the reverse order of dismantling, with special attention to the following points:
a) Lap in each valve in turn using coarse, followed by fine, grinding paste until a gas-tight seal is obtained at the seat. This will be indicated by a continuous matt-grey ring around the valve face and seat. When this has been achieved, clean all traces of paste from the cylinder head and valves - this is most important.

b) Lubricate the valve guides and valves with SAE 90 Hypoid Oil before installing the valves.
c). The valve stem seal must always be renewed. Cover the collet grooves in the end of the valve stem with adhesive foil or tape to avoid damaging the seal during installation (Fig. C:7). Lubricate the seal with oil to make fitting easier. Remove the foil once the seal is in position.
d) Ensure that the valve stem is not damaged by the spring retainer when compressing the valve spring, and that the split tapered collets engage correctly in the valve stem and spring retainer when the spring is released.
e) If the rocker assembly was dismantled, reassemble it in reverse order. If the end plugs were removed, install new plugs in each end of the shaft. The shaft must be positioned so that the oil feed holes in the shaft for rocker lubrication point downwards to the cylinder head. The bolt holes in the rocker shaft support pillars must be located on the same side as the adjusting screws in the rocker arms. The rocker arms are 'handed' and must be fitted on the shaft with the rocker pads inclined towards the support pillars. Install the split pins at the ends of the shaft with their heads upwards, and bend over their legs to secure.
f) When refitting the inlet manifold assembly, apply sealing compound to both sides of the manifold gasket at the central water way.

CRANKSHAFT FRONT OIL SEAL........[4]

Replacement

The crankshaft front oil seal is one of the most common sources of oil leakage on the engine but need not be tolerated as replacement is relatively simple.

The radiator must first be removed to allow access to the front of the engine. See **Cooling System** section for details.

Slacken the alternator mounting bolts and remove the fan belt. Detach the cooling fan and drive pulley from the water pump hub.

Remove the centre-bolt from the end of the crankshaft and withdraw the crankshaft pulley, using levers or a suitable puller (Fig. C:8).

Withdraw the oil seal from its location in the front cover, using the special tool shown in Fig. C:9, or by prising it out carefully with a screwdriver. Ensure that the bore in the cover is clean and undamaged. Apply a light film of oil to the sealing lip and outer surface of the new seal. Press the seal into position in the cover bore, using the special tool in conjunction with the crankshaft pulley and centre-bolt, as shown in Fig. C:10. If care is taken, the seal can also be pressed into place using a suitable size of socket, but bear only on the outer diameter of the seal during this operation.

Remove the Installer Tool and refit the crankshaft pulley and cooling fan. Refit the fan belt and adjust the tension to give a free-play of approximately 0.5 in (13 mm) at the midway point between the alternator and fan pulleys. Refit the radiator and refill the cooling system.

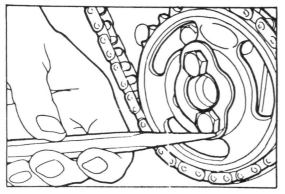

Fig. C:17 Bend back lock plate tabs and remove camshaft sprocket complete with timing chain

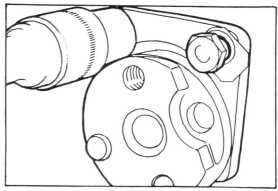

Fig. C:18 Camshaft can be withdrawn after removing thrust plate from front face of block

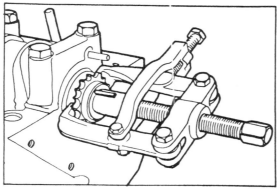

Fig. C:19 If required, sprocket can be pulled off crankshaft using suitable two-legged puller

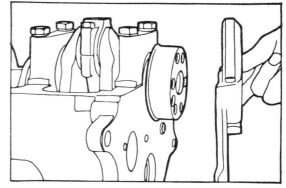

Fig. C:20 Rear oil seal is located in detachable carrier which is bolted to rear face of block

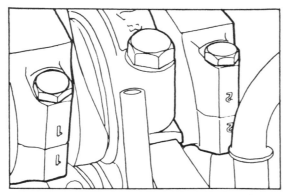

Fig. C:21 Check that markings on connecting rods and caps match before removing

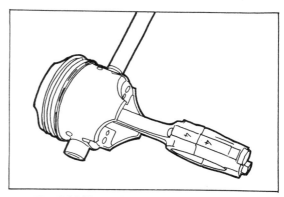

Fig. C:22 Piston pin can be tapped out after removing circlips from each end of bore

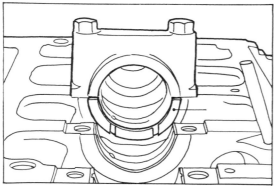

Fig. C:23 Position of half thrust washers at centre main bearing

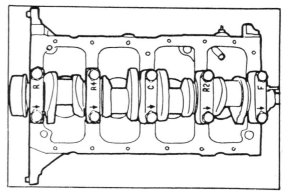

Fig. C:24 Ensure that main bearing caps are fitted correctly with arrows pointing forwards

Engine (OHV)

CRANKSHAFT REAR OIL SEAL . . . . [5]

Replacement

It is not really a practical proposition to attempt to replace the crankshaft rear oil seal while the engine is still installed in the car, as the abutment flange on the seal carrier must first be cut away to allow the old oil seal to be withdrawn. A special cutter tool is required to remove the abutment flange and this is not an item which is generally available. Also, special tools are required to remove and install the actual seal.

As an alternative, the complete carrier can be detached from the rear of the cylinder block, and a new seal fitted to the carrier while it is removed. In this case, great care must be taken when refitting the carrier to ensure that the gasket joint at the sump is correctly re-sealed.

OIL PUMP. . . . . [6]

Removal

Place a suitable container directly under the oil pump to catch any oil spilled during removal.

Unscrew the oil filter cartridge from the mounting pad on the underside of the pump. A strap wrench may be required to release the filter, if tight. See Fig. A:3 in the **Routine Maintenance** section.

Remove the three bolts securing the pump to the side of the cylinder block, and detach the pump assembly together with its gasket (Fig. C:11).

Installation

Ensure that the joint surfaces on the pump and cylinder block are clean and free from old gasket material.

If a new or overhauled oil pump is being fitted, it should be filled with oil and turned by hand through a complete rotation prior to installation.

Locate a new gasket on the pump mounting flange and fit the pump assembly to the cylinder block. Secure with the three retaining bolts.

Fit a new filter cartridge to the pump. Wet the seal on the cartridge with clean engine oil, then screw the cartridge onto the threaded adaptor by hand until the seal just contacts the pump housing. Tighten the cartridge by a further three quarters of a turn.

When installation is complete, check the engine oil and top us as necessary. Finally, run the engine and check for oil leaks at the pump and filter.

If leakage does occur, stop the engine immediately. Remove the pump and check the gasket position.

Overhaul

In most cases of wear or damage to the components of the oil pump, it will be more economical to obtain a complete new pump, rather than attempt to overhaul and fit new parts to the existing unit. The pump should be dis-

mantled and inspected to determine its condition as follows:

Hold the pump body with the cover end uppermost, then unbolt and remove the cover plate. Extract the rubber sealing ring from the groove in the pump body (Fig. C:12). Withdraw the outer rotor from the housing.

The rotors are a matched pair, and it is important that the outer rotor be fitted the correct way round. It should therefore be suitably marked on its outer face before removing it, to ensure it will be installed in its original position.

Wash the interior of the pump with petrol, using a brush to remove any metal or dirt particles, if necessary.

Inspect the inside of the pump housing and the rotors for damage or signs of excessive wear or scoring. Inspect the inside face of the pump cover for scores, grooves, or other signs of wear; if present, the cover must be replaced.

Refit the outer rotor, correctly orientated, in the pump body. Check the clearance between the outer rotor and the pump housing with feeler gauges. The wear limit is 0.011 in (0.27 mm).

Check the clearance between the lobes of the inner and outer rotors. The wear limit in this case is 0.005 in (0.13 mm).

Check the rotor end-float by placing a straight-edge across the face of the pump body, and measuring the clearance between the straight-edge and the end of the rotors. The clearance must not exceed 0.0025 in (0.064 mm). If the end-float is excessive, but the other clearances are within the wear limits, the pump face can be carefully lapped in on a flat surface to bring the end-float within the limit.

If any of the other clearances are excessive, the pump should be replaced as an assembly.

To reassemble the pump, locate a new sealing ring in the groove in the pump body. Lubricate the rotors and pump housing liberally with engine oil, then fit the cover plate with the machined face towards the rotors, and secure with the retaining bolts.

The pressure relief valve is located in the pump mounting face and will not normally require attention. However, if necessary, the valve and spring can be withdrawn for inspection after carefully extracting the spring seat which is a press fit in the pump body.

ENGINE REMOVAL & INSTALLATION . . . [7]

Removal

1. Disconnect the battery.
2. Remove the bonnet (4 bolts). It will facilitate refitting if the positions of the bonnet hinges are first marked by scribing a line around them.
3. Where fitted, remove the splash shield from under the engine compartment. The shield is secured in position by 4 bolts and 4 clips.
4. Drain the cooling system and remove the radiator, as detailed in the **Cooling System** section.
5. Drain the engine oil from the sump. Refit the sump plug after draining.
6. Remove the air cleaner assembly after prising the

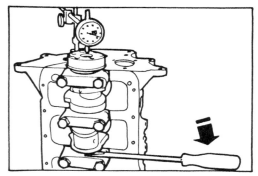

Fig. C:25 Crankshaft end-float can be checked using a dial indicator or with feeler gauges

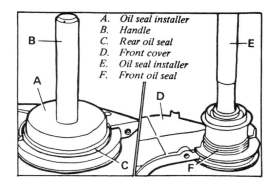

A. Oil seal installer
B. Handle
C. Rear oil seal
D. Front cover
E. Oil seal installer
F. Front oil seal

Fig. C:26 Install oil seals in rear carrier and timing cover, using Special Tools shown

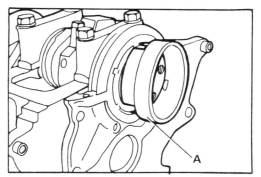

Fig. C:27 Special Tool is used to centralise rear oil seal carrier. If tool is not available this can be done by eye

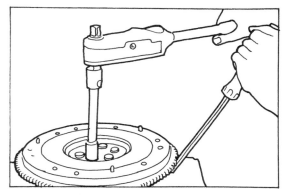

Fig. C:28 Lock flywheel with screwdriver, as shown, when tightening retaining bolts

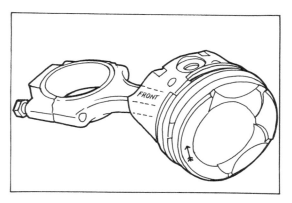

Fig. C:29 Piston must be assembled to connecting rod in relationship shown

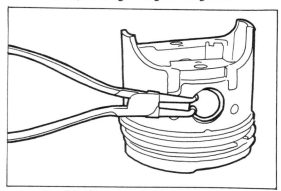

Fig. C:30 Ensure circlips locate correctly in grooves in piston bore

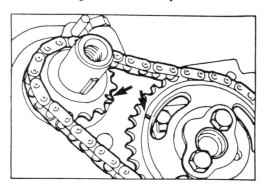

Fig. C:31 Fit camshaft sprocket so that timing marks on gears are aligned

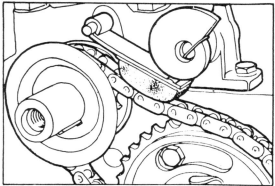

Fig. C:32 After fitting tensioner arm, release tensioner wheel so that spring pressure moves arm into correct position

Engine (OHV)

three mounting stays clear of the cleaner body.

7.   Disconnect the heater hoses from the water pump and inlet manifold connections.

8.   Disconnect the choke cable at the carburettor. Disconnect the throttle cable from the throttle linkage and the abutment bracket on the engine (Fig. C:2). If difficulty is encountered in detaching the cable, refer to 'THROTTLE CABLE - Replacement' in the **Fuel System** section for details.

9.   Disconnect the fuel supply hose at the fuel pump.

10. Disconnect the wiring multi-plug connector from the rear of the alternator, and the wiring from the temperature sender unit at the cylinder head and the oil pressure switch on the cylinder block. Also disconnect the engine earth strap.

11. Disconnect the distributor LT lead and the HT lead from the ignition coil.

12. Disconnect the brake servo vacuum hose at the inlet manifold connection.

13. Disconnect the starter motor lead, remove the starter motor retaining bolts and withdraw the starter motor.

14. Disconnect the exhaust down pipe from the exhaust manifold.

15. Detach the cover plate from the bottom of the clutch housing.

16. Attach a suitable sling or lifting brackets to the engine and support the weight with lifting tackle.

17. Remove the rubber insulators from between the engine mountings and the suspension crossmember at each side of the car.

18. Remove the bolts securing the engine to the transmission.

19. Suitably support the transmission, then draw the engine forwards to disengage it from the transmission and carefully lift it out of the engine compartment.

Installation

Installation is a simple reversal of the removal procedure, but special attention should be paid to the following points:

a)   Two locating dowels are provided on the engine rear flange to help locate the engine adaptor plate. If these were left behind in the transmission housing when the engine was removed, they must be transferred to their correct locations in the cylinder block.

b)   If the adaptor plate is a loose fit on the dowels, it can be temporarily secured to the cylinder block with two nuts and bolts to prevent it being dislodged during engine installation. Fit the bolts through the holes immediately above each of the tubular dowels, with the bolts head facing forwards, and secure with the nuts. Once the engine has been located securely on the transmission, the bolts can then be removed.

c)   Lightly grease the splines of the transmission input shaft before installing the engine. Also ensure that the clutch release lever is correctly positioned in the clutch housing. When installing the engine, it may be necessary to turn the engine over slowly to allow the splines on the gearbox input shaft to mesh with the clutch disc hub.

d)   Tighten the engine to transmission bolts evenly, so

that the engine is pulled squarely into place.

e)   Set the clutch cable adjustment as detailed in the **Routine Maintenance** section.

f)   Set the throttle cable adjustment, as detailed in the **Fuel System** section.

g)   Refill the engine with the recommended grade of oil. Approximately 6.2 pts (3.6 litres) of oil will be required, including the capacity of the oil filter.

h)   When installation is complete, run the engine and check for leaks.

i)   Finally, check the ignition timing and engine idle setting as detailed in the **Tune-Up** section at the beginning of the manual.

ENGINE OVERHAUL . . . . [8]

Dismantling

1.   Disconnect the fuel supply hose and the distributor vacuum pipe at the carburettor. Also disconnect the engine breather hose from the oil separator by withdrawing the vent valve.

2.   Disconnect the HT leads from the spark plugs, detach the leads from the clip on the rocker cover and remove the distributor cap, complete with the leads. Remove the spark plugs.

3.   Remove the rocker cover and gasket. Detach the water outlet housing from the front of the cylinder head and lift out the thermostat.

4.   Release the rocker shaft retaining bolts evenly and lift off the rocker assembly (Fig. C:3). Lift out the push rods. Retain them in their correct order to ensure they are not interchanged during reassembly.

5.   Release the cylinder head bolts evenly, in the reverse sequence to that shown in Fig. C:5, and lift off the cylinder head, complete with the inlet and exhaust manifolds. Remove the head gasket.

6.   Remove the clutch pressure plate and clutch disc from the flywheel.

7.   Slacken the alternator mounting bolts, pivot the alternator towards the cylinder block and remove the fan belt. Detach the alternator, complete with its mounting bracket, from the cylinder block (Fig. C:13).

8.   Detach the cooling fan and drive pulley from the water pump hub. Remove the three bolts securing the water pump to the front face of the block, and detach the pump, together with its gasket (Fig. C:15). Note that the alternator adjusting link is also secured by one of the pump bolts.

9.   Remove the bolt securing the oil separator to the cylinder block, and prise the separator out of its location, using a screwdriver (Fig. C:14).

10. Remove the two bolts securing the fuel pump, and detach the pump together with its insulating spacer from the block.

11. Unscrew the distributor clamp plate bolt and withdraw the distributor from the cylinder block.

12. If not already drained, drain the engine oil. Refit the sump plug after draining.

13. Unscrew the oil filter cartridge. A strap wrench may

be required to release the filter, if tight. Remove the three bolts securing the oil pump, and detach the pump from its mounting pad.

14. If required, unscrew the oil pressure switch from its location next to the oil pump mounting pad.

15. Remove the centre-bolt from the front of the crankshaft and withdraw the crankshaft pulley, using levers or a suitable puller (Fig. C:8).

16. Remove the sump securing bolts and detach the sump from the lower face of the cylinder block. This should be done while the cylinder block is still mounted upright to prevent sludge and swarf from getting into the crankcase.

17. Invert the engine. A tray or other suitable container should be placed under the block to catch the remaining oil and coolant which will be released.

18. Remove the bolts securing the timing cover to the front of the cylinder block and detach the cover. Remove the oil slinger from the crankshaft (Fig. C:16).

19. Remove the bolt securing the oil pick-up pipe to the base of the crankcase and, moving the pipe to and fro, withdraw it from the cylinder block.

20. Unbolt the timing chain tensioner from the lower face of the cylinder block, then withdraw the tensioner arm from the pin on the front main bearing cap (Fig. C:32).

21. Release the lock plate tabs at the camshaft sprocket, (Fig. C:17), remove the two retaining bolts and detach the sprocket complete with the timing chain.

22. Turn the camshaft through one complete turn to move all the cam followers away from the cam lobes. Bend back the lock plate tabs and unscrew the two bolts securing the camshaft thrust plate (Fig. C:18). Remove the thrust plate and withdraw the camshaft from the cylinder block.

23. Extract the cam followers from their locations in the cylinder block, keeping them in their installed order to ensure correct assembly.

24. If required, withdraw the timing chain sprocket from the front end of the crankshaft, using a sutiable puller (Fig. C:19).Extract the woodruff key from the keyway in the crankshaft.

25. Check that the big end bearing caps and rods are suitably marked with their respective cylinder numbers (Fig. C:21). Turn the crank shaft as necessary to bring each connecting rod in turn to the bottom of its travel. Remove the big end bearing cap, together with its bearing shell. Push the piston and connecting rod assembly up the cylinder bore and carefully withdraw it from the top of the block. Remove the bearing shells from the cap and rod, and suitably identify them if they are to be re-used.

26. If required, remove the piston rings from the pistons by easing them up over the crown of the piston.

27. Detach the flywheel from the crankshaft flange. Remove the engine adaptor plate from the rear face of the cylinder block.

28. Unbolt and remove the rear oil seal carrier, together with its gasket, from the cylinder block (Fig. C:20).

29. Check that the main bearing caps are suitably marked with their respective locations. Release the cap retaining bolts and detach the main bearing caps together with their bearing shells. Carefully lift the crankshaft out of the

crankcase. Note the position of the two half thrust washers at the centre main bearing and mark them accordingly (Fig. C:23). Remove the bearing shells and thrust washers from the crankcase and bearing caps. Identify the shells if they are to be re-used.

30. Remove the crankshaft oil seals from the timing cover and rear oil seal carrier.

Inspection & Overhaul

The cylinder block and components should be inspected for obvious wear, scoring or other damage.

Excessively worn cylinder bores should be rebored oversize. Check the crankshaft, and the camshaft lobes using a micrometer.

The components of the cylinder head assembly have already been dealt with under the heading 'CYLINDER HEAD'.

Cylinder Bores

In production, the standard bore diameter is graded into six tolerance groups, the smallest diameter being identified by the grade letter 'A', and the largest by the letter 'F'. The grade size of each bore is stamped on the push rod side of the cylinder block, adjacent to the top face. Pistons are selected and fitted to correspond to the cylinder bore grading, thus giving the correct working clearance. The piston grade identification is marked on the piston crown.

Pistons & Connecting Rods

Service pistons are available in standard and oversize. When selecting a replacement piston in this case, measure the cylinder bore at a point 2.338 in (59.39 mm) from the cylinder block top face across the crankshaft axis. Measure the piston skirt diameter at a point 2.314 in (58.78 mm) from the piston crown at right-angles to the piston pin bore.

The piston pins are of the fully-floating type and are retained in position by circlips installed in grooves at each end of the piston pin bore. The pistons can be easily separated from the connecting rods by extracting the two piston pin circlips and pushing the piston pin out of the piston (Fig. C:22). It may be necessary to warm the piston slightly by immersing it in warm water to enable the pin to be removed. Suitably identify the various components of each assembly.

When reassembling the piston and connecting rod, ensure that they are fitted in the correct relationship to each other. The 'FRONT' marking on the rod must point in the same direction as the notch or arrow on the piston crown (Fig. C:29). Again heat the piston in water to expand it, then insert the piston pin, lightly oiled, through the piston and connecting rod. Ensure that the two retaining circlips engage correctly in their grooves in the piston bore (Fig. C:30).

Oil Pump

Inspection of the oil pump assembly has already been

covered under its own heading earlier in this section.

Auxiliary Shaft

An auxiliary shaft is not fitted in this engine, the oil pump, distributor and fuel pump being driven directly from the camshaft in the cylinder block.

Camshaft

Inspect the cam lobes and journals for signs of scoring or abnormal wear. Lobe wear characteristics may result in slight pitting in the general area of the lobe toe, but this is not detrimental to the operation of the camshaft, and the camshaft need not therefore be replaced unless the lobe lift loss exceeds 0.005 in (0.127 mm).

Check the teeth of the skew gear on the camshaft for wear or damage. If damaged, the camshaft must be replaced. In this case, the skew gears on the oil pump and distributor should also be checked.

The camshaft runs in three steel-backed white metal bearings in the cylinder block. If one or more of these bearings are worn or damaged, all three bearings should be replaced, otherwise camshaft alignment may be affected. Replacement should be entrusted to a Specialist Engineering Firm, as special service tools are required to ensure correct alignment of the bearings during installation.

Check the cam followers for wear or scoring. Followers which are only slightly worn on their lower face may be used again with the original camshaft, but replacement is preferable. New cam followers must always be used when fitting a new camshaft.

Timing Gear

Inspect both the camshaft and crankshaft timing sprockets for cracks and worn or damaged teeth.

Inspect the timing chain for wear or looseness at the link pins.

Inspect the rubber pad on the tensioner arm. In use, the chain links wear two grooves in the pad so that the chain runs directly on the roller. Do NOT dress the surface of the pad in an attempt to remove the grooves. If necessary, the arm should be replaced.

Reassembly

1. Install the selected main bearing shells dry in the crankcase and main bearing caps. Ensure that the locating tab on each shell correctly engages the corresponding notch in the housing.
2. Install the two half thrust washers on each side of the centre main bearing housing, with the oil grooves facing away from the centre bearing (Fig. C:23).
3. Lubricate the bearing surfaces of the bearing shells and crankshaft journals liberally with oil, then carefully lower the crankshaft into position in the crankcase.
4. Fit the main bearing caps in their respective locations (Fig. C:24). The cast arrows on the caps must point towards the front of the engine. The intermediate and rear main bearing caps are identical, but must NOT be inter-

changed. Normally these are marked by a number '2' cast beside the letter 'R' on the front intermediate cap (No. 2 bearing), and '4' on the rear intermediate cap (No. 4 bearing). The rear cap has only an 'R' cast. The front and centre bearing caps are marked 'F' and 'C' respectively. Tighten the cap bolts evenly to their specified torque of 57 lb ft (8.0 kgm), then check that the crankshaft rotates freely and smoothly.
5. Check the crankshaft end-float. This can be done using either a dial indicator, as shown in Fig. C:25, or with feeler gauges. If feeler gauges are being used, lever the crankshaft fully forwards to take up the endfloat in one direction, then measure the gap between the thrust washer at the front of the centre main bearing and the crankshaft web. The end-float should be 0.003 - 0.011 in (0.08 - 0.28 mm). If it exceeds the upper limit, the thrust washers must be replaced with new ones, or ones of suitable oversize, to bring the figure within the limits.
6. Press new crankshaft seals into the timing cover and rear seal carrier as shown in Fig. C:26. Lubricate the outside diameter of the seals to facilitate installation.
7. Lubricate the sealing lip of the crankshaft rear oil seal. Position a new gasket on the rear face of the cylinder block and slide the rear seal carrier over the crankshaft. The use of Carrier Centraliser Tool 21 - 029, shown in Fig. C:27, will ensure correct alignment of the carrier, but if this is not available the seal should be centred on the crankshaft flange by eye. Ensure that the carrier is in line with sump mating surface on the block.
8. Position the engine adaptor plate on the rear face of the block. Check that the mating surfaces on the crankshaft rear flange and flywheel are perfectly clean, then locate the flywheel squarely on the flange and tap it into place. Apply oil resistant sealer to the threads of the retaining bolt, then fit and tighten the bolts to their specified torque of 53 lb ft (7.5 kgm). The crankshaft can be locked in position, using a screwdriver as shown in Fig. C: 28, when tightening the bolts. Re-use only bolts which are in good condition. If any bolts are suspect, they should be renewed.
9. Assemble the piston rings on the pistons, following the instructions supplied with the new rings. The rings must be fitted from the top of the piston. The rings will normally be marked 'TOP' on one face, and this side should face towards the piston crown. Service rings for use in worn bores normally have a stepped top ring to avoid the wear ridge at the top of the bore. If is most important that these rings be fitted with the stepped portion uppermost, otherwise breakage of the rings will result when the engine is run.

Where possible, proper piston ring pliers should be used to expand the rings when installing them as this will eliminate the possibility of ring breakage or damage to the piston.
10. For each piston and connecting rod assembly in turn:
a) Check that the piston is correctly assembled to its respective connecting rod (Fig. C:29).
b) Lubricate the cylinder bore and piston rings liberally with engine oil.
c). Install the piston assembly in its correct respective bore, with the notch or arrow on the piston crown point-

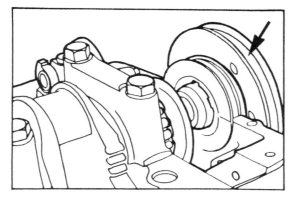

Fig. C:33 Use crankshaft pulley to centre front cover before fitting retaining bolts

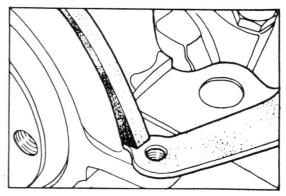

Fig. C:34 Apply sealing compound at joints of timing cover and rear seal carrier

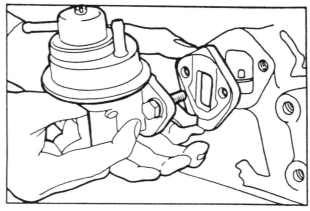

Fig. C:35 Ensure pump operating arm lies on camshaft eccentric when pump is installed on block

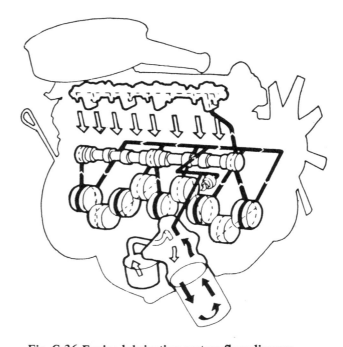

Fig. C:36 Engine lubrication system flow diagram

Engine (OHV)

ing towards the front of the block.

d) Position the bottom piston ring so that the gap is to the rear of the piston. The centre ring should be positioned with the gap at 90° to this, and the top ring gap a further 90° round.

e) Compress the piston rings using a proper ring compressor tool, such as that shown in Fig. D:39 in the **OHC Engine** section. Do NOT attempt to fit the pistons by hand, otherwise breakage of the rings may result. Carefully tap the piston into the cylinder bore, using the handle end of a hammer, until the piston crown is slightly below the top of the cylinder. Take great care to avoid the connecting rod hitting the crankshaft journal.

f) Fit the bearing shells dry in the connecting rod and cap. Ensure that the retaining tab on each shell correctly engages the corresponding notch in the bearing housing.

g) Coat the crankshaft journal and bearings liberally with engine oil, then pull the connecting rod assembly down firmly onto the crankshaft journal and fit the cap to the rod. Check that the identification numbers on the cap and rod match, and are on the same side of the assembly (Fig. C:22). Ensure that the cap is correctly located on the two dowel pins, then tighten the cap bolts to their specified torque of 33 lb ft (4.8 kgm). Check that the connecting rod has sufficient end-float on the crankpin.

11. If removed, refit the woodruff key in the nose of the crankshaft and press on the crankshaft sprocket.

12. Lubricate the cam followers and insert them into their respective locations in the cylinder block. If the existing followers are being re-used, they must be refitted in their original bores.

13. Lubricate the camshaft journals, lobes and bearings thoroughly with engine oil. Insert the camshaft into the cylinder block, taking great care to avoid damaging the bearing inserts in the block. Fit the camshaft thrust plate, and secure to the block face using a new locking plate. Secure the two bolts with the lock plate tabs.

14. Check the camshaft end-float by measuring the clearance between the camshaft flange and the thrust plate, using feeler gauges. The end-float should be 0.0025 - 0.0075 in (0.064 - 0.191 mm). If the clearance is excessive, renew the thrust plate.

15. Turn the crankshaft until the timing mark on the crankshaft sprocket is pointing towards the camshaft centre. Temporarily fit the camshaft sprocket and turn the camshaft until the timing mark on the sprocket is adjacent to, and in line with, the crankshaft timing mark (Fig. C:31). Remove the camshaft sprocket, without moving the camshaft, and fit the timing chain to the sprocket. Locate the chain around the crankshaft sprocket and refit the sprocket on the camshaft flange. Check that the timing marks are still correctly aligned. Fit the camshaft sprocket retaining bolts with a new locking plate, tighten the bolts and secure by bending up the locking plate tabs.

16. Locate the chain tensioner arm on the pivot pin at the front main bearing cap. Pre-load the spring of the tensioner assembly and secure the tensioner in place with the two retaining bolts. Release the tensioner spring. This will automatically load the chain to its correct tension (Fig. C:32).

17. Fit the oil slinger on the front of the crankshaft with the concave side facing outwards. Lubricate the lip of the crankshaft front oil seal in the timing cover and slide the crankshaft pulley through the seal. Locate the timing cover together with the pulley on the front of the engine and fit the cover retaining bolts (Fig. C:33). This will ensure that the cover is correctly centred on the crankshaft. Ensure that the cover is in line with the sump mating surface on the block. Tighten the timing cover bolts and the crankshaft centre-bolt.

18. Apply suitable metal jointing compound to the oil pick-up pipe and press it into position in the bottom face of the cylinder block. Fit and tighten the retaining bolt.

19. Position the two halves of the sump gasket on the cylinder block flange, using jointing compound at each end of the two sections. It will help locate the gaskets if they are smeared with grease before fitting. Fit new sealing strips in the grooves in the lower face of the timing cover and rear oil seal carrier. With the chamfered edge of the seals into the grooves. The tabs on the ends of the sump gasket must be located under the cut-outs in the sealing strips, as shown in Fig. C:34.

20. Fit the sump in position on the block and install the retaining bolts. Tighten the bolts evenly, staring with the four end ones, then working down one side of the sump and up the other. Finally, retighten in the reverse order to their specified torque on 7 lb ft (1.1 kgm). Fit a new sealing ring to the sump drain plug and tighten securely.

21. If removed, screw and oil pressure switch into the tapped hole next to the oil pump mounting pad.

22. If a new or overhauled oil pump is being fitted, it should be filled with engine oil, then turned through a complete rotation by hand before installing it. Fit the oil pump, using a new gasket, and secure in position with the three retaining bolts. Wet the sealing ring on the oil filter cartridge with engine oil and screw the cartridge onto the threaded adaptor by hand until the seal just contacts the pump flange, then further tighten three quarters of a turn.

23. Insert the oil separator unit in its location in the cylinder block up to the stop, and secure with the retaining bolt.

24. Fit the fuel pump to the cylinder block, using a new insulating spacer, if necessary. Ensure that the pump operating arm lies on the camshaft eccentric (Fig. C:35). Secure with the two retaining bolts.

25. Locate the water pump with a new gasket on the front face of the cylinder block and secure in position with the three retaining bolts. Note that the alternator adjusting link is also secured by one of the pump fixing bolts. Tighten this bolt only finger-tight at this stage. Refit the cooling fan and drive pulley to the water pump hub.

26. Position the alternator on the side of the cylinder block and fit and tighten the mounting bracket retaining bolts. Fit the fan belt and adjust the tension so that a total free-movement of 0.5 in (13 mm) is present at the midway point between the alternator and fan pulleys.

27. Refit the cylinder head assembly, using a new head gasket. The use of two guide studs, made up and screwed into the cylinder head bolt holes, as shown in Fig. C:4, will facilitate correct alignment of the head gasket during installation. Once the head is installed, the studs can then

be replaced by the proper bolts.

28. Tighten the head bolts finger-tight initially. It should be noted that two of the head bolts are shorter than the others. Ensure that these are fitted in their correct respective positions. Tighten the head bolts evenly, following the sequence and stages of tightening shown in Fig. C:5. Note that the final stage of tightening will have to be carried out once the engine is installed in the car.

29. Dip the ends of the push rods in engine oil and install them in their original positions. Position the rocker shaft assembly on the cylinder head, ensuring that the arm adjusting screws locate correctly in the cupped ends of their respective push rods. Tighten the shaft pedestal bolts evenly to 28 lb ft (4.0 kgm).

30. Check the valve clearances, as detailed under the appropriate heading previously, and adjust if necessary.

31. Refit the rocker cover, using a new gasket. Ensure that the tabs on the outside of the gasket are correctly located in the notches in the cover.

32. Install the thermostat in its location in the cylinder head. Ensure that the thermostat is correctly located, as shown in Fig. C:6, otherwise overheating of the engine will result. Position a new gasket on the housing flange, fit the water outlet housing over the thermostat, with the outlet neck pointing to the rear, and secure with the two retaining bolts.

33. Crank the engine to bring No. 1 cylinder to TDC on its firing stroke. Position the distributor on the engine with the vacuum unit pointing to the rear and approximately 35° out from the engine. Turn the rotor arm until the electrode is immediately over the condenser cannister. Insert the distributor into the engine and secure the clamp plate to the block with the retaining bolt. Refit the distributor cap.

34. Refit the spark plugs and reconnect the spark plug leads. The firing order is 1 - 2 - 4 - 3.

35. Reconnect the engine breather hose to the inlet manifold and fit the vent valve into the grommet at the oil separator.

36. Reconnect the fuel supply hose and the distributor vacuum line to the carburettor.

37. Place the clutch disc in position on the flywheel. Ensure the disc is fitted the correct way round. Normally, the flywheel side of the disc is appropriately marked near the centre. Align the disc, using a suitable centralising tool, and locate the pressure plate assembly on the flywheel. Fit the clutch assembly retaining bolts and tighten evenly to 15 lb ft (2.0 kgm). Remove the centraliser tool.

Technical Data

GENERAL	HC	HC Economy
Identification code	J2	JS
Bore/stroke	80.98/62.99 mm	80.98/62.99 mm
Capacity	1297 cc	1297 cc
Compression ratio	9.2:1	9.2:1
Output (DIN)	58 BHP at 5,500 rev/min	50 BHP at 5,000 rev/min
	43 KW at 5,500 rev/min	37 KW at 5,000 rev/min
Torque (DIN)	67 lb ft at 3,000 rev/min	64 lb ft at 3,000 rev/min
	9.3 kgm at 3,000 rev/min	8.8 kgm at 3,000 rev/min
Idling speed	800 ± 25 rev/min	800 ± 50 rev/min
Max. engine speed:		
Continuous	5800 rev/min	5800 rev/min
Intermittent	6100 rev/min	6100 rev/min
Fuel octane requirement (RM)	97 (4 star-UK)	97 (4 star-UK)
Firing order	1 - 2 - 4 - 3	1 - 2 - 4 - 3

CYLINDER BLOCK

Cylinder bore diameter (Std) . . . . .80.947 - 81.007 mm (6 grades, A to F)
Bore ovality (max) . . . . .0.001 in (0.025 mm)
Bore taper (max) . . . . .0.001 in (0.025 mm)

CRANKSHAFT

Number of main bearings 5
Main bearing journal diameter:
    Standard . . . . .53.983 - 54.003 mm
    Undersize
        0.010 in (0.254 mm) . . . . .53.729 - 53.749 mm
        0.020 in (0.508 mm) . . . . .53.475 - 53.495 mm
        0.030 in (0.762 mm) . . . . .53.221 - 53.241 mm

Main bearing clearance . . . . 0.0004-0.0022 in (0.010-0.057 mm)
Crankpin diameter:
    Standard . . . . 49.195 - 49.215 mm
    Undersize
        0.010 in (0.254 mm) . . . . 48.941 - 48.961 mm
        0.020 in (0.508 mm) . . . . 48.687 - 48.707 mm

PISTONS

Piston diameter (Std) . . . . 80.944 - 80.974 mm (3 grades, D to F)
Oversize
    0.0025 in (0.064 mm) . . . . 80.978 - 81.038 mm
    0.015 in (0.38 mm) . . . . 81.294 - 81.354 mm
    0.030 in (0.76 mm) . . . . 81.674 - 81.734 mm
Piston to bore clearance . . . . 0.0009-0.0017 in (0.023-0.043 mm)

PISTON RINGS

Ring end gap
    (fitted in block) - ALL . . . . 0.009-0.014 in (0.23-0.36 mm)
Ring gap position:
    Bottom ring . . . . Aligned with piston pin
    Centre ring . . . . 90° to bottom ring gap
    Top ring . . . . 180° to bottom ring gap

        0.030 in (0.762 mm) . . . . 48.433 - 48.453 mm
Big-end bearing clearance . . . . 0.0002-0.0024 in (0.006-0.061 mm)
Thrust washer thickness:
    Standard . . . . 2.311 - 2.362 mm
    Oversize . . . . 2.502 - 2.553 mm
Crankshaft end-float . . . . 0.003-0.011 in (0.075-0.279 mm)

VALVE TIMING

Inlet valve
    Opens . . . . 21° BTDC
    Closes . . . . 55° ABDC
Exhaust valve
    Opens . . . . 70° BBDC
    Closes . . . . 22° ATDC

VALVE CLEARANCES

Inlet valves . . . . 0.008 in (0.20 mm)
Exhaust valves . . . . 0.022 in (0.55 mm)

LUBRICATION SYSTEM

Oil pump clearances:
    Rotor to casing . . . . 0.006-0.011 in (0.140-0.267 mm)
    Inner to outer rotor . . . . 0.002-0.005 in (0.051-0.127 mm)
    Rotor to end cover . . . . 0.001-0.0025 in (0.025-0.064 mm)
Relief valve opens at . . . . 35-40 lb/sq in (2.46-2.81 kg/cm^2)
Oil pressure warning light operates at . . . . 6 ± 1.5 lb/sq in (0.4 ± 0.1 kg/cm^2)
Minimum oil pressure at:
    750 rev/min . . . . 8.5 lb/sq in (0.6 kg/cm^2)
    2000 rev/min . . . . 21 lb/sq in (1.5 kg/cm^2)
Maximum oil pressure, above 2000 rev/min . . . . 71 lb/sq in (5.0 kg/cm^2)

ENGINE
Trouble Shooter

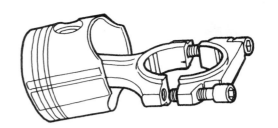

FAULT	CAUSE	CURE
Noisy tappet (with correct clearance)	1. Wear in rocker pad face and/or rocker sleeve and shift (OHV). 2. Worn cam follower (OHC).	1. Reface pad surface, replace rockers or shaft (OHV). 2. Fit new followers (OHC).
Lack of compression	1. Faulty valve seat, excessive wear in stem or guide. 2. Faulty head gasket. 3. Worn pistons, rings and bores.	1. Recut seat and valve, fit new guide and valve. 2. Fit new gasket or reface head. 3. Either fit new rings, pistons and rings and rebore. If engine badly worn then recon. engine.
Smoke from exhaust. Lack of power	1. As above. 2. Blocked crankcase breather.	1. As above. 2. Check breathing apparatus as above.
Piston slap	1. As above (except blocked breather).	1. As above
Big-end knock	1. Wear between big-end shell and crankcase. Wrong torque on bolts.	1. Depending on wear, fit new shells, regrind crankshaft and check torque.
Mains rumble	1. Wear between main bearing shells and crankshaft.	1. As above.
Cam follower tap	1. Camshaft worn or follower dished.	1. Examine and replace followers or camshaft. Or both.
Knocking when clutch depressed. Movement at crank pulley	1. Excessive crankshaft end-float. Wear between crank and thrust washer.	1. Fit new thrust washers and recheck clearance.
Clattering from front of engine	1. Worn or slack timing chain, worn chain tensioner.	1. Fit new chain and tensioner. Adjust chain where necessary.
Small-end or gudgeon pin knock	1. Excessive wear between gudgeon pin and con-rod.	1. Fit new bush to con-rod.
Lack of oil pressure	1. Excessive wear in crankshaft journals. 2. Faulty oil pump. 3. Blocked oil pick-up strainer. 4. Faulty pressure-relief valve. 5. Blocked oil filter. 6. Lack of Oil.	1. Overhaul engine. 2. Fit new pump. 3. Clean pick-up. 4. Fit new relief valve. 5. Fit new filter. 6. Install fresh oil.
Oil leaks	1. Sump gaskets or packings. 2. Front and rear crankshaft oil seal. 3. Rocker or camshaft gasket. 4. Oil filter.	1. Fit new gaskets. 2. Fit new seals. 3. Fit new gasket. 4. Check filter seal.
Lack of power (engine in good condition)	1. Faulty ignition timing. Faulty sparking plugs, points or condenser. Wrong valve clearance.	1. Tune engine.

Engine-ohc

OVERHAUL PROCEDURES . . . . [1]

The engine must be removed from the car to enable any major overhaul work to be carried out on the cylinder block. The cylinder head can, however, be removed while the engine is still in place.

Removal and installation or replacement of the camshaft requires that the cylinder head be removed as the camshaft can only be withdrawn from the rear of the head. However, the cam followers and the camshaft oil seal can be replaced without removing the head.

The auxiliary shaft oil seal and crankshaft from oil seal can be replaced while the engine is still in the car, but the timing belt must first be removed first.

A special puller (Tool No. 21-008-A) will be required to withdraw the crankshaft front oil seal because of its difficult location. Similarly, a special installer tool (No. 21-009-A) will be required to fit the new seal. The same tools are used to replace the camshaft oil seal.

The removal and installation of the engine ancillary components, i.e. water pump, distributor, alternator, etc., are not specifically covered in this section as these are included in the relevant sections later in the manual.

As with most engines, overhaul operations will require the use of special tools which can be hired or bought locally. Similarly, any machining work is best left to a local auto machinist who will have the necessary equipment for the job.

Tools you will need to remove the cylinder head or replace the timing belt are socket set adaptors to fit the internally splined heads of the bolts, a different size being required for each of these jobs. However, such adaptors are generally available from most motor accessory shops.

VALVE CLEARANCES . . . . [2]

To check the valve clearances, the air cleaner and rocker cover must first be removed. It will facilitate turning over the engine if the spark plugs are also removed.

The clearances should be checked statically at least half an hour after the engine has been switched off:

Rotate the crankshaft until the toe of the cam for the valve being checked is positioned facing upwards, then check the clearance between the upper face of the rocker arm and the cam (Fig. D:1). If required, the clearances can be checked, two at a time, by positioning the cam lobes for each respective pair upwards, so as to form a 'V' configuration, then measuring the clearances for both valves.

In either case, the clearances should be:-
Inlet . . . . 0.008 in (0.20 mm)
Exhaust . . . . 0.010 in (0.25 mm)

The setting is correct when the appropriate thickness of feeler gauge is a neat sliding fit between the rocker arm and the cam lobe.

The valve arrangement, from the front, is exhaust then inlet alternately.

If adjustment is necessary, slacken the ball pin locknut then turn the ball pin at the rocker arm pivot until the correct gap is obtained. Recheck the clearance after tightening the locknut.

Repeat for the other valves. Crank the engine in the direction of rotation only, during this procedure.

When adjustment is complete, refit the rocker cover, using a new gasket if necessary. Ensure that the dove-tail at the gasket joint is correctly engaged, and that the tabs on the outside of the gasket are correctly located in the cover recesses. Tighten the cover retaining bolts in stages following the sequence shown in Fig. D:2.
1st Stage, tighten bolts 1-6 . . . . 4 lb ft (0.6 kgm)
2nd Stage, tighten bolts 7 & 8 . . . . . 1.5 lb ft (0.25 kgm)
3rd Stage, tighten bolts 9 & 10. . . . . . 4 lb ft (0.6 kgm)
4th Stage, retighten bolts 7 & 8 . . . . . . 4 lb ft (0.6 kgm)

CAMSHAFT DRIVE BELT. . . . . [3]

Replacement

Firstly, disconnect the battery leads. Detach the fan belt after first slackening the alternator mounting bolts and pivoting the alternator towards the engine. Remove the four bolts securing the timing belt cover and detach the cover from the front of the engine (Fig. D:3).

Turn the crankshaft until the TDC mark on the crankshaft pulley is in line with the pointer on the front cover (see Fig. B:7 in the TUNE-UP section) and the pointer on

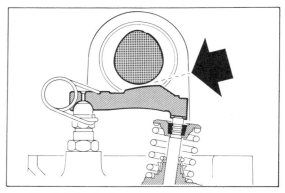

Fig. D:1 Check clearance with cam lobe pointing upwards

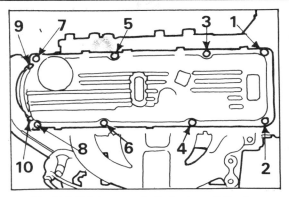

Fig. D:2 Tighten cover bolts in stages following the sequence shown

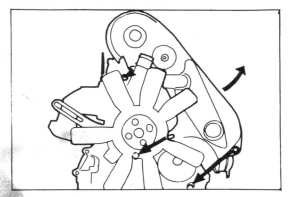

Fig. D:3 Locations of belt guard mounting points are indicated by dotted lines

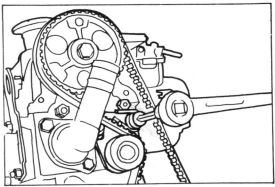

Fig. D:4 Special adaptor will be required to fit internal splined head of belt tensioner pivot bolt

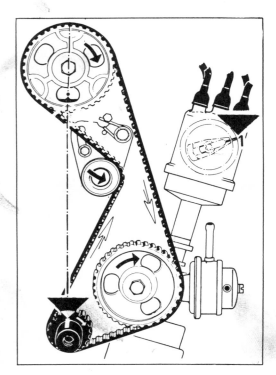

Fig. D:5 Distributor and timing gears must be aligned as shown

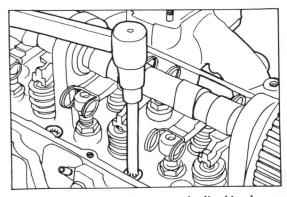

Fig. D:6 Head bolts have internal splined heads, needing an adaptor to unscrew them

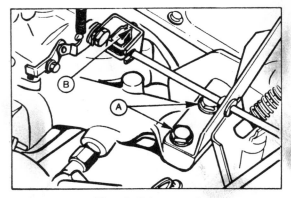

Fig. D:7 Throttle linkage attachment at carburettor and inlet manifold

the camshaft pulley backing plate is in line with the mark on the cylinder head (Fig. D:5). Remove the distributor cap and check that the rotor arm is pointing towards the No. 1 electrode position in the cap. The engine must remain in this position while the toothed belt is removed.

Remove the bolt securing the 'V' belt pulley to the crankshaft and take off the pulley together with its thrust washer. Note that the thrust washer is cup-shaped and is fitted with the dished side facing the pulley

Slacken the locking bolt at the tensioner plate and release the timing belt tension by pivoting the tensioner assembly clockwise against the spring pressure (Fig. D:4). Retighten the lock bolt to hold the tensioner in the released position. A special adaptor will be required for this operation as the tensioner pivot bolt has an internal splined head.

The timing belt can now be removed by disengaging it from the camshaft, auxiliary shaft and crankshaft sprockets.

If after removal of the timing belt it is found that the camshaft and crankshaft marks are not in correct alignment, under no circumstances must the camshaft or crankshaft be rotated through 360° to achieve alignment of the marks, otherwise damage to the valves and pistons will result. Choose the shortest travel to the mark, ensuring that the pistons and valves are not fouling.

Check that the crankshaft, camshaft and distributor are positioned as described above, then fit the new timing belt.

Slacken the tensioner plate locking bolt to release the tensioner roller onto the timing belt. Turn the engine over twice in its direction of normal rotation, then retighten the plate locking bolt. This will automatically load the belt to its correct tension.

Refit the crankshaft pulley together with its thrust washer, ensuring that the thrust washer is correctly positioned, and tighten the centre-bolt to its specified torque of 42 lb ft (6.0 kgm). Refit the timing belt guard. Refit the fan belt and adjust to achieve a total free-movement of 0.5 in (13 mm) midway between the alternator and fan pulleys. Finally, reconnect the battery leads.

CYLINDER HEAD....................[4]

Removal

1.   Disconnect the battery earth lead.
2.   Drain the cooling system by disconnecting the bottom hose from the radiator and opening the cylinder block drain plug. Also remove the radiator cap.
3.   Remove the air cleaner after removing the four screws at the top cover and prising the mounting stays clear of the cleaner body
4.   Disconnect the radiator top hose at the water outlet elbow on the front of the cylinder head. Also disconnect the heater hose from choke water housing on the carburettor. The other water hose to the inlet manifold connection need not be disconnected.
5.   Disconnect the fuel supply hose (and fuel return

hose, where fitted) at the carburettor. If the original crimped-type hose clamp is used, this must be cut off and a new screwed-type used on reassembly. Where a vent tube is fitted to the top of the carburettor float chamber, this also must be disconnected.
6.   Disconnect the engine breather hose at the oil separator. Also disconnect the distributor vacuum line at the carburettor, and the servo unit vacuum hose at the inlet manifold. On models with automatic transmission the transmission vacuum hose must also be disconnected from the inlet manifold connection.
7.   Disconnect the throttle linkage by removing the cable support bracket with the throttle cable still attached from the cylinder head. Release the spring clip securing the throttle linkage rod to the carburettor, then remove the two bolts securing the support bracket to the inlet manifold (Fig. D:7). Position the cable and bracket to one side out of the way. On models with automatic transmission, the down-shift cable will also be attached to the throttle linkage assembly.
8.   Disconnect the HT leads from the spark plugs and the ignition coil. Remove the distributor cap and the spark plugs.
spark plugs.
9:   Disconnect the water temperature sender unit lead.
10.   Remove the two nuts securing the exhaust pipe clamp to the exhaust manifold.
11.   Detach the timing belt cover from the front of the engine (Fig. D:3).
12.   Slacken the locking bolt at the tensioner plate and release the timing belt tension by pivoting the tensioner assembly clockwise against the spring pressure (Fig. D:4). A special adaptor will be required for this operation as the tensioner pivot bolt has an internal splined head. Retighten the plate lock bolt to hold the tensioner in the released position. Detach the toothed belt from the camshaft sprocket.
13.   Remove the securing bolts and lift off the rocker cover together with its gasket.
14.   Unscrew the cylinder head bolts, using a suitable adaptor to fit the internal splines of the bolt heads (Fig. D:6). Release the bolts evenly, following the reverse sequence to that shown in Fig. D:9.
15.   Lift off the cylinder head and remove the gasket. After removal, the cylinder head should not be laid down on its mating face, otherwise damage may be caused to those valves which are in the fully open position.

Installation

Installation is a reversal of the removal procedure, with special attention to the following points:-
a)   Ensure that all mating surfaces on the cylinder head and block are perfectly clean and free from old gasket material.
b)   If the cylinder head was removed to replace a leaking or blown head gasket, check the mating faces on both the head and block for distortion before reassembling.
c)   Use only new gaskets. The head gasket mut be fitted without the use of sealing compound of any type.

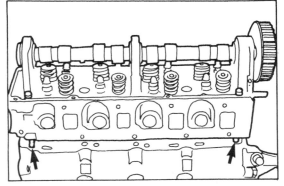

Fig. D:8 Use of locating studs will help retain gasket in correct position when refitting head

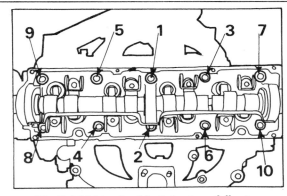

Fig. D:9 Tighten head bolts in stages following the sequence shown

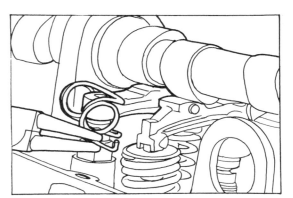

Fig. D:10 Cam finger is secured to pivot pin by a spring clip

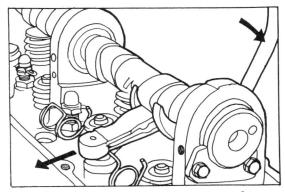

Fig. D:11 Valve spring must be compressed to allow removal of cam finger

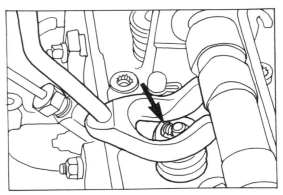

Fig. D:12 Compress valve spring with suitable compressor tool and remove split collets

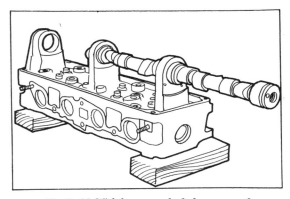

Fig. D:13 Withdraw camshaft from rear of cylinder head

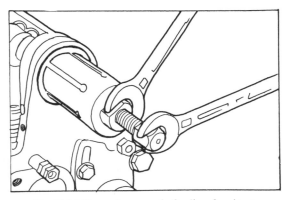

Fig. D:14 Removing cam shaft oil seal, using a drift or Special Tool 21-008-A

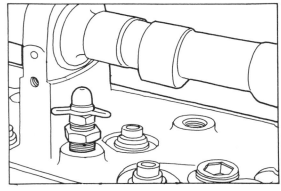

Fig. D:15 Fit ball pin complete with locknut and retaining clip

d) In order to avoid damage to the valves and pistons when installing the cylinder head, it is essential that the crankshaft be positioned with the No. 1 cylinder at TDC and the camshaft positioned with the sprocket aligned on the cylinder head mark (Fig. D:5). With the camshaft and crankshaft thus positioned, the distributor rotor arm should point towards the position of the No. 1 electrode in the distributor cap.

e) Tighten the cylinder head bolts evenly, using the special splined adaptor (Fig. D:6). The bolts should be tightened in stages, following the sequence shown in Fig. D:9.

1st Stage . . . . .30-40 lb ft (4.0-5.5 kgm)
2nd Stage. . . . . .45-50 lb ft (6.0-7.0 kgm)
3rd Stage
(after 10-15 minutes wait). . . . 65-80 lb ft (9.0-11.0 kgm)

f) The head bolts must be retightened to the final setting after running the engine for 15 minutes at fast idle (1.000 rpm).

g) Before fitting the toothed drive belt onto the camshaft sprocket, check that the crankshaft, camshaft and distributor are still correctly positioned, as shown in Fig. D:5. Once the belt is in position, slacken the tensioner plate locking bolt to release the tensioner roller onto the timing belt. Turn the engine over twice in its normal direction of rotation, then retighten the plate locking bolt. This will automatically load the belt to its correct tension.

h) Check the valve clearances, as detailed under the appropriate heading previously, and adjust if necessary. Also refit the rocker cover as detailed under that heading.

i) When installation is complete, refill the cooling system, then run the engine and check the ignition itming and carburettor idle setting as detailed in the TUNE-UP section.

Dismantling

1. Support the cylinder head assembly on two blocks of wood, one at either end, to prevent damage to the valves.
2. Detach the inlet manifold, complete with the carburettor, from the cylinder head. Similarly, detach the exhaust manifold.
3. At each cam follower arm, unhook the retaining spring securing the arm to its ball pin (Fig. D:10). Compress the valve spring the valve spring and withdraw the cam follower arm (Fig. D:11). Special Tool 21-005 is shown in the illustration, but any normal valve spring compressor tool can be used. Keep the followers in their correct order if they are to be re-used, as their positions must not be interchanged on reassembly.
4. If required, the camshaft assembly can be removed from the head as detailed under the appropriate heading later in this section.
5. Remove all carbon deposits from the combustion chambers and valve heads, using a suitable scraper such as a blunt screwdriver, but take great care to avoid damaging the surface of the cylinder head. Also remove any carbon from the piston crowns and the cylinder block.
6. At each valve in turn, compress the valve spring with a suitable spring compressor tool and extract the two split tapered collets from around the valve stem (Fig. D:12). Release the compressor tool and remove the spring retainer and valve spring. Withdraw the valve from the head and prise the valve stem oil seal out of its seat at the top of the valve guide. Suitably mark the valve and associated components to identify their positions in the cylinder head.

Inspection and Overhaul

Inspect the valves and associated components in a similar manner to that detailed for OHV engines in the previous chapter.

Inspect the camshaft, cam follower arms and pivot ball studs for wear or damage as detailed under the subsequent 'CAMSHAFT' heading.

Reassembly

Reassemble the components to the cylinder head in the reverse order of dismantling, with special attention to the following points:-

a) Lap in each valve in turn using coarse, followed by fine grinding paste until a gas-tight seal is obtained at the seat. This will be indicated by a continuous matt-grey ring around the valve face and seat. When this has been achieved, clean all traces of paste from the cylinder head and valve - this is most important.

b) Lubricate the valve guides and valves with SAE 90 Hypoid Oil before installing the valves.

c) The valve stem oil seals must always be renewed. Lubricate the seal with oil to make fitting easier.

d) Ensure that the valve stem is not damaged by the spring retainer when compressing the valve spring, and that the split tapered collets engage correctly in the valve stem and spring retainer when the spring is released.

e) If the camshaft was removed, refit it was detailed under the 'CAMSHAFT' heading later in this section.

f) If the existing cam followers are being refitted, ensure that they are installed in their original locations. Secure the followers to their respective ball pins with the retaining clips (Fig. D:15).

g) When refitting the inlet manifold assembly, apply sealing compound to both sides of the manifold gasket at the central water way (Fig. D:19).

CAMSHAFT . . . .[5]

If the valve gear is noisy in use, even when the rocker clearances are correctly adjusted, the cam followers and cam lobes should be inspected for wear or damage.

Follower arms should only be replaced individually if they are found to be damaged, or causing unacceptable noise without showing signs of wear. When changing a follower, the respective pivot ball stud must also be changed. If one or more followers show signs of excessive wear, a complete set of new components (i.e. camshaft, all followers, ball studs and oil feed pipe) should be fitted.

When investigating noisy or worn valve gear, check

OHC Engines

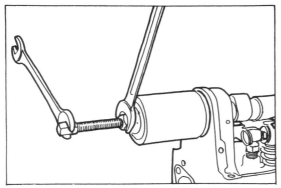

Fig. D:16 Press in a new oil seal at front of camshaft, or use Special Tool 21-009-A

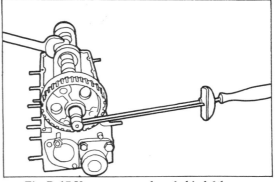

Fig. D:17 Use spanner on boss behind 6th cam to hold camshaft while tightening sprocket bolt

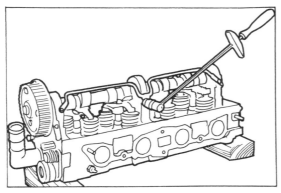

Fig. D:18 Fitting oil feed pipe in position on cylinder head

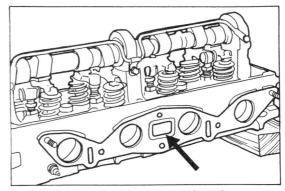

Fig. D:19 Apply sealant around the gasket water-way when refitting inlet manifold

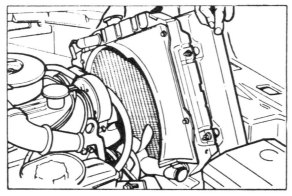

Fig. D:20 Remove radiator complete with mounting panel and shroud

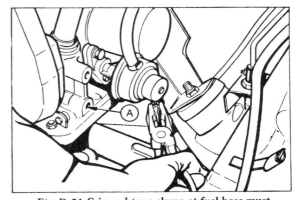

Fig. D:21 Crimped-type clamp at fuel hose must be cut off and a new clip used on reassembly.

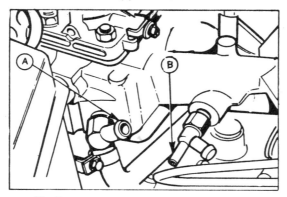

Fig. D:22 Brake servo (A) and auto. trans. (B) vacuum connections on inlet manifold

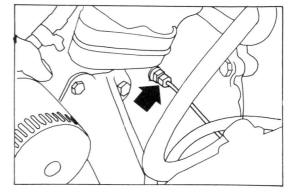

Fig. D:23 Oil pressure line connection

the operation of the valve gear oil feed pipe before starting to dismantle the assembly. Run the engine and observe the oil feed from each nozzle. If it is found that the nozzles do not direct oil onto the cam lobes, the oil feed pipe should be renewed.

If either the camshaft or a cam follower is renewed, the engine oil and filter should also be changed.

Replacement

The cylinder head must be removed from the car to replace the camshaft as the shaft is withdrawn from the rear of the head.

Support the cylinder head assembly on two blocks of wood, one at either end, to prevent damage to the valves. Detach the water outlet elbow from the front face of the cylinder head. Detach the valve gear oil feed pipe from the camshaft bearing supports.

At each cam follower arm, unhook the retaining spring securing the arm to its ball pin (Fig. D:10). Compress the valve spring and withdraw the cam follower (Fig. D:11). Keep the followers in their removed order if they are to be re-used, as their positions must not be interchanged on reassembly.

Hold the camshaft in position, using an open-ended spanner on the flats behind the 6th cam, and unscrew the sprocket centre-bolt (Fig. D:17). Remove the sprocket, together with its backing plate.

Detach the camshaft retaining plate from the rear bearing and withdraw the camshaft from the rear (Fig. D: 13). Extract the oil seal from its location at the front bearing.

It should be noted that the camshaft oil seal can be removed with the camshaft still in position, using Tool 21-008, as shown in Fig. D:14.

If the pivot ball pins are being replaced, release the locknut and unscrew the ball pin from the cylinder head (Fig. D:15). Screw the new ball pins, complete with locknuts, into position in the head and fit the spring clip into the groove in each pin.

Coat the three bearing journals on the new camshaft liberally with SAE 90 Hypoid Oil and carefully insert the camshaft into the cylinder head from the rear. Secure the camshaft in position with the locating plate.

Check the camshaft end-float by measuring the clearance of the thrust plate in the camshaft groove. The permissible end-float is 0.0016 - 0.0047 in (0.04 - 0.12 mm). If the end-float is outside these limits, renew the thrust plate.

Lubricate the outer surface and sealing lip of the new oil seal with engine oil, and press it into position at the front bearing using the Seal Installer Tool shown in Fig. D:16.

Compress each valve spring in turn and fit the cam follower arm into position on the pivot pin and valve. If the old followers are being re-used, ensure they are refitted in their original positions. Secure each arm to its respective ball pin with the retaining clip (Fig. D:10). Lubricate the cam lobes and followers liberally with SAE Hypoid Oil.

Refit the camshaft sprocket, together with its backing plate. The backing plate is fitted with the reinforced side

facing outwards. Tighten the sprocket centre-bolt to 35 lb ft (5.0 kgm) while holding the camshaft in position with the open-ended spanner (Fig. D:17).

Fit the valve gear oil feed pipe in position on the cam bearing supports and secure with the three retaining bolts (Fig. D:18). The operation of the oil feed pipe should be checked once the cylinder head is refitted on the engine to ensure that each cam lobe is receiving an adequate flow of oil from its respective nozzle.

After replacement of the camshaft and/or any follower, the engine should be run for 10 - 15 minutes at fast idle before putting the oil feed pipe back into permanent use.

ENGINE REMOVAL & INSTALLATION . . . [6]

Removal

1. Disconnect the battery leads and remove the battery from its location at the left-hand side of the engine compartment.
2. Remove the bonnet (4 bolts). It will facilitate refitting if the position of the bonnet hinges is first marked on the underside of the bonnet panel by scribing a line around them.
3. Drain the cooling system by disconnecting the bottom hose from the radiator and opening the cylinder block drain plug. Also remove the radiator cap.

If the engine is goind to be overhauled or exchanged, remove the sump plug and drain the engine oil into a suitable container. Refit the plug when all the oil has drained out.
5. Remove the air cleaner assembly after removing the four screws at the top cover and prising the mounting stays clear of the cleaner body
6. Disconnect the radiator bottom hose. On models with automatic transmission, disconnect the two oil cooler pipes from the base of the radiator. Plug the pipe ends to prevent loss of fluid and the ingress of dirt. Remove the four bolts securing the radiator mounting panel to the body and carefully lift out the radiator assembly, complete with the mounting panel and fan shroud (Fig. D:20).
7. Disconnect the two heater hoses either from the matrix at the heater box, or from the connection on the water pump and the automatic choke housing respectively. In either case, tie the hoses up out of the way so that they will not interfere during engine removal.
8. Disconnect the brake servo unit hose from its connection on the inlet manifold (Fig. D:22). On models with automatic transmission, also disconnect the transmission vacuum hose from the manifold.
9. Disconnect the throttle linkage by removing the two bolts securing the throttle cable support bracket to the inlet manifold and releasing the spring clip securing the linkage rod to the carburettor (Fig. D:7). Position the cable and bracket to one side out of the way. On models with automatic transmission, the transmission down-shift cable will also be attached to throttle linkage assembly.
10. Disconnect the fuel feed pipe from the fuel pump inlet. If the original crimped-type hose clamp is used, this

must be cut off and a new screwed-type used on reassembly (Fig. D:21). Plug the pipe end to prevent loss of fuel and minimise fire danger.

11. Disconnect the wiring from the following items on the engine:-

a)   Starter motor, with the pre-engaged type starter note the positions of the connections at the solenoid, making a diagram if necessary.

b)   Temperature sender unit; On cylinder head.

c)   Oil pressure switch; where applicable.

d)   Alternator; withdraw multi-plug from rear.

e)   Distributor; disconnect HT lead from coil tower and LT lead from coil terminal.

f)   Engine earth strap; adjacent to fuel pump 26).

12. On models with an oil pressure gauge, disconnect the oil pressure pipe from its union above the dipstick (Fig. D:23). Plug the pipe end to prevent the ingress of dirt.

13. Disconnect the clamp plate securing the exhaust down pipe to the exhaust manifold. Allow the clamp to slide down the pipe, then separate the pipe from the manifold and withdraw the sealing ring.

14. Working from underneath the car, remove the starter motor from its location on the flywheel/converter housing.

15. On models with automatic transmission, remove the bolts securing the engine drive plate to the torque converter. These are accessible, one at a time, through the cut-out at the starter motor aperture in the converter housing (Fig. D:24). The cut-out is sealed with a rubber grommet which must first be removed.

16. Attach a suitable sling or lifting brackets to the engine and support the weight with lifting tackle.

20. Remove the nut securing the engine front mounting rubber to the suspension crossmember on each side of the car. Prise both insulators out of their respective brackets using a suitable lever. Engine removal may be found easier if one of the rubber insulators is detached completely from its engine mounting bracket.

21. Remove the bolts securing the engine to the transmission.

22. Suitably support the transmission, then draw the engine forwards to disengage it from the transmission and carefully lift it out of the engine compartment.

Installation

Installation is carried out in the reverse order of removing, but special attention should be paid to the following points:-

a)   Two locating dowels are provided on the engine rear flange to help locate the engine adaptor plate. If these were left behind in the transmission housing when the engine was removed, they must be transferred to their correct locations in the cylinder block.

b)   On manual transmission models, lightly grease the splines of the gearbox input shaft before installing the engine. Also ensure the clutch release lever and bearing is correctly positioned in the clutch housing.

c)   When installing the engine it is most important that no strain be put on the gearbox input shaft. The engine must not be allowed to hang on the shaft when only partly engaged. It, may be necessary to turn the engine over slowly to allow the splines on the shaft to engage with the clutch disc.

d)   As soon as the engine is properly mated to the transmission and fully up to the transmission flange, fit the securing bolts and tighten them evenly so that the engine is pulled squarely into place.

e)   Use a suitable lever to engage the engine mounting insulator studs in the cross member brackets, then secure with the nuts and spring washers.

f)   On automatic models, turn the engine as necessary to align the bolt holes in the converter with those in the drive plate. After fitting and tightening the bolts, refit the grommet to the cut-out in the starter aperture (Fig. D: 24).

g)   On manual models, set the clutch cable adjustment as detailed in the ROUTINE MAINTENANCE section.

h)   When reconnecting the exhaust pipe to the manifold, insert the sealing ring, then ensure that the down pipe is seating squarely on the manifold outlet and that the pipe clamp is parallel with the manifold face before tightening the nuts.

i)   If drained, refill the engine with the appropriate quantity of fresh engine oil.

j)   On models with automatic transmission, check the transmission fluid level and top up if necessary.

k)   When installation is complete, run the engine and check for leaks.

l)   Finally, check the ignition timing and carburettor idle setting as detailed in the TUNE-UP section.

ENGINE OVERHAUL . . . . [7]

1.   Unscrew the oil filter cartridge from the side of the cylinder block.

2.   Detach the clutch pressure plate and clutch disc from the flywheel, where applicable.

3.   Slacken the alternator mounting bolts, pivot the alternator towards the cylinder block and detach the fan belt. Remove the alternator, complete with its mounting bracket, from the engine.

4.   Detach the cooling fan and drive pulley from the water pump boss, then unbolt and remove the water pump together with the alternator adjusting bracket from the front face of the block.

5.   Remove the four attaching bolts and withdraw the timing belt cover to the left-hand side of the engine (Fig. D:3).

6.   Remove the bolt securing the 'V' belt pulley to the crankshaft and take off the pulley together with its thrust washer. Also remove the centre-bolt from the auxiliary shaft sprocket.

7.   Release the timing belt tension by slackening the locking bolt at the tensioner plate and pivoting the tensioner assembly clockwise against the spring pressure (Fig. D:4). A special splined adaptor will be required to fit the socket head of the tensioner pivot bolt. Re-tighten the plate lock bolt to hold the tensioner in the released position. The timing belt can now be detached from the cam-

shaft, auxiliary shaft and crankshaft sprockets.

8. Disconnect the fuel supply hose and distributor vacuum pipe at the carburettor. Also disconnect the engine breather hose from the oil separator by withdrawing the vent valve.

9. Disconnect the HT leads from the spark plugs, detach the leads from the clip on the rocker cover and remove the distributor cap, complete with leads. Mark the No. 1 spark plug lead with tape to identify it. Remove the spark plugs.

10. Remove the ten securing bolts and lift off the rocker cover together with its gasket.

11. Slacken the cylinder head bolts evenly, following the reverse sequence to that shown in Fig. D:9. A special adaptor will again be required to fit the internal splines of the bolt heads (Fig. D:6). Lift off the cylinder head complete with the inlet and exhaust manifolds, and detach the gasket. After removal, the cylinder head should not be laid on its mating face, otherwise damage may be caused to those valves which are is the fully open position.

12. Remove the bolt securing the distributor clamp plate to the cylinder block and withdraw the distributor, complete with the vacuum line (Fig. D:25). It will facilitate subsequent installation of the distributor if the position of the rotor arm at the No. 1 firing point is marked on the distributor body. Turn the crankshaft until the rotor arm is almost opposite the position of the No. 1 cylinder segment in the distributor cap. Align the TDC (last) line on the crankshaft pulley with the pointer on the front cover, then scribe a line on the distributor body in line with the centre-line of the rotor arm.

13. Remove the two bolts securing the fuel pump and detach the pump complete with the fuel line. Withdraw the pump push rod from the block (Fig. D:26).

14. Prise the oil separator from its location in the block above the oil filter pad (Fig. D:27). If required, the oil pressure switch, or oil pressure line connector, can be unscrewed from its location at the dipstick tube.

15. Remove the sump securing bolts and detach the sump from the lower face of the cylinder block. This should be done while the cylinder block is still mounted upright to prevent sludge and swarf from getting into the crankcase.

16. Invert the engine. A tray or other suitable container should be placed under the block to catch the remaining oil and coolant which will be released.

17. Remove the three bolts securing the oil pump and lift out the pump and its drive shaft from the crankcase (Fig. D:28). A special adaptor, the same size as that for the timing belt tensioner, will be required to fit these bolts.

18. Remove the auxiliary shaft and crankshaft sprockets. If the crankshaft sprocket is difficult to remove, a suitable puller such as that shown in Fig. D:29, will be required to withdraw it. Remove the bolts securing the auxiliary shaft front cover and crankshaft front cover, and detach the covers from the cylinder block. Remove the two screws securing the auxiliary shaft retaining plate and withdraw the auxiliary shaft.

19. Check that the big end bearing caps and rods are suitabley marked with their respective cylinder numbers (Fig. D:30). Turn the crankshaft as necessary to bring each connecting rod in turn to the bottom of its travel. Remove the big end bearing cap and push the piston and connecting rod assembly up the cylinder bore and carefully withdraw it from the top of the block. Remove the bearing shells from the cap and rod, and suitably identify them if they are to be re-used.

20. Detach the flywheel from the rear end of the crankshaft. Use the handle of a hammer to prevent the crankshaft turning while loosening the bolts (Fig. D:31). On automatic models a drive plate, reinforcing plate and spacer are fitted in place of the flywheel.

21. Check that the main bearing caps are suitably marked with their respective locations. Release the cap retaining bolts and remove the main bearing caps together with their bearing shells. Carefully lift the crankshaft out of the crankcase and remove the rear oil seal from the rear end of the shaft. Note the position of the half thrust washers on each side of the centre main bearing and mark them accordingly (Fig. D:32). Remove the bearing shells and thrust washers from the crankcase and bearing caps. Identify the shells if they are to be re-used.

Inspection & Overhaul

The components of the cylinder head assembly have already been dealt with under the heading 'CYLINDER HEAD' and reference should be made for details.

The components of the cylinder block assembly should be inspected in a similar manner to that described for the OHV engines in the previous chapter, except where stated otherwise below.

Pistons & Connecting Rods

The pistons and rods should be inspected for wear and any other signs of damage and replaced as necessary.

In this case, when selecting replacement pistons for use in used bores, the bores should be measured at a point 2.75 in (70 mm) from the block top face.

As for OHV engines, the piston pins are a press fit in the connecting rod small end and the connecting rods must be heated up to the same specified temperature to allow the pin to be fitted.

Each piston must be assembled to its respective connecting rod with the notch or arrow or the piston crown positioned to the front, and the oil squirt hole in the connecting rod to the right-hand side of the assembly (Fig. D:33).

Auxiliary Shaft

The auxiliary shaft serves only to provide the drive for the distributor (and oil pump) and the fuel pump. Inspect the shaft journals for scoring or signs of abnormal wear. Also check the teeth of the skew gear for wear, or damage. If wear is present, the shaft must be replaced. In this case, the skew gear on the distributor should also be checked. Inspect the shaft thrust plate for wear, and renew if necessary.

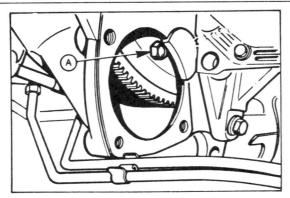

Fig. D:24 Torque converter bolts (A) are accessible through starter motor aperture

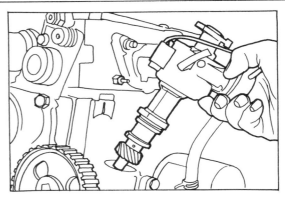

Fig. D:25 Removing distributor

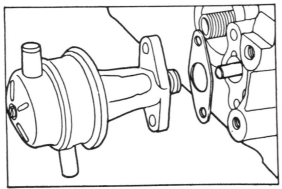

Fig. D:26 Withdraw push rod from block after removing fuel pump

Fig. D:27 Remove oil separator by levering it up with a screwdriver

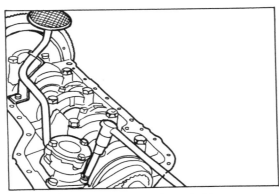

Fig. D:28 Special adaptor is needed to remove pump bolts with socket heads

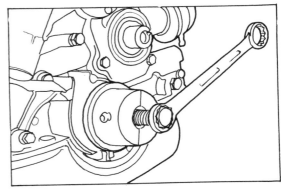

Fig. D:29 Special puller (21-028) may be required to remove crankshaft sprocket

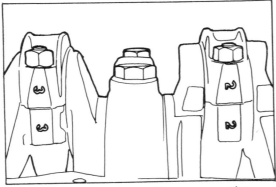

Fig. D:30 Check that markings on connecting rods and caps match before removing

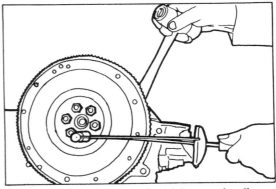

Fig. D:31 Lock crankshaft with hammer handle while loosening or tightening flywheel bolts

Oil Pump

The oil pressure pump on the OHC engine is of the eccentric bi-rotor type and the internal components can be inspected after removing the cover plate. However, it should be noted that in most cases of wear or damage to the components of the pump, it will be more economical to obtain a complete new pump, rather than attempt to overhaul and fit new parts to the existing unit. The pump should be dismantled for inspection as follows:

Remove the two bolts securing the oil pick-up pipe to the pump body, and detach the pipe together with its gasket. Unbolt the end cover plate and withdraw both rotors from the housing.

The inner and outer rotors are a matched pair and must only be fitted one way round. To ensure that they will be installed in their original positions, they should be suitably marked on their outer face before removing them.

Inspect the components of the pump and check the rotor clearances in the same manner as described for the OHV type pump; the wear limits are the same in this case.

If required, the oil pressure relief valve spring and plunger can be removed from the pump body after extracting the valve sealing plug. To remove the plug, punch a hole in the centre and screw in a self-tapping screw of appropriate diameter. The plug can then be levered out of the relief valve bore, and the spring and plunger removed. Use a brush to clean the inside of the relief valve bore.

To reassemble the valve, fit the plunger and spring into the bore in the pump body and lubricate lightly with engine oil. Drive in a new sealing plug, flat side outwards, until it is flush with the pump face.

When reassembling the pump, lubricate the rotors and pump housing liberally with engine oil before fitting the pump cover. Fit the intermediate shaft into the rotor drive shaft and check for free rotation of the rotors. Use a new gasket when refitting the oil pick-up pipe, and ensure that the pipe is correctly orientated in relation to the pump body.

Reassembly

1. Install the selected main bearing shells dry in the crankcase and main bearing caps. Ensure that the hole in the upper bearings aligns with the oil feed hole the crankcase. Locate the thrust washers on each side of the centre main bearing housing and bearing cap, with the oil grooves facing away from the bearing (Fig. D:32).
2. Lubricate the bearing surfaces of the bearing shells and crankshaft journal liberally with oil, then carefully lower the crankshaft into position in the crankcase.
3. Fit the main bearing caps in their respective locations. Apply a light film of sealing compound to the rear of the contact face on the rear main bearing cap before fitting (Fig. D:35). Locating dowels are provided at the centre and rear main bearings to ensure correct alignment of the caps (Fig. D:34). Once fitted, the cast arrows on the caps should all point to the front of the engine. Tighten the cap bolts of all, except the rear bearing cap to their specified torque of 70 lb ft (10 kgm).

4. Screw the bolts into the rear bearing cap, finger-tight only. Push the crankshaft first to the rear abutment, then slowly, but positively, to the front abutment, and retain in this position. This procedure is necessary to ensure that both bearing shells in the rear main bearing are loaded evenly. Now tighten the rear bearing cap bolts to their specified torque.
5. Check the crankshaft end-float. This can be done using either a dial indicator, as shown in Fig. D:36, or with feeler gauges. If feeler gauges are being used, move the crankshaft fully forwards to take up the end-float in one direction, then measure the gap between the thrust washer at the front of the centre main bearing and the crankshaft web. The endfloat should be 0.003 - 0.011 in (0.08 - 0.28 mm). If it exceeds the upper limit, the thrust washers must be replaced with new ones of standard or suitable oversize to bring the figure within the limits.
6. Lubricate the lips of the new rear oil seal with engine oil. Fit the seal onto the Installer Tool, then drive it into its seat in the rear main bearing until it rests against the abutment (Fig. D:37).
7. Coat the two rear main bearing cap sealing strips with sealing compound and press them into position at each side of the bearing cap, using a blunt screwdriver (Fig. D: 38). The rounded face of the strips has a red colour marking and should be fitted pointing towards the bearing cap.
8. Check that the mating faces on the crankshaft flange and flywheel are perfectly clean, then locate the flywheel squarely on the flange and tap it into place. Tighten the retaining bolts evenly to 50 lb ft (7.0 kgm). The crankshaft can be locked in position with the handle of a hammer, as shown in Fig. D:31, when tightening the bolts. On models with automatic transmission, fit the drive plate, reinforcing plate and spacer in place of the flywheel.
9. Assemble the piston rings on the pistons, following the instructions supplied with the new rings. The rings must be fitted from the top of the piston. The rings will normally be marked 'TOP' on one face, and this side should face towards the piston crown. Service rings for use in worn bores normally have a stepped top ring to avoid the wear ridge at the top of the bore. It is most important that these rings be fitted with the steptted portion uppermost, otherwise breakage of the rings will result when the engine is run.

Where possible, proper piston ring pliers should be used to expand the rings when fitting them as this will eliminate the possibility of ring breakage or damage to the piston.

10. For each piston and connecting rod in turn:
a) Check that the piston is correctly assembled to its respective connecting rod (Fig. D:33).
b) Lubricate the cylinder bore and piston rings liberally with engine oil.
c) Install the piston assembly in its correct respective bore, making sure the notch or arrow on the piston crown is pointing towards the front of the block.
d) Position the piston rings so that their gaps are spaced at 120° to each other. The bottom ring should be positioned so that the gap in the spreader ring is to the rear of the piston, with the centre and top ring gaps at 120° on

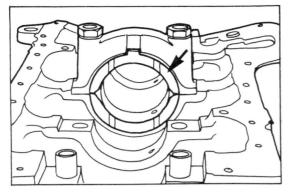

Fig. D:32 Thrust washers are fitted with oil groove facing outwards

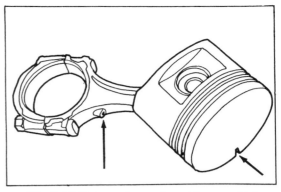

Fig. D:33 Piston and conrod must be assembled in the correct relationship

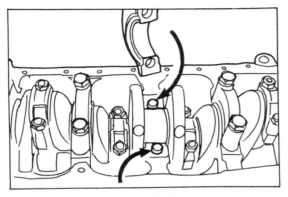

Fig. D:34 Dowels are provided to locate rear and centre main bearing caps

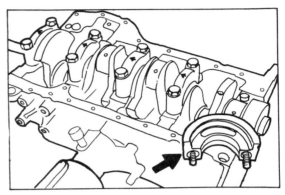

Fig. D:35 Apply sealant to contact face on rear main bearing cap before fitting

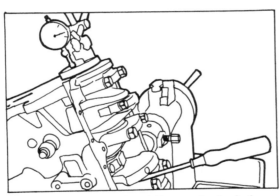

Fig. D:36 Crankshaft end-float can be checked using a dial indicator or feeler gauges

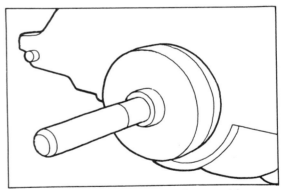

Fig. D:37 Drive new rear oil seal into position using wood block or installing tool

Fig. D:38 Press rear bearing cap seals into position using a BLUNT screwdriver

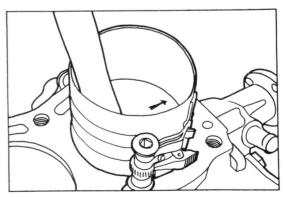

Fig. D:39 Use a proper ring compressor tool when re-installing pistons

either side.

e) Compress the rings using a proper piston ring compressor tool, such as that shown in Fig. D:39. Do not attempt to fit the rings by hand, otherwise breakage of the rings may result. Carefully tap the piston down into the cylinder bore, using the handle end of a hammer, until the piston crown is slightly below the top of the cylinder. Take great care to avoid the connecting rod hitting the crankshaft journal.

f) Fit the bearing shells dry in the connecting rod and cap.

g) Coat the crankshaft journal and bearings shells liberally with engine oil, then pull the connecting rod assembly down firmly onto the crankshaft journal and fit the cap to the rod. Check that the identification numbers on the cap and rod match, and are on the same side of the assembly (Fig. D:33). Ensure that the cap is correctly located, then tighten the cap retaining nuts to their specified torque of 33 lb ft (4.8 kgm). Check that the connecting rod has sufficient end-float on the crankpin.

11. Press a new oil seal into position in the crankshaft front cover from the front. Lightly oil the outer surface of the seal to facilitate installation. Fit the cover in position on the front of the cylinder block with a new gasket, and secure it in place with the retaining bolts. Ensure the cover is centred in relation to the crankshaft and is in line with the sump mating surface on the block. The use of Special Tool 21-009-A will avoid damage to the seal lip and ensure correct centring of the cover (Fig. D:42). Fit the crankshaft sprocket with the chamfered part facing inwards.

12. Lubricate the journals of the auxiliary shaft with engine oil and carefully insert the shaft into the cylinder block. Fit the shaft thrust plate and secure with the two cross-head screws. Check the shaft end-float. This should be 0.0016 - 0.0047 in (0.04 - 0.12 mm). If excessive, fit a new thrust plate. Tap the old oil seal out of the shaft cover plate (Fig. D:41). Press a new seal into position so that it is level with the outer face of the cover. Lubricate the lip of the new seal and fit the cover plate, using a new gasket. Ensure that the cover is correctly centred in relation to the auxiliary shaft. The use of the special tool, shown in Fig. D:40, will avoid the possibility of damage to the seal when installing the cover. Fit the timing sprocket on the shaft with the reinforcing ribs towards the cylinder block (Fig. D:43). Tighten the sprocket centre-bolt to 35 lb ft (5.0 kgm).

13. Fit the oil pump drive shaft into its location in the crankcase first, then fit the oil pump, ensuring that the locating bush is positioned in the block. Tighten the pump retaining bolts to 14 lb ft (2.0 kgm), using the special splined adaptor as for removal

14. If a new or overhauled oil pump is being fitted, it should be filled with engine oil first, then turned through a complete rotation by hand before installing it.

15. Fit new rubber seals in the grooves in the lower face of the front cover and rear main bearing cap. Apply sealing compound at the joints at the front cover and rear cap and the cylinder block. Position the two halves of the sump gasket on the block flange and slide the tabs on the ends of the gasket under the cut-outs in the rubber sealing strips (Fig. D:44). It will help locate the cork gasket if it is smeared with grease before fitting. Place the sump in position on the block, then fit and tighten the retaining bolts evenly in stages.

1st Stage, starting with bolt 'A' . . . . . 1 lb ft (0.2 kgm)
2nd Stage, starting with bolt 'B' . . . . . 5 lb ft (0.8 kgm)
3rd Stage, starting with bolt 'A' . . . . . 7 lb ft (1.0 kgm)

The last stage of tightening should be done after the engine has been run for about 20 minutes.

16. Turn the cylinder block upright and insert the oil separator into its location in the block above the oil filter pad. If removed, refit the oil pressure switch, or oil pressure connector, at the tapped hole below the fuel pump mounting pad.

17. Lubricate the sealing ring on the oil filter cartridge with clean engine oil then screw the cartridge onto the threaded adaptor by hand until the seal just contacts the mounting face, tighten it a further three-quarters of a turn.

18. Fit the cylinder head, using a new gasket. The use of two guide studs, made up and screwed into the cylinder head bolt holes, as shown in Fig. D:8, will facilitate correct alignment of the cylinder head and gasket during installation. Once the head is installed, the studs are then replaced by the proper cylinder head bolts.

In order to avoid damage to the valve and pistons when installing the cylinder head, it is essential that the crankshaft be positioned with the No. 1 piston at TDC and the camshaft be positioned with the sprocket aligned on the cylinder head mark, see Fig. D:5.

Fit the cylinder head bolts and tighten them evenly, using the special splined adaptor (Fig. D:6). The bolts should be tightened in the stages, following the sequence shown in Fig. D:9.

1st Stage . . . . .30-40 lb ft (4.0-5.5 kgm)
2nd Stage. . . . . .45-50 lb ft (6.0-7.0 kgm)
3rd Stage
(after 10-15 minutes wait). . . .65-80 lb ft (9.0-11.0 kgm)

Note that the head bolts must be retightened to the final setting after the engine has been run for about 15 minutes at fast idle (1.000 rpm).

19. Check that the crankshaft and camshaft are still positioned as shown in Fig. D:5, then fit the camshaft drive belt. The position of the auxiliary shaft sprocket is unimportant. Slacken the tensioner plate locking bolt to release the tensioner roller onto the timing belt. Turn the engine over twice in its normal direction of rotation, then retighten the plate locking bolt. This will automatically load the belt to its correct tension.

20. With the crankshaft and camshaft still positioned as above, install the distributor. Position the distributor on the engine so that the rotor arm will be in line with mark made on the distributor body prior to removal once the drive gear is engaged. If no mark was made, or an other distributor is being fitted, refer to the ENGINE ELECTRICS section for details of the installation procedure.

21. If required, check the valves clearances, as detailed under the appropriate heading previously, and adjust if necessary.

22. Fit the rocker cover with a new gasket. Ensure that

OHC Engines

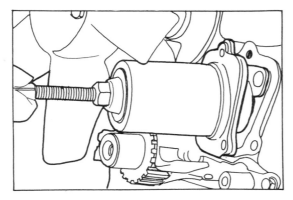

Fig. D:40 Centre front cover with alignment tool or use crankshaft sprocket

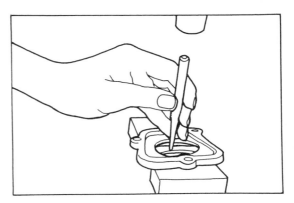

Fig. D:41 Tap old seal out of auxiliary shaft cover, using a drift

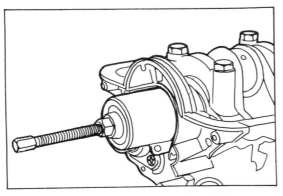

Fig. D:42 Using centring tool will avoid damaging sealing lip when re-fitting shaft cover

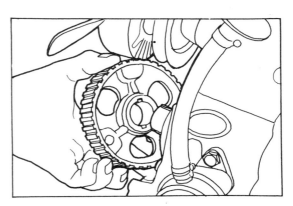

Fig. D:43 Webs on auxiliary shaft sprocket must face to rear

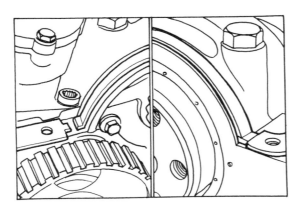

Fig. D:44 Engage gasket tabs under recesses in rubber seals

Fig. D:45 Use centring tool to align clutch disc

the dove-tail at the gasket joint is correctly engaged, and that the tabs on the outside of the gasket are correctly located in the recesses in the cover. Tighten the cover retaining bolts in the stages and sequence shown in Fig. D:2.

1st Stage, tighten bolts 1-6 . . . . 4 lb ft (0.6 kgm)
2nd Stage, tighten bolts 7 & 8 . . . . . 1.5 lb ft (0.25 kgm)
3rd Stage, tighten bolts 9 & 10. . . . . . 4 lb ft (0.6 kgm)
4th Stage, retighten bolts 7 & 8 . . . . 4 lb ft (0.6 kgm)

23. Refit the distributor cap. Install the spark plugs and reconnect the spark plug leads. The firing order is 1 - 3 - 4 - 2. Also reconnect the distributor vacuum pipe to the carburettor.

24. Fit the thrust washer and 'V' belt pulley on the crankshaft and tighten the pulley centre-bolt to 42 lb ft (6.0 kgm). The thrust washer is cup-shaped and should be fitted with the hollow side facing the pulley. Refit the timing belt cover.

25. Fit the water pump to the front face of the cylinder block, using a new gasket. Note that one of the pump retaining bolts also secures the alternator adjusting link. Assemble the cooling fan and drive pulley on the water pump hub.

26. Position the alternator on the side of the cylinder block and fit and tighten the mounting bracket retaining bolts. Fit the fan belt and adjust the belt tension so that a total free-movement of about 1/2 in (13 mm) is present at the midway point between the alternator and fan pulleys.

27. Insert the fuel pump push rod into its location in the cylinder block, then fit the fuel pump using a new gasket (Fig. D:26). Reconnect the fuel supply hose to the carburettor. Also reconnect the engine breather hose by pushing the vent valve into the grommet in the top of the oil separator.

28. On manual models, assemble the clutch disc and pressure plate to the flywheel, using a suitable centring tool to align the clutch disc (Fig. D:45). Tighten the retaining bolts evenly, working diagonally across the clutch. Finally withdraw the centring tool.

Technical Data

Identification code	Standard version NE, Economy NS
Capacity	1993 cc
Bore	90.82 mm
Stroke.	76.95 mm
Compression ratio	9.2:1
Firing order	1 - 3 - 4 - 2
Location of No. 1 cylinder	Adjacent to radiator

CYLINDER BLOCK

Bore diameter	
standard (4 grades, 1 to 4).	90.800-90.840 mm
oversizes (3 grades, A to C)	91.310-91.340 mm
Bore taper and ovality - maximum	0.001 in (0.025 mm)
Piston dia	
standard (4 grades, 1 to 4).	90.755-90.795 mm
service oversizes	0.020; 0.040 in (0.5; 1.0 mm)
Piston to bore clearance	0.001-0.024 in (0.025-0.060 mm)
Piston rings - end gap (fitted in block)	
compression rings	0.015-0.022 in (0.38-0.58 mm)
oil control rings.	0.016-0.055 in (0.4-1.4 mm)

CRANKSHAFT AND MAIN BEARING

Main bearing journal dia	
standard	56.970-56.990 mm
undersizes	0.010; 0.020; 0.030; 0.040 in (0.25; 0.50; 0.75; 1.00 mm)
clearance (Brgs 1 and 5)	0.0005-0.0018 in (0.014-0.048 mm)
clearance (Brgs 2, 3 and 4)	0.0009-0.0022 in (0.024-0.058 mm)
Big-end bearing journal ida	
standard	51.980-52.000 mm
undersizes	0.010; 0.020; 0.030; 0.040 in (0.25; 0.50; 0.75; 1.00 mm)
clearance (aluminium shells)	0.0005-0.0022 in (0.014-0.058 mm)
clearance (composite shells).	0.0005-0.0024 in (0.014-0.062 mm)
Crankshaft end-float	0.003-0.011 in (0.08-0.28 mm)

CAMSHAFT

Camshaft end-float . . . . 0.0016-0.0047 in (0.04-0.12 mm)
Thrust plate thickness
    type 1 . . . . .4.01 mm
    type 2 . . . . .3.98 mm

AUXILIARY SHAFT

End-float . . . . 0.0016-0.0047 in (0.04-0.12 mm)

VALVE TIMING

Inlet valve
    opens . . . . 24° BTDC
    closes . . . . 64° ABDC
Exhaust valve
    opens . . . . 70° BBDC
    closes . . . . 18° ATDC

CYLINDER HEAD

Identification mark (cast in) 20
Combustion chamber volume . . . . 48.6-50.1 cc
Valve seat angle . . . . 44°30′ - 45°
Valve oversizes available . . . . 0.008; 0.016; 0.024; 0.032 in
    (0.2; 0.4; 0.6; 0.8 mm)
Valve stem to guide clearance . . . . 0.0008-0.0025 in (0.020-0.063 mm)
Valve springs - free length . . . . 44 mm + – 3 mm
Valve clearance
    inlet (cold) . . . . 0.008 in (0.20 mm)
    exhaust . . . . 0.010 in (0.25 mm)

OIL PUMP

Rotor to casing clearance . . . . 0.006-0.012 in (0.15-0.30 mm)
Inner to outer rotor . . . . 0.002-0.008 in (0.05-0.20 mm)
Rotor to end cover . . . . 0.001-0.004 in (0.03-0.10 mm)
Pressure relief valve opens at . . . . .58-68 psi (4.0-4.7 kg/cm^2)
Oil pressure warning light operates at . . . . 4.4-8.7 psi (0.3-0.6 kg/cm^2)
Minimum oil pressure at 80 deg C
    750 rpm . . . . 30 psi (2.1 kg/cm^2)
    2000 rpm . . . . 35 psi (2.4 kg/cm^2)
Sump capacity
    initial fill with filter . . . . 7.0 pints (4.0 litres)
    oil change, including filter . . . . 6.6 pints (3.75 litres)
    oil change, excluding filter . . . . .5.72 pints (3.25 litres)
Recommended lubricants . . . . See 'SERVICE DATA' at the end
of ROUTINE MAINTENANCE section

Engine Electrics

CHARGING CIRCUIT TEST . . . . [1]

Dynamo System

1. Check that the generator drive belt is correctly adjusted. The battery should be in good condition and its terminals clean and tight, also the leads and connections in the rest of the charging circuit should be clean and making good contact.
2. Disconnect both leads ('D' and 'F') from the rear of the dynamo and connect a voltmeter between a good earth point and the 'D' terminal (the large one) on the rear of the dynamo. Start the engine and gently increase its speed to about 2500 - 3000 rpm. At this speed, the voltmeter reading should be between 2 and 3 volts.

If the reading is outside these limits, check the brushes condition first. If the brushes are in good order, a replacement dynamo is probably needed.

With the voltmeter still connected to the 'D' terminal, connect an ammeter between the two dynamo 'D' and 'F' terminals. Start the engine and increase its speed until the voltmeter reads 12 volts; the ammeter should then read not more than 2 amperes. If the ammeter reading is more, or less than 2 amperes, a replacement dynamo is probably needed.

3. If the above tests show that the dynamo and its connections are apparently in order, then any fault will probably be with the voltage regulator unit. Adjustment of the regulator unit is not really a DIY proposition as special tools and conditions are necessary apart from the economics involved - an exchange unit should be obtained from a Ford dealer or local auto electrician.

Alternator System

1. Check that the generator drive belt is correctly adjusted. The battery should be in good condition and its terminals clean and tight, also the connections and leads in the rest of the charging system should be clean and making good contact.

2. Disconnect the cable plug from the rear of the alternator, then connect the negative side of a voltmeter to a good earth and switch the ignition on. Connect the other voltmeter lead to each of the disconnected alternator cables in turn. If a battery voltage is not recorded at the 'Brown' and 'Yellow' 'IND' cable, then check the warning light circuit and the bulb.

If a battery voltage is not recorded at the main charging lead, check the wiring and the connections between the battery and the alternator.

If all is well, reconnect the alternator cables and then disconnect the 'Brown' cable on the starter motor solenoid. Connect an ammeter between the 'Brown' cable and the terminal on the starter solenoid, also connect a voltmeter between the battery terminals.

If, with the engine idling, the ammeter reads zero, then the alternator is probably at fault. If the ammeter reads less than 10 amperes and the voltmeter reads between 13.6 and 14.4 volts, with the battery in a low state of charge, then suspect the alternator. If the ammeter reads more or less than 10 amperes and the voltmeter more or less than 13.6 volts then suspect the voltage regulator.

Most faults allied to the charging system are usually due to either worn brushes or to a defective voltage regulator.

Replacement of both the brushes and the integral regulator unit on alternators is detailed under the appropriate headings. If anything more involved such as the rectifier diodes, slip rings bearings etc., are faulty then it is recommended that any repairs are given to an auto electrical specialist or an exchange unit obtained.

In most cases, the latter will be found to be the most economical and convenient solution rather than attempt to obtain parts and repair an alternator or dynamo.

It should be noted that with an alternator, the battery should ALWAYS be disconnected before starting work on the charging system to avoid any possibility of damage to the semi-conductor devices in the rectifier and diode units.

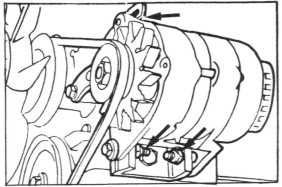

Fig. E:1 The generator mounting bolts arrowed
- alternator type shown

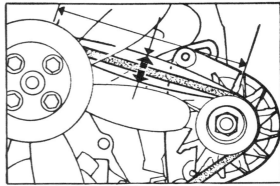

Fig. E:2 Adjust the drive belt tension to give 0.5
in (13 mm) deflection

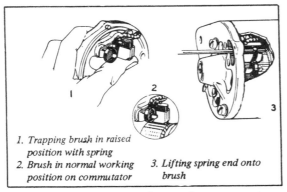

1. Trapping brush in raised
   position with spring
2. Brush in normal working
   position on commutator
3. Lifting spring end onto
   brush

Fig. E:3 Fitting the brushes on the commutator
when reassembling the end bracket

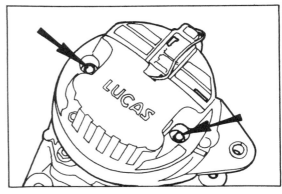

Fig. E:4 Box spanner or socket will be needed to
undo alternator cover bolts - Lucas

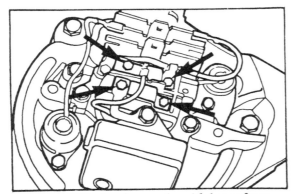

Fig. E:5 The brushes can be withdrawn from
brush box by undoing four screws - Lucas

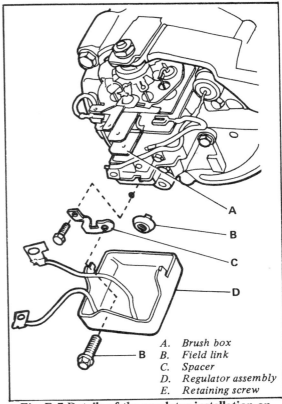

A. Brush box
B. Field link
C. Spacer
D. Regulator assembly
E. Retaining screw

Fig. E:7 Details of the regulator installation on
Lucas type alternators

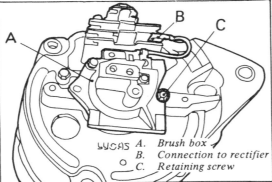

A. Brush box
B. Connection to rectifier
C. Retaining screw

Fig. E:6 To remove brush box, undo two screws
and disconnect rectifier lead

GENERATOR...................[2]

Removal - Dynamo/Alternator

1. Disconnect the battery and then detach the multiplug from the rear of the alternator or the two wires 'D' and 'F' at the rear of the dynamo.
2. Slacken the three generator mounting bolts and swing the unit towards the engine to detach the fan belt from the pulley. Remove the mounting bolts and detach the generator from the engine (Fig. E:1).

Installation - Alternator/Dynamo

a) If the dynamo or alternator is being exchanged for a new one, the drive pulley and cooling fan must be removed from the shaft and transferred to the new unit, as these parts are not normally supplied with an exchanged unit. The shaft locating key must also be transferred, but it is good practice to use a new key anyway when assembling the components to the new unit.

b) Install the generator in the reverse order of removal but leave all fixings and the adjuster slack.

c) Refit the drive belt using hand pressure only, and pull it tight. The belt tension is correct when moderate thumb pressure at the centre of the longest belt run deflects the belt by 0.5 in (13 mm). If a lever is needed, make sure the pressure is applied only to the drive end bracket part of the generator. Do not overtighten the belt (Fig. E:2).

DYNAMO BRUSHES..................[3]

Removal and Replacement

Remove the dynamo from the engine as detailed earlier, then unscrew the two through-bolts at the rear of the dynamo and withdraw the commutator end bracket from the main body. Lever the brush springs to one side and withdraw the brushes from their holders and the end bracket (Fig. E:3).

Inspect the brushes for wear - brushes which are worn to, or are approaching the wear minimum length of 0.32 in (8 mm) must be renewed as a set. Check too, the commutator surface for deep scoring, excessive wear and oil contamination. If the commutator is blackened, dirty and has only slight surface scoring, then it can be cleaned either with a petrol moistened cloth or rubbed with very 'fine' grade glass paper. Do not use emery cloth or similar abrasive. If the commutator surface is badly worn or deeply scored, then either it should be skimmed by a specialist or the unit replaced.

To renew the brushes, undo the screw and lock washer securing each brush lead to its holder, and detach the brushes.

Ensure that the replacement brushes are of the correct type and length, then secure the leads of the new brushes to their respective holders.

Check the new brushes for freedom of movement in the holders. Sticking brushes can usually be freed by lightly polishing the sides with a 'fine' file.

To reassemble the brush gear, position the brush springs so that the ends are just resting on the outer edge of the brush holders and holding the brushes clear of the commutator. Check that the fibre thrust washers are fitted on the commutator end of the armature shaft, then refit the commutator end bracket

Ensure that the locating dowel in the flange of the bracket engages in the notch on the dynamo body. Refit the through-bolts and tighten securely.

Insert a thin screwdriver through the ventilation hole at the rear of the end bracket and gently move the brush springs so that they release the brushes, then place the spring end so it is bearing on the brush end and pushing the brush onto the commutator.

DYNAMO REGULATOR...............[4]

Replacement

A two or three-bobbin voltage control regulator unit is used to control the dynamo output and this is mounted in the engine compartment. As explained earlier, if there is a charging fault and the generator is found to be working correctly, then it is likely that the regulator is at fault.

Rather than attempt to clean or adjust the unit, which requires special conditions and tools it is advised that the unit is exchanged at a Ford or Lucas dealer or auto electrician.

To replace the voltage regulator, disconnect the battery and disconnect the various leads to the regulator unit - noting which lead goes where. Undo the two screws attaching the unit to the side of the engine compartment and fit the new unit using the same screws.

Reconnect the leads making sure that the EARTH lead is making good contact, then reconnect the battery.

ALTERNATOR - LUCAS...............[5]

Regulator Replacement

The voltage regulator can be replaced with the alternator still attached to the engine but if this type of work has not been tackled before, then it is recommended that the alternator is removed first.

Remove the black plastic cover from the rear of the alternator. This is secured by two retaining screws with hexagon heads and a small box spanner or socket will be needed to undo them (Fig. E:4).

Disconnect the regulator wiring connections, one on the top of the brush box and one on the side. Note their respective positions for assembly. Remove the single screw securing the regulator to the brush box and remove the regulator assembly. To do this, it may be necessary to slacken the field link retaining screw to allow the link to be moved aside. Note the small plastic spacer fitted between the regulator and brush box (Fig. E:7).

Position the new regulator in the rear of the alternator and secure it in position, ensuring that the plastic

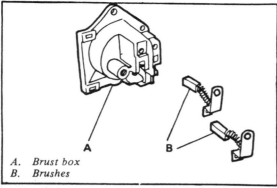

A. Brust box
B. Brushes

Fig. E:8 An exploded view of the brush box
assembly - Lucas type

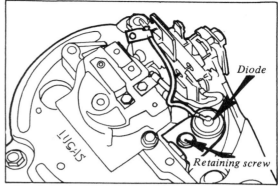

Diode

Retaining screw

Fig. E:9 The surge protection diode installation
on Lucas alternator

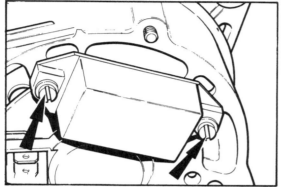

Fig. E:10 The regulator/brush assembly is
attached by two screws - Bosch type

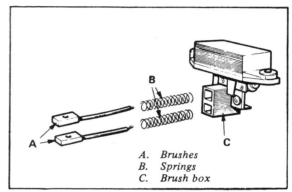

A. Brushes
B. Springs
C. Brush box

Fig. E:11 Details of the brush box assembly
on Bosch alternators

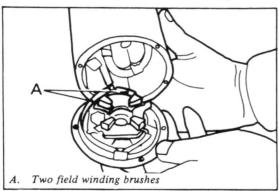

A. Two field winding brushes

Fig. E:12 Removing the brush end plate on
Lucas M35J type starters

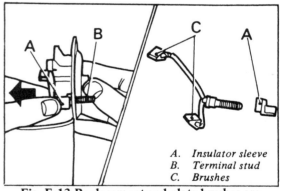

A. Insulator sleeve
B. Terminal stud
C. Brushes

Fig. E:13 Replacement end plate brushes are
attached to terminal stud

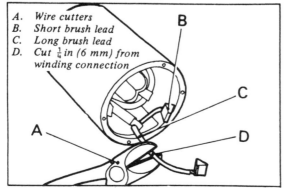

A. Wire cutters
B. Short brush lead
C. Long brush lead
D. Cut ¼ in (6 mm) from
   winding connection

Fig. E:14 Note the short and long leads when
replacing the field winding brushes

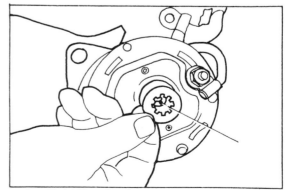

Fig. E:15 Use chisel to remove armature shaft
retaining clip - Lucas M100 type

spacer and connecting link are correctly fitted. Reconnect the regulator wiring and refit the end cover (Fig. E:0).

The slip ring brushes are located in the brush box at the rear of the alternator and can easily be replaced if they are worn. Although this can be done with the alternator still in the car, it is easier if the unit is removed from the engine first as detailed earlier.

Remove the black plastic cover from the rear of the alternator. This is secured by two retaining screws with hexagon heads and a small box spanner or socket will be needed to undo them (Fig. E:4).

Undo and remove the four screws securing the two brush retaining plates and withdraw the brush assemblies from the brush box (Fig. E:5).

NOTE: It is as well to make a note that the brush connecting lead to the rectifier pack and the regulator unit are attached to the outer brush plate screws; the regulator field link is attached to one of the inner brush plate screws. Remember to refit the leaf spring at the side of the inner brush.

Fit the new brush assemblies into the brush box and secure them in position with the screws. Ensure that the various leads are reconnected as before, then refit the alternator end cover.

Alternatively, the complete brush box assembly - together with the regulator unit - can be removed from the slip ring end bracket. The advantage of this is so that the condition of the slip ring and the brush holders can be checked.

In this case, remove the end cover as detailed earlier, then remove the single screw attaching the surge protection diode to the slip ring end bracket, - detach the diode complete with the brush box assembly - then disconnect the brush box lead from the rectifier pack (Fig. E:6).

Remove the two screws securing the brush box flange to the slip ring end bracket and lift off the complete assembly (Fig. E:8).

Note that the regulator earth lead is alos secured by one of these screws.

Inspect the brushes for wear. With both brushes in the free position, measure the amount by which they protrude beyond the brush box moulding. The brush length when new is 0.5 in (13 mm). If the amount protruding is worn down to or is approaching the limit of 0.2 in (5 mm), the brushes should be replaced.

Remove the old brushes from the brush box and fit the new ones as detailed earlier.

Check the new brushes for freedom of movement in their holders and use a 'fine' file to relieve one that is sticking.

Inspect the surface of the slip ring on the end of the rotor. If it shows signs of roughness, this can be cleaned off with 'fine' grade glass paper. Do not use emery cloth or similar abrasive.

Before refitting the brush box, clean off any dirt that may have collected around the slip ring end bracket or the apertures in the plastic end cover.

Check that the brushes are correctly located in their holders, then locate the brush box assembly on the alternator end bracket and secure with the two retaining screws. Make sure that the regulator earth lead is secured by one of the screws. Secure the surge protection diode in position on the end bracket, then reconnect the outer brush lead to the terminal on the rectifier pack. Finally, refit the alternator end cover.

ALTERNATOR (BOSCH). . . . . [6]

Regulator

The voltage regulator is mounted on the rear of the alternator and can be easily detached after removing the two retaining screws. The brush box assembly is in unit with the regulator and is removed with it. (Fig. E:10).

If defective, the regulator must be renewed as an assembly with the brush holder and brushes.

Fit the new regulator in position on the rear of the alternator and secure with the two retaining screws.

Brushes

As stated above, the brush assembly is removed together with the regulator.

When new, the brushes protrude 0.4 in (10 mm) beyond the brush housing. If the brushes are worn out, or are approaching, the wear limit of 0.2 in (5 mm), they should be renewed.

To replace the brushes, first unsolder the existing brush leads from the terminals on the brush holder, and remove the worn brushes and their springs. Install the new brushes and springs in the brush box and solder their leads to the terminals (Fig. E:11).

Refit the brush holder assembly and regulator unit as detailed previously.

STARTER MOTOR . . . . [7]

Removal and Installation - Inertia and Pre-Engaged Types

First of all, as a safety precaution, disconnect the battery. Disconnect the leads from the starter motor terminal - one on inertia types, and three on the pre-engaged type.

Remove the nuts and/or bolts on some models attaching the starter to the engine, noting the earth lead on some models. Withdraw the starter from the engine.

Replacement is a straight reversal of the removal procedure.

STARTER BRUSHES. . . . . [8]

Brush Replacement - Lucas M35J - Inertia Type

Remove the starter motor from the car as detailed above, remove the plastic cap and detach the retaining pin/washers from the armature shaft. Remove four screws securing the commutator end plate to the starter yoke.

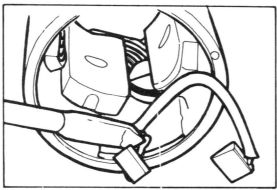

Fig. E:16 Solder the new brush leads to terminal on field windings - Lucas M100 type

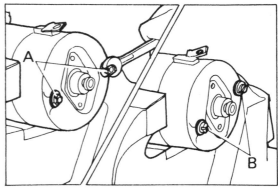

Fig. E:17 Bosch commutator end housing attachments, nuts (A) or through-bolts (B)

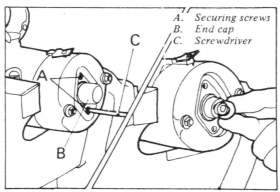

A. Securing screws
B. End cap
C. Screwdriver

Fig. E:18 'C' clip and shims can be removed after detaching end cap - Bosch type

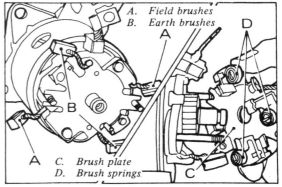

A. Field brushes
B. Earth brushes
C. Brush plate
D. Brush springs

Fig. E:19 Details of the brushes and brush plate removal on Bosch starters

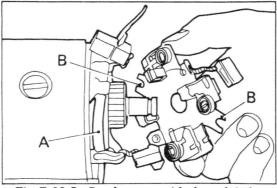

Fig. E:20 On Bosch starter with through-bolts, align cut-outs (B) with loops (A)

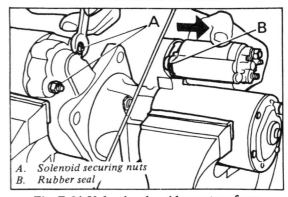

A. Solenoid securing nuts
B. Rubber seal

Fig. E:21 Unhook solenoid armature from actuating arm to remove it - Lucas type

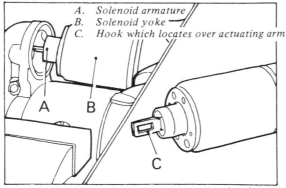

A. Solenoid armature
B. Solenoid yoke
C. Hook which locates over actuating arm

Fig. E:22 Remove two screws and unhook solenoid armature from actuating arm - Bosch

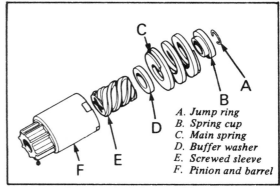

A. Jump ring
B. Spring cup
C. Main spring
D. Buffer washer
E. Screwed sleeve
F. Pinion and barrel

Fig. E:23 An exploded view of inertia starter pinion components

Withdraw the end plate sufficiently to allow the two field brushes to be removed from their holders, then remove the end plate complete with the brush box moulding. Care should be taken to avoid damaging the end plate gasket during removal (Fig. E:12).

Inspect the brushes for wear. Brushes which are worn to, or are approaching, their wear limit of 0.32 in (8 mm) should be renewed as a set.

Inspect the brush contact face on the end of the commutator for signs of oil contamination; if present, the brushes should be renewed. If the commutator surface is blackened or dirty, clean it with a petrol-moistened cloth. If there is evidence of burning, this can be cleaned off with very fine glass paper. On NO account must emery cloth or similar abrasive be used for this purpose.

Replacement brushes for the commutator end plate come complete with the terminal stud (Fig. E:13). To renew the brushes, first remove the nut, washer and insulator sleeve from the terminal stud. Push the stud and second insulator through the end plate, unhook the two attached brushes from the brush box, and remove the stud and brushes as an assembly. Fit the terminal stud of the new brush assembly, together with the insulator bush, through the hole in the end plate and secure the stud with the second insulator, washer and nut.

The field winding brushes must be cut off and the new brush leads soldered to the stubs of the original leads. Cut the old leads about 0.25 in (6 mm) from the field winding connection (Fig. E:14).

Note the arrangement of the long and short brush leads. Clean the ends of the original leads and solder the new brush leads to them, ensuring a perfect soldered joint. Also ensure the long and short leads are fitted in their original positions and their correct lengths are maintained. The insulating sleeving on the new leads must provide maximum coverage consistent with satisfactory soldering.

Fit the brushes into their respective channels in the brush box, ensuring that the fitting arrangement of the long and short leads with respect to the end bracket is the same as it was for the original brushes. Check the brushes for freedom of movement in their holders. Sticking brushes can be freed by cleaning the brushes and holders with a petrol-moistened cloth, or by lightly polishing the brush sides with a smooth file if necessary.

Ensure that the thrust washer is in position on the end of the armature shaft, then assemble the end plate to the starter yoke and secure in position with the four retaining screws. Clip the plastic cap onto the end plate.

Brush Replacement - Lucas M 100 Pre-Engaged Type

Remove the starter from the engine as detailed earlier, then remove the plastic cap from the commutator end plate.

Use a thin cold chisel to remove the 'star' retaining washer from the end of the armature shaft (Fig. E:15). Discard the washer after removal.

Undo and withdraw the two through bolts and withdraw the end cover from the motor body sufficiently to allow the two field brushes to be removed from their

holders in the brush box moulding on the commutator end-plate.

Inspect the brushes for wear. Brushes which are worn down to, or are approaching the wear limit length of 0.375 in (10 mm) should be renewed as a set.

Check the commutator contact face on the end of the armature shaft for signs of scoring or dirt. This can usually be cleaned off using 'fine' grade glass paper until the commutator face is bright copper coloured. On no account should emery cloth be used for this purpose.

Replacement brushes for the commutator end-plate come complete with terminal and rubber grommet. Withdraw the old brushes from the end-plate and fit the new ones in the original order. Check that both brushes are free to move in their holders.

The field winding brushes must be cut off and the new brush leads soldered to the stud ends. Cut the old leads about 0.25 in (6 mm) from the field winding connection - noting the arrangement of the long and the short leads.

Clean the ends of the field winding leads in meths or white spirit and solder the new brush leads to them and insulate the joint (Fig. E:16).

Ensure that the long and short leads are fitted in their original positions and that their correct lengths are maintained.

Check that the field winding brushes are also free to move in their holders then replace the brush assembly end cover, securing it with the through bolts and a new 'star' retaining washer on the armature shaft.

Brush Replacement - M35J/5M90 Types

The brush replacement procedure on the pre-engaged starter is the same as that for the M35J inertia-type detailed earlier.

Brush Replacement - Bosch Pre-Engaged Type

Remove the two screws securing the protective end cap to the commutator end bracket and detach the cap and rubber seal (Fig. E:17).

Wipe the grease from the end of the armature shaft, then extract the 'C' clip and remove the shims from the shaft. Unscrew the two through-bolts (or nuts and washers on certain motors) and withdraw the commutator end housing (Fig. E:18).

Withdraw the two field brushes from their holders on the brush plate and remove the brush plate complete with the two earth brushes (Fig. E:19).

Inspect the brushes for wear. Brushes which are worn to, or are approaching their wear limit of 0.4 in (10 mm) should be renewed as a set.

Inspect the brush contact face on the side of the commutator for signs of oil contamination; if present, the brushes should be renewed. If the commutator surface is blackened or dirty, clean it with a petrol-moistened cloth. If there is evidence of burning, this can be cleaned off with very fine glass paper. On no account must emery cloth or similar abrasive be used for this purpose.

To renew the brushes, cut the original brush leads at a point midway between their base and the brush leads to the original connections, ensuring a good soldered joint.

Check the brushes for freedom of movement in their respective holders. Sticking brushes can be freed by cleaning the brushes and holders with a petrol-moistened cloth, or by lightly polishing the sides of the brushes with a smooth file, if necessary.

If possible, check the brush spring pressure with a pull-type spring scale. A minimum reading of 31.5 oz (900 grams) should be obtained. If the spring pressures are low, the springs should be renewed.

Fit the brush holder plate over the end of the armature shaft, aligning the cut-outs in the plate with either the fixing studs or the 'loops' in the field windings, as applicable (Figs. E:19 and E:20).

Position the four brushes in their respective holders and retain with the brush springs. Position the spring ends on the brushes and check that the brushes seat correctly on the commutator.

Refit the commutator end housing, ensuring that the rubber insulator engages correctly in the cut-out in the end housing

Secure the end housing with either the two through-bolts or the two nuts and spring washers, as applicable. Fit the shims and 'C' clip on the end of the armature shaft. Check the end-float of the shaft by sliding it axially in its bearings. The end-float should be 0.004 - 0.012 in (0.1 - 0.3 mm). If necessary, the end-float can be adjusted altering the thickness of the shim pack under the 'C' clip.

Smear a quantity of lithium-based grease on the end of the armature shaft, then refit the protective end cover with its sealing ring and secure with the two retaining screws.

SOLENOID . . . . [9]

Replacement M35J Type

Remove the starter motor from the engine as detailed earlier in this section. The solenoid is mounted on the drive-end housing of the starter motor and is easily removed for replacement.

Disconnect and remove the field connecting link from the field terminal on the starter motor and the solenoid by removing the two nuts and washers (Fig. E:21).

Remove the two nuts and washers securing the solenoid mounting studs to the drive end housing and draw the solenoid away from the housing (Fig. E:21).

Unhook the solenoid armature from the actuating lever inside the housing by moving the solenoid upwards and away from the lever. Note the rubber sealing plug fitted between the drive end housing and the starter yoke at the solenoid location.

To refit the solenoid, locate the solenoid armature on to the actuating lever inside the drive end housing. Guide the solenoid yoke over the solenoid armature and locate the yoke securing stud through the drive end housing. Secure the solenoid in position with the two retaining nuts and washers.

Refit the connecting link between the solenoid and

the starter field terminal and secure with the two nuts and washers.

Replacement Lucas M 100 Type

Remove the starter motor from the engine as described earlier in this section.

The solenoid is mounted on the drive-end housing of the starter motor and it is easily removed for replacement.

Disconnect the link wire between the starter motor and the solenoid terminal 'STA'

Undo and remove the two screws attaching the solenoid to the drive end bracket, then withdraw the solenoid outer casing away from the interior plunger.

Lift the solenoid plunger upwards to separate it from the actuating lever and withdraw the block shaped rubber grommet from between the drive end bracket and the starter motor yoke.

Withdraw the return spring, spring seat and dust excluder from the plunger body.

To refit the solenoid, replace the return spring assembly into the plunger body, refit the block shaped grommet between the drive end bracket and the yoke - if removed.

Insert the plunger assembly into the drive end housing and engage it with the end of the actuating lever.

Slide the solenoid body into position over the plunger and secure it with the two screws. Reconnect the link wire to the solenoid 'STA' terminal.

Replacement - Bosch 0,7, 1 PS Type

The solenoid is mounted on the drive end housing of the starter motor and is easily removed for replacement.

Disconnect the field connecting link from the lower terminal on the solenoid. Remove the two screws securing the solenoid to the drive end housing and draw the solenoid away from the housing. Unhook the solenoid armature from the actuating lever inside the housing by moving the solenoid upwards and away from the lever (Fig. E:22).

To refit the solenoid, locate the hook on the solenoid armature over the end of the actuating lever inside the drive end housing. Secure the solenoid in position with the two retaining screws. Reconnect the field lead to the solenoid terminal.

DRIVE PINION . . . . [10]

Replacement - Inertia Type

If difficulty is experienced with the starter motor pinion not meshing correctly with the ring gear, it may be that the drive assembly requires cleaning. The pinion barrel assembly should move freely on the screwed sleeve. If there is any dirt or other foreign matter on the sleeve, it should be washed off with petrol or paraffin. If required, the drive assembly can be lubricated with a silicone-based aerosol lubricant, but on NO account must grease or oil be used as this would attract dirt.

If required, the pinion assembly can be replaced as

follows, but a special compressor tool will be required to compress the drive spring.

Such tools are relatively inexpensive to buy and should be available from most of the good motor accessory shops.

Compress the drive spring sufficiently to expose the jump ring which can then be sprung from its groove in the armature shaft. The spring cup, drive spring, thrust washer and drive pinion assembly can then be removed from the armature shaft. You may find it necessary to depress the pinion assembly and turn it slightly to disengage it from the shaft splines (Fig. E:24).

The pinion and barrel is serviced as a complete assembly with the screwed sleeve and no attempt should be made to dismantle the pinion assembly (Fig. E:23).

Fit the new pinion assembly on the armature shaft, with the pinion teeth towards the starter motor. Assemble the thrust washer, drive spring and spring seat on the shaft, then compress the drive spring and fit the jump ring. Ensure that the ring is correctly seated.

Replacement - Lucas Pre-Engaged Types

Replacement of the drive pinion assembly involves dismantling most of the starter motor.

Remove the solenoid and commutator end plate as detailed previously. Remove the two screws securing the drive end housing to the starter yoke, and separate the housing and armature assembly from the yoke. Withdraw the armature from the drive end housing, at the same time unhooking the solenoid actuating lever from the drive pinion assembly (Fig. E:25).

The lever fork engages in the groove in the drive assembly clutch.

A suitably dimensioned tube will be required to remove the drive pinion assembly from the armature shaft (Fig. E:26).

Secure the armature in a vice with soft jaws and, using the piece of tube, tap the thrust collar down the shaft to expose the jump ring. Extract the jump ring from its groove in the armature shaft and slide the thrust collar and drive pinion assembly up off the shaft.

The drive pinion and clutch assembly are serviced as a complete unit and no attempt should be made to repair or even separate them.

Refitting is a reversal of the removal procedure.

Replacement - Bosch Pre-Engaged Types

Replacement of the drive pinion assembly involves dismantling most of the starter motor.

Remove the solenoid, commutator end housing and brush plate as detailed previously.

Separate the drive end housing and armature from the yoke by tapping them apart.

On starter motors which have fixing studs, unscrew the studs to release the drive pinion clutch stop bracket (Fig. E:27).

Withdraw the armature assembly from the drive end housing at the same time uncoupling the actuating arm from the locating flange on the drive pinion assembly (Fig. E:28).

A suitably dimensioned tube will be required to remove the drive pinion assembly from the armature shaft

Secure the armature in a vice with soft jaws and, using the piece of tube, tap the thrust collar down the shaft to expose the jump ring. Extract the jump ring from its groove in the armature shaft and slide the thrust collar and drive pinion assembly up off the shaft.

The drive pinion and clutch assembly are serviced as a complete unit and no attempt should be made to repair or even separate them.

Slide the new drive pinion assembly and thrust collar onto the armature shaft. On starters with a separate clutch stop bracket, ensure the bracket is in place on the armature shaft before fitting the new drive pinion assembly. Fit the jump ring into the groove in the shaft, then pull the thrust collar up over the ring, using a two-legged puller

Insert the armature assembly into position in the drive end housing, at the same time engaging the actuating arm fork onto the drive pinion flange (Fig. E:28).

On starters which use fixing studs in place of through-bolts, align the clutch retaining bracket with the drive end housing and secure in position with the two fixing studs (Fig. E:27).

Ensure that the rubber sealing block is in position at the actuating lever in the drive end housing, then assemble the starter yoke to the drive end housing and tap it home.

Assemble the brush plate, commutator end housing and solenoid to the starter yoke as detailed previously.

DISTRIBUTOR (OHV ENGINE) . . . . [11]

Removal

Remove the distributor cap and note or mark the position of the No. 1 segment in the distributor cap relative to the distributor body.

Rotate the crankshaft until the rotor arm is pointing approximately to the position of the No. 1 segment, and the notch in the crankshaft pulley is in line with the TDC mark on the timing scale (Fig. E:31).

Disconnect the plug leads by grasping the moulded cap of each lead, then twisting and pulling the cap off the plug. Do NOT pull on the lead, otherwise the connection inside the cap may become separated.

Disconnect the distributor LT lead from the terminal on the side of the distributor body, and the HT lead from the ignition coil tower. Disconnect the vacuum pipe at the distributor.

Remove the bolt securing the distributor clamp plate to the cylinder block, and carefully withdraw the distributor, allowing the rotor arm to turn as the shaft gear dis-engages from the camshaft. The shaft will rotate approximately 35 - 40° anti-clockwise. After removal, mark the position of the rotor arm relative to the distributor body as this will facilitate installation.

Installation

Ensure that the engine is at TDC position with No. 1

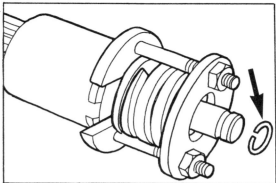

Fig. E:24 Using special tool to compress pinion spring and release circlip (arrowed)

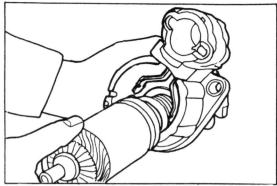

Fig. E:25 Removing armature from drive-end housing and actuating arm. Lucas PE type

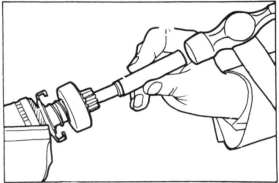

Fig. E:26 Removing drive pinion. Drift collar down shaft to remove 'jump' ring

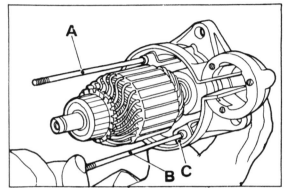

Fig. E:27 Unscrew studs (A) and (B), release clutch stop (C) - Bosch type with fixing studs

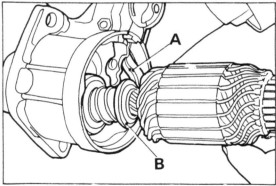

Fig. E:28 Uncouple actuating arm (A) from locating flange (B) on drive pinion

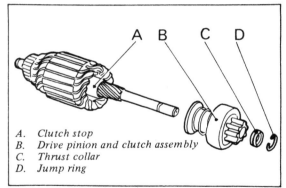

A. Clutch stop
B. Drive pinion and clutch assembly
C. Thrust collar
D. Jump ring

Fig. E:29 Armature/drive pinion assembly - Bosch starters with through - bolts

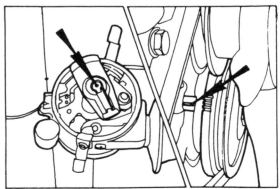

Fig. E:30 Distributor rotor position with No. 1 piston at TDC - OHC engine

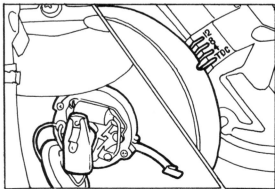

Fig. E:31 Distributor rotor position with No. 1 piston at TDC - OHV engine

cylinder on its compression stroke. Align the rotor arm with the scribed mark on the distributor body made on removal, and insert the distributor into the cylinder block. As the gears mesh, the rotor will rotate clockwise slightly into its correct position.

If no mark was made on removal, or if a new distributor is being fitted, align the distributor as follows: Position the distributor on the engine with the vacuum unit pointing to the rear and approximately 35° out from the engine. Turn the rotor arm until the electrode is immediately over the end of the condenser cannister. Insert the distributor into the engine.

Fit and tighten the clamp plate securing bolt. Refit the distributor cap. Reconnect the LT, HT and spark plug leads. Ensure that the plug leads are refitted in their correct respective positions (see TUNE-UP). The firing order is 1 - 2 - 4 - 3, No. 1 cylinder being at the front of the engine. Reconnect the vacuum line.

Finally, check the contact breaker gap or dwell angle, and the ignition timing setting, as detailed in the TUNE-UP section previously.

Overhaul

In most cases of wear or damage to the main components of the distributor (distributor shaft, cam assembly, advance weights, bearings, etc.,) and especially after considerable mileage, it will probably be more economical and convenient to exchange the complete distributor assembly for a new or reconditioned unit, rather than attempt to repair it.

DISTRIBUTOR (OHC ENGINE) . . . . [12]

Removal

Remove the distributor cap and note or mark the position of the No. 1 segment in the distributor cap relative to the distributor body.

Rotate the crankshaft until the rotor arm is pointing approximately to the position of the No. 1 segment, and the TDC mark on the crankshaft pulley is in line with the timing pointer on the front cover (Fig. E:30).

Disconnect the plug leads by grasping the moulded cap of each lead in turn, then twisting and pulling the cap off the plug. Do NOT pull on the lead, otherwise the connection inside the cap may become separated.

Disconnect the distributor LT lead from the terminal on the ignition coil, and the HT lead from the coil tower. Disconnect the vacuum pipe at the distributor.

Remove the bolt securing the distributor clamp plate to the cylinder block, and carefully withdraw the distributor, allowing the rotor arm to turn as the shaft disengages from the auxiliary shaft. The shaft will rotate approximately 35 - 40° clockwise. After removal, mark the position of the rotor arm relative to the distributor body as this will facilitate installation.

Installation

Ensure that the engine is at TDC position with No. 1 cylinder on its compression stroke. Align the rotor arm with the scribed mark on the distributor body made on re moval, and insert the distributor into the cylinder block. As the gears mesh, the rotor will rotate anti-clockwise slightly into its correct position.

If no mark was made on removal, or if a new distributor is being fitted, align the distributor as follows: Position the distributor on the engine with the vacuum unit pointing to the rear and in line with the engine centre-line.

IGNITION COIL. . . . . [13]

The ignition coil is a special low voltage type for use with a ballast resistor, and is mounted on the left-hand side of the front panel. The ballast resistor is in the form of a special wire connected between the ignition switch and the coil. The wire is colour coded grey and has a predetermined resistance of 1.5 ohms which limits the battery voltage to the coil during normal running to approximately 7 volts. During starting, the ballast resistor wire is by-passed allowing full battery voltage to be applied to the coil to facilitate starting.

When fitting a replacement coil, it is MOST important that the correct type be obtained, otherwise the complete ignition system will be adversely affected. Also, if the resistance wire becomes damaged or defective it MUST be replaced by a similar high resistance wire, not any old piece of wire.

Technical Data

LUCAS ALTERNATOR

Type.	15 ACR or 17 ACR
Earth polarity.	Negative
Brush length (above holder):	
New	0.5 in (13 mm)
Wear limit	0.2 in (5 mm)

BOSCH ALTERNATOR

Type. . . . . .G1-28A or K1-35A
Earth polarity. . . . . .Negative
Brush length (above holder):
   New . . . . 0.4 in (10 mm)
   Wear limit . . . . 0.2 in (5 mm)

LUCAS STARTER MOTOR - INERTIA TYPE

Type. M35J
Maximum draw. . . . . 380 amps
Minimum brush length . . . . 0.4 in (10 mm)
Brush spring pressure . . . . .28.8 oz (0.8 kg)
Armature end-play. . . . . 0.010 in (0.25 mm)

LUCAS STARTER MOTOR - PRE-ENGAGED TYPE

Type. . . . . .M35J, M90 or M100
Maximum draw. . . . . 440 amps
Minimum brush length . . . . 0.4 in (10 mm)
Brush spring pressure . . . . .35.2 oz (1.0 kg)
Armature end-play. . . . . 0.010 in (0.25 mm)

BOSCH STARTER MOTOR - PRE-ENGAGED TYPE

Type. . . . . 0.7, 0.8 or 1.0 PS (Pre-engaged)
Maximum draw. . . . . 340 amps
Minimum brush length . . . . 0.4 in (10 mm)
Brush spring pressure . . . . .43.2 lb (1.2 kg)
Minimum diam. of commutator . . . . 1.3 in (33.5 mm)
Armature end-play. . . . . 0.004-0.012 in (0.1-0.3 mm)

DISTRIBUTOR - 1300, 1600 OHV

Make. . . . . Motorcraft
Contact breaker gap. . . . . 0.025 in (0.65 mm)
Dwell angle . . . . Early - 38° to 40° Later 48° to 52°
Condenser capacity . . . . 0.21 - 0.25 mfd
Rotor rotation . . . . .Anti-clockwise

DISTRIBUTOR - 1600 OHC

Make. . . . . Motorcraft
Contact breaker gap. . . . . 0.025 in (0.65 mm)
Dwell angle . . . . Early 38° to 40° Later 48° to 52°
Condenser capacity . . . . 0.21 - 0.25 mfd
Rotor rotation . . . . .Clockwise

DISTRIBUTOR - 2000 OHC

Make. . . . . Motorcraft
Contact breaker gap. . . . . 0.025 in (0.65 mm)
Dwell angle . . . . Early - 38° to 40° Later 48° to 52°
Condenser capacity . . . . 0.21 - 0.25 mfd
Rotor rotation . . . . .Clockwise

ÍGNITION COIL

Make. . . . . .Motorcraft, Lucas, Bosch
Type. . . . . .Low voltage for use with 1.5 ohm ballast resistor

Cooling

DRAINING & REFILLING .... [1]

Draining

A drain point is provided on the side of the cylinder block, but to completely drain the system it will also be necessary to remove the drain plug from the bottom of the radiator, or disconnect the radiator bottom hose where no drain plug is provided, and drain out the coolant (Fig. F:1).

If a splash shield is fitted under the engine compartment, this will have to be removed to gain access to the bottom hose and allow it to drain.

Before opening the drain point or detaching the hose, ensure that the cooling system is not pressurised by removing the radiator cap. If the system is warm, allow it to cool before removing the cap. Muffle the cap with a thick cloth to protect the hands against scalding and turn the cap slowly anti-clockwise to the first stop to release the pressure in the system before completely removing the cap.

If the system contains anti-freeze and it is required for re-use, the coolant should be drained into a clean container.

If the car is to be left standing with the cooling system drained, it will be advisable to leave a reminder to this effect on the vehicle.

Refilling

When refilling the system, water alone should never be used as this will cause corrosion. A proprietary brand of corrosion inhibitor may be added during the summer months, but it is recommended that an inhibited all-season anti-freeze be used permanently in the system to prevent corrosion and the formation of scale. Details were given in the ROUTINE MAINTENANCE section at the beginning of the manual.

To refill the system, close the engine drain point and reconnect the bottom hose. Check all other hose connections. Dilute the anti-freeze or corrosion inhibitor in accordance with the manufacturer's instructions and add the coolant through the radiator filler neck. Fill the system slowly to avoid air locks. Run the engine for several minutes with the radiator cap off to release any air trapped in the system.

Check the coolant level and top up as necessary to bring the level approximately 1 in (25 mm) below the bottom of the radiator filler neck.

After the engine has been run for several minutes at fast idle the coolant level may drop by as much as 2 pints (1 litre) due to the displacement of trapped air. In this case, top up the system to the correct level.

Flushing

If overheating is experienced and it is suspected that this is due to a build-up of sludge, rust, or other foreign material in the cooling system, then the system should be flushed out.

The use of a proprietary brand of radiator cleanser is recommended as a first step, as even if this does not clear the system it will help to loosen any deposits present. Follow the solvent manufacturer's instructions.

If the solvent does not satisfactorily clean the system, the system should be pressure flushed with a high pressure water hose. Reverse flushing, where the flow is in reverse direction to the normal coolant flow, is normally the most satisfactory method of cleaning the system.

To reverse flush the complete system, remove the thermostat housing and thermostat and insert the hose into the thermostat location on the engine.

In extreme cases, the various components of the cooling system (engine, radiator, heater matrix) should be flushed separately. The radiator should be removed to flush it. With the radiator cap in position, turn the radiator upside-down and insert the pressure hose into the bottom hose location.

RADIATOR .... [2]

Removal

Open the bonnet and disconnect the battery. Where a splash shield is fitted under the engine compartment, this must be removed.

Remove the drain plug from the bottom of the radiator, or disconnect the radiator bottom hose where no drain plug is provided, and drain out the coolant. Disconnect the radiator top hose.

On models with automatic transmission from mid-1974 onwards a transmission oil cooler is incorporated in the radiator bottom tank and the two oil pipes must be disconnected from their unions at the base of the radiator. Clean the unions before undoing them, then plug the pipe ends to prevent the ingress of dirt. A clean tray should be positioned under the radiator during this opera-

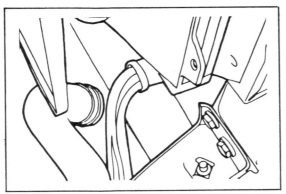

Fig. F:1 Drain the cooling system by disconnecting the bottom radiator hose

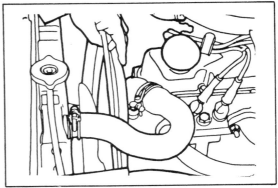

Fig. F:2 Remove the protective shroud over the fan blades before removing the radiator

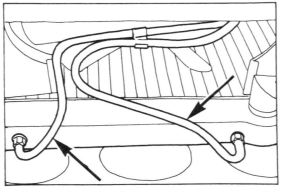

Fig. F:3 On auto transmission models, disconnect the oil cooler pipes from the rad

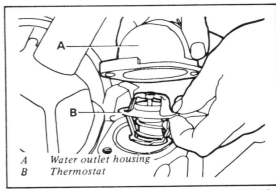

A Water outlet housing
B Thermostat

Fig. F:4 The thermostat location on the 1300/ 1600 OHV engine

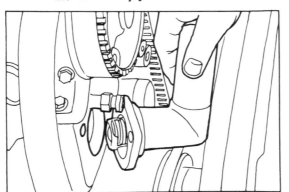

Fig. F:5 The thermostat is located inside the outlet neck on OHC engines

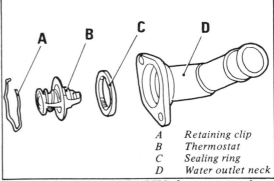

A Retaining clip
B Thermostat
C Sealing ring
D Water outlet neck

Fig. F:6 To remove the OHC thermostat, prise out the retaining clip

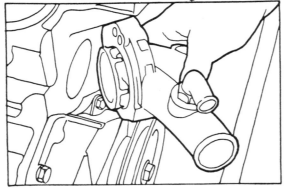

Fig. F:7 Removing the water pump from the OHV engine

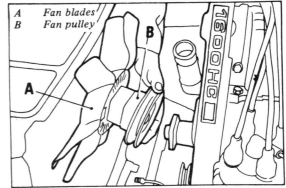

A Fan blades
B Fan pulley

Fig. F:8 To remove the OHC water pump, first detach the cooling fan

tion to catch any spilt transmission fluid (Fig. F:3).

A protective shroud may be fitted over the fan on later 1600 and all 2000 models, and where the shroud is completely circular without a cut-out at the bottom the shroud must be unbolted from the radiator and positioned over the fan blades out of the way before the radiator can be removed. On models where there is sufficient clearance, the radiator can be removed complete with the shroud and the radiator mounting plate (Fig. F:2).

When lifting out the radiator, take great care to avoid damaging the matrix on the fan blades.

Installation

Install the radiator in the reverse order of removing, but pay special attention to the following points:
a) If a replacement radiator is being fitted, the overflow pipe and clips should be transfered to the new radiator.
b) Inspect the radiator hoses carefully for cuts, splits, perishing, etc., and renew if required. Also check the condition of the hose clips.
c) When installation is completed, close the drain point (where applicable) then refill the system. Fill it slowly to avoid air locks. Run the engine for several minutes with the radiator cap off to release any air trapped in the system. Recheck the coolant level after the engine has been run for several minutes at fast idle.
d) On automatic models, check the fluid level in the transmission and top up as required.
e) Finally, run the engine up to normal operating temperature and check for leaks.

THERMOSTAT . . . . [3]

Replacement (OHV Engines)

The thermostat is located in the water outlet housing on the cylinder head and is easily replaced.

Disconnect the radiator bottom hose and drain the cooling system sufficiently to bring the level below that of the water outlet housing.

Loosen the top hose connection at the radiator. Remove the two bolts securing the outlet housing to the cylinder head and lift up the housing clear of the cylinder head. Remove the thermostat from its location in the head (Fig. F:4).

Clean all old gasket material from the surfaces of the housing and cylinder head. Also ensure the thermostat seating in the head is clean.

Install the new thermostat in the head as shown in Fig. F:4. It is important that the thermostat be correctly positioned in the engine, otherwise overheating will result. Position a new gasket on the head face, locate water outlet housing over the thermostat and secure with the two retaining bolts. Secure the top hose connection at the radiator.

Reconnect the bottom hose and top up or refill the system as detailed previously.

Run the engine up to normal operating temperature and check for leaks. Recheck the coolant level once the engine has cooled down.

Replacement (OHC Engines)

On the OHC engines, the thermostat is located in the water outlet neck at the front of the cylinder head and can be removed once the outlet neck is detached.

Disconnect the radiator bottom hose and drain the cooling system sufficiently to bring the level below that of the outlet neck.

Disconnect the radiator top hose at the water outlet neck. Remove the two bolts securing the outlet neck and detach the assembly from the cylinder head (Fig. F:5).

Prise out the retaining clips from the groove inside the neck and extract the thermostat and sealing ring (Fig. F:6).

Clean all old gasket material from the surfaces of the outlet neck and cylinder head.

Reassemble the sealing ring and thermostat in the outlet neck and secure with the retaining clip. Ensure the thermostat is positioned as shown in Fig. F:5, otherwise overheating will result.

Refit the assembly in position on the cylinder head, using a new gasket, and secure with the two retaining bolts. Reconnect and secure the top hose.

Reconnect the bottom hose and top up or refill the cooling system as detailed previously.

Run the engine up to normal operating temperature and check for leaks. Recheck the coolant level once the engine has cooled down.

Testing

Inspect the thermostat for obvious faults. If the valve is stuck in the open position the thermostat is defective and must be renewed.

To test the operation of the thermostat, suspend it fully submerged along with a suitable thermometer in a container of water. Both the thermostat and the thermometer should be suspended in such a way that they do not touch the sides of the container.

Heat the water gradually and observe the action of the thermostat valve. Note the temperature at which the valve opens. The thermostat should start to open at 85 - 89°C and be fully open at 99 - 102°C. The nominal temperature at which the thermostat opens is normally stamped on the base of the thermostat bulb.

If the thermostat does not function correctly, it must be replaced with a new unit.

WATER PUMP . . . . [4]

Removal - OHV Engines

Drain the cooling system and remove the radiator as detailed above. Slacken the bolt securing the adjusting link to the generator, and the two bolts securing the generator to its mounting bracket. Press the generator towards the engine and detach the fan belt from the pulleys. Remove the four bolts securing the cooling fan and drive pulley to the water pump hub, and detach the fan and pulley.

Disconnect the heater hose at the water pump. Disconnect and detach the bottom hose from the water

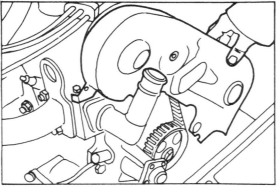

Fig. F:9 Detach the timing belt cover to gain access to the OHC water pump

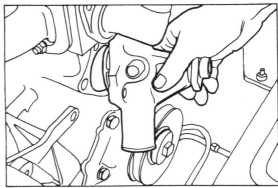

Fig. F:10 Removing the water pump from the OHC engine

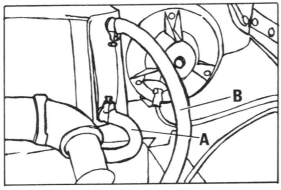

Fig. F:11 Note the position of the heater feed (A) and return (B) pipes before disconnecting

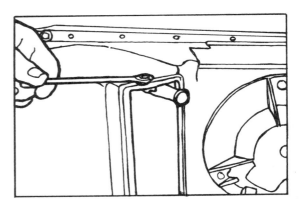

Fig. F:12 The heater matrix cover plate is secured by an upper and lower screw

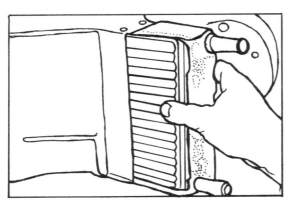

Fig. F:13 Withdraw the matrix from the heater housing. Note foam sealing gasket

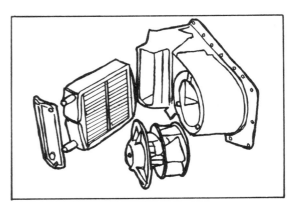

Fig. F:14 The components of the heater housing assembly

pump. Remove the three bolts securing the pump to the front face of the cylinder block and detach the pump together with its gasket (Fig. F:7).

Installation

Clean all old gasket material from the mating faces of the pump and cylinder block. Position a new gasket on the cylinder block face, using grease to retain it in position. Locate the water pump on the engine and secure with the three retaining bolts. Note the generator adjusting arm is also secured by one of the pump fixing bolts.

Reconnect the heater hose. Refit the drive pulley and cooling fan on the water pump hub. Fit the fan belt and adjust the tension so that a total free movement of 0.5 in (13 mm) is present at a point midway between the alternator and water pump pulleys

Install the radiator, reconnect the hoses and refill the cooling system. Run the engine up to normal operating temperature and check for leaks.

Removal - OHC Engines

Disconnect the battery, then drain the cooling system and remove the radiator assembly as detailed previously.

Slacken the alternator mounting bolts, press the alternator towards the engine and detach the fan belt. Remove the four bolts securing the cooling fan and drive pulley to the water pump hub and detach the fan and pulley (Fig. F:8).

Detach the timing belt cover from the front of the engine (Fig. F:9). Disconnect the heater hose and radiator bottom hose from the water pump. Remove the three bolts securng the pump to the front face of the cylinder block and detach the pump together with its gasket (Fig. F:10).

Installation

Clean all old gasket material from the mating face on the cylinder block (and pump, if original is to be refitted). Position a new gasket on the cylinder block face, using grease to retain it in position.

Locate the water pump on the engine and secure with the three retaining bolts (don't forget the alternator adjusting link).

Reconnect the heater hose and radiator bottom hose at the pump. Refit the cooling fan and drive pulley on the water pump hub. Fit the fan belt and adjust the tension so

that a total free movement of approximately 1/2 in (13 mm) is present at the midway point between the alternator and fan pulley.

Install the radiator and refill the cooling system, then run the engine up to normal operating temperature and check for leaks.

INTERIOR HEATER . . . . [5]

Heater Matrix

If leaking, the heater matrix can be easily removed without having to remove the complete heater assembly. Access is from inside the engine compartment.

Disconnect the two water hoses from the heater connections (Fig. F:11). Remove the lower hose first and drain the coolant into a suitable container, then pull off the upper hose. Once disconnected, position both hoses with their ends facing upwards, as high as possible. This will ensure that only a minimum of coolant is lost.

Remove the two bolts securing the heater cover plate (Fig. F:12), and detach the cover plate from the heater housing.

Withdraw the heater matrix, together with its foam sealing gasket, from the heater housing (Fig. F:13).

Installation is a simple reversal of the removal procedure. Use a new foam sealing gasket on the matrix, if required. Ensure that the water hoses are reconnected in their correct respective positions (inlet manifold or carburettor feed hose at bottom, water pump return hose at top), Fig. F:11.

Finally, top up the cooling system as required.

TEMPERATURE SENDER UNIT. . . . . [6]

Replacement

The temperature gauge sender unit is located on the left-hand side of the cylinder head, at the front. The loom connector is a push fit on to the unit terminal.

Before unscrewing the unit from the cylinder head, ensure that the cooling system is not pressurised by removing and refitting the radiator cap (this latter move will minimise coolant loss while the unit is removed).

Smear sealer on to the threads of the new switch before screwing it into position.

Technical Data

Cooling system capacity (inc. heater):
1300. . . . . 8.7 pt (5.0 litres)
1600. . . . . 10.1 pt (5.8 litres)
2000. . . . . 10.8 pt (6.2 litres)
Radiator cap rating . . . . 13 psi (0.9 kg/cm^2)
Thermostat:
Starts to open. . . . . 82 - 92°C (180 - 198°F)*
Fully open . . . . 99 - 102°C (210 - 216°F)*
* Add ± 3°C (5°F) for a used thermostat
Anti-freeze. . . . . To Ford specification
SM-97B-1002A

COOLING
Trouble Shooter

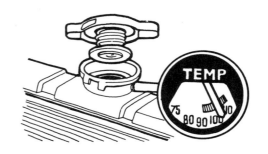

FAULT	CAUSE	CURE
Loss of coolant	1. Damaged radiator 2. Leak at heater connection or plug 3. Damaged cylinder head gasket 4. Cracked cylinder block. 5. Cracked cylinder head. 6. Loose cylinder head bolts	1. Repair or replace radiator. 2. Repair or replace. 3. Replace gasket. Check engine oil and refill as necessary. 4. Replace cylinder block. Check engine oil in crank-case for mixing with water. 5. Replace cylinder head. 6. Tighten cylinder head bolts.
Poor circulation	1. Restriction in system 2. Insufficient coolant 3. Inoperative water pump 4. Loose fan belt 5. Inoperative thermostat	1. Check hoses for crimping. Clear the system of rust and sludge. 2. Replenish. 3. Replace water pump. 4. Adjust for belt. 5. Replace thermostat.
Corrosion	1. Excessive impurity in water 2. Infrequent flushing and draining of system	1. Use soft, clean water. 2. Flush thoroughly at least twice a year.
Overheating	1. Inoperative thermostat 2. Radiator fin choked with mud, leaves etc. 3. Incorrect ignition and valve timing 4. Dirty oil and sludge in engine 5. Inoperative water pump 6. Loose fan belt 7. Restricted radiator 8. Inaccurate temperature gauge 9. Impurity in water	1. Replace thermostat. 2. Clean out air passage. 3. Tune engine. 4. Change engine oil and filter. 5. Replace (or check-electrical). 6. Adjust tension. 7. Flush radiator. 8. Replace temperature gauge. 9. Use soft, clean water.
Overcooling	1. Inoperative thermostat 2. Inaccurate temperature gauge	1. Replace thermostat. 2. Replace temperature gauge.

Fuel System

INTRODUCTION . . . . [1]

Two types of carburettor are used on the Cortina, both the OHV and 1600 OHC models are equipped with a Ford single barrel down-draught carburettor. On later 1300 cc OHV and 1600 cc OHC models a Motorcraft 'increased severity emission' carburettor is fitted which incorporates a 'by-pass' idle system. It is visually similar to the earlier Ford carburettor and can be identified by comparing the number of screws retaining the upper body. The new unit has seven screws, the earlier model six. Servicing procedure is identical to the earlier Ford carburettor.

1600 GT and 2000 OHC vehicles have a Weber dual-barrel down-draught carburettor. On later 1600 and 2000 cc OHC models a Weber 'by-pass' carburettor is fitted, features of which are two independent idling systems. These systems are referred to as 'by-pass' idle and 'basic' idle. It is not necessary to service the 'basic' system at regular intervals - only when overhaul of the carburettor has been completed, or if correct idle cannot be achieved using the 'by-pass' adjuster.

The new carburettor can be easily identified by a plastic cap which is fitted to the 'basic' idle screw.

Also fitted to the later models is a fuel return flow line incorporated into the Weber carburettor and linked to the fuel tank. Identification is by cast housing on top of the carburettor at the supply pipe. Flow is indicated by two arrows and one outlet is blanked off.

The Ford carburettor has a semi-automatic strangler type choke, or on 1600 auto. trans. models, a fully automatic choke. Carburettor model number identification is stamped on the float chamber.

On models with automatic choke, the choke assembly is attached to the upper body and is operated by water temperature direct from the cylinder head.

The Weber carburettor may have either a manual or a fully automatic strangler-type choke, operated by water temperature from the cylinder head. The carburettor model identification is stamped on the lower part of body mounting flange.

Throttle plate opening arrangement is progressive, the primary plate starting to open first, followed by the secondary, both plates reaching the fully-open position simultaneously. The primary barrel, venturi and throttle plate is smaller than that of the secondary, whilst the auxilary venturi size is identical for both the primary and secondary. The accelerator pump discharges into the primary barrel.

Four types of fuel pump may be fitted: two types on the OHV engines (1300 & 1600), and two types on the OHC engines (1600/GT & 2000). In each case, the pump is of the mechanical, diaphragm-type, and incorporates a filter screen and sediment cap.

On the OHV engine, the fuel pump is mounted on the R.H. side of the engine, and is driven by an eccentric on the camshaft. On OHC engines, the pump is mounted on the L.H. side of the cylinder block, and is driven by the auxiliary shaft through a short push rod.

A separate in-line fuel filter is incorporated between the pump and the carburettor to provide additional filtration. The filter is a one-piece assembly and must be replaced if found to be clogged or restricted.

The fuel tank is located below the luggage compartment, and is secured with two straps. Fuel tank ventilation is via the filler cap. The fuel outlet is incorporated in the fuel gauge sender unit, in the front face of the tank.
NOTE: Later models have an additional fuel return pipe to the tank from the carburettor.

FUEL FILTER . . . . [2]

The in-line fuel filter is fitted in the fuel line between the carburettor and fuel pump.
1. To remove the filter, slacken the hose clamps, and disconnect the fuel hoses from each side of the filter. Blow through the filter in the reverse direction of the fuel flow, indicated by the arrow on the filter housing. If it is found to be clogged or restricted, it should be replaced.
2. Ensure that the arrow points in the direction of the

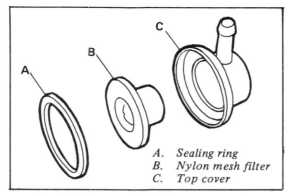

A. Sealing ring
B. Nylon mesh filter
C. Top cover

Fig. G:1 Remove the fuel pump cover for cleaning. Check condition of sealing ring (A)

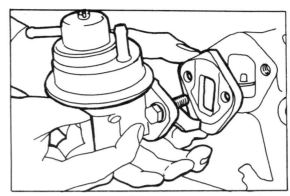

Fig. G:2 Removing the fuel pump assembly from the OHV engine

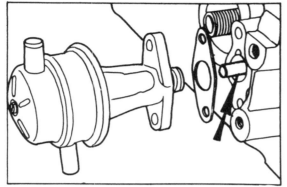

Fig. G:3 Removing the fuel pump from OHC engine. Note push rod arrowed

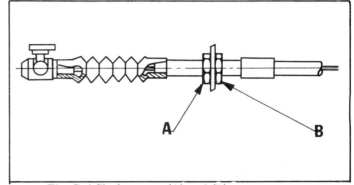

Fig. G:4 Slacken nuts (A) and (B), screw up nut (B) to remove all cable slackness. Tighten nut (A)

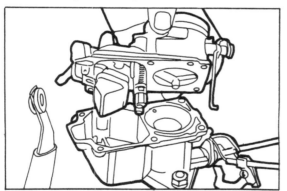

Fig. G:5 Removing the carburettor upper body -manual choke type shown

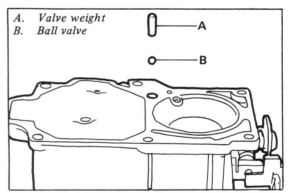

A. Valve weight
B. Ball valve

Fig. G:6 The Motorcraft type carburettor accelerator pump ball valve components

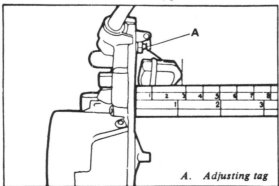

A. Adjusting tag

Fig. G:7 Check float level setting. Adjust by bending tag (A) - Motorcraft type

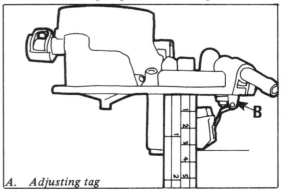

A. Adjusting tag

Fig. G:8 Checking float travel. Adjust by bending tag (B) - Motorcraft type

fuel flow when refitting the filter. Tighten the hose clamps securely and check for leaks.

FUEL PUMP . . . . [3]

Cleaning

1. Remove the centre-screw and 'O' ring seal or unscrew the knurled nut as applicable, then detach the sediment cap, filter screen, and sealing ring (Fig. G:1).
2. Blow the cap and filter screen clean of all sediment, or wash them in petrol. Inspect the sealing ring, and renew it if perished or worn, or otherwise damaged.
3. Carefully refit the filter screen, sealing ring, and sediment cap, and secure with the knurled nut, or centre-screw and 'O' ring as applicable.

Delivery Pressure Check

1. Fill the carburettor float chamber with petrol, so the engine will run with the fuel pipe disconnected.
2. Disconnect the fuel line from the fuel pump at the carburettor, and connect a suitable pressure gauge to the end of the supply pipe.
3. Start the engine, and observe the pressure reading with the engine running at idling speed. Momentarily race the engine, and check that the pressure reading indicated is as specified.
4. Stop the engine and disconnect the pressure gauge, then reconnect the fuel line.

Removal

1. Disconnect the fuel supply and delivery pipes at the fuel pump. Plug the pipe ends to prevent loss of fuel and the ingress of dirt.
2. Remove the two retaining bolts and detach the pump from the cylinder block. On OHV engines, also remove the insulating block fitted between the pump and cylinder block. On OHC engines, remove the gasket and withdraw the pump push rod from the engine block (Figs. G:2 & 3).

Installation

1. Clean all old gasket remains from the mating faces of both the pump and mounting pad on the engine block.
2. On OHC engines, insert the pump push rod into its guide bore in the engine block. Fit the pump, using a new gasket, or spacer, as applicable.
3. On OHV engines, ensure that the pump operating arm is positioned on top of the camshaft eccentric and not underneath it. Secure with the two retaining bolts, then reconnect the fuel pipes. Start the engine and check for fuel leaks.

Overhaul

In each case the pump is a sealed unit and, with the exception of cleaning the filter assembly, the pump cannot be overhauled. It must therefore be serviced as a complete assembly if defective or worn.

ACCELERATOR LINKAGE. . . . . [4]

Adjustment

1. Slacken the two outer cable locknuts at the abutment bracket on the engine (Fig. G:4).
2. Turn the throttle linkage until the throttle plate is in the fully open position, and hold it there with one hand. With the other hand, adjust the nut nearest the outer cable until all slackness is removed from the inner cable and the throttle plate is just maintained in the fully open position.
3. Tighten the other nut to secure the cable, and re-check the setting. Check the operation of the throttle linkage.

Cable Replacement

1. Disconnect the inner cable from the throttle shaft lever, by sliding the spring clip off the joint and pulling the cable socket off the lever ball.
2. Slacken the two outer cable locknuts at the abutment bracket on the engine, then screw the nut off the end of the threaded sleeve, and disconnect the cable from the bracket.
3. Remove the spring clip, and disconnect the inner cable from the lever on the accelerator pedal shaft.
4. Remove the screw securing the outer cable flange to the engine compartment bulkhead, and withdraw the cable.

Install the new throttle cable in the reverse order of removal. Adjust the cable, as described above.

FORD/MOTORCRAFT CARBURETTOR . . . [5]

Float Level Adjustment

1. Remove the air cleaner, and disconnect the fuel line. On automatic choke models, partially drain the cooling system and disconnect the water hoses at the auto-choke housing. Remove the pivot screw retaining the fast idle cam and link rod to the lower body.
2. Remove the upper body retaining screws and lift off the upper body, simultaneously disengaging the choke link from the fast idle cam (manual choke models only). Note that the manual choke cable braket is also retained by the rear left-hand cover screw (Fig. G:5).
NOTE: Once the upper body is removed, the accelerator pump discharge valve will be exposed in its bore in the top face. Care should be taken when operating the throttle linkage, otherwise the valve and weight may be ejected. This would cause serious damage if the valve enters the engine (Fig. G:6).
3. Hold the upper body in the vertical position with the float hanging down, and measure the distance from the upper body face to the bottom of the float with a depth gauge or similar instrument (Fig. G:7)
4. If the float level is outside specification, adjust by bending the tab resting against the needle valve.
5. Turn the upper body upside down and again measure

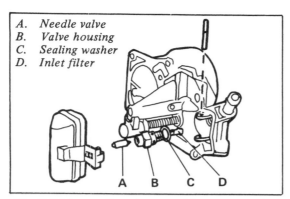

A. Needle valve
B. Valve housing
C. Sealing washer
D. Inlet filter

A B C D

Fig. G:9 The needle valve assembly components - Motorcraft type

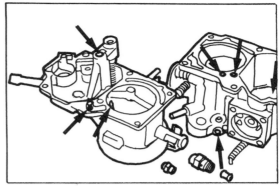

Fig. G:10 The main items to be cleaned when the carb is dismantled - Motorcraft type

Fig. G:11 Checking manual choke plate pull down, adjust at tag arrowed - Motorcraft type

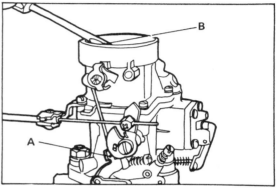

Fig. G:12 Checking fast idle setting. Choke plate open (B) Adjust at tag (A) - Motorcraft type

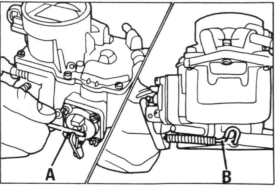

A B

Fig. G:13 Checking accelerator pump lever (A) Adjust at rod (B) - Motorcraft type

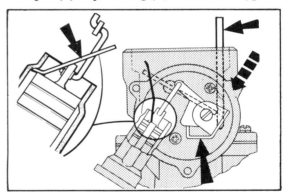

Fig. G:14 Checking automatic choke plate pull down setting - Motorcraft type

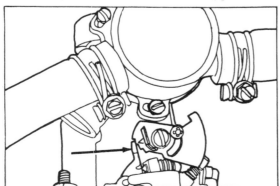

Fig. G:15 Set auto-choke to fast idle setting. 'V' mark must be aligned with throttle lever top

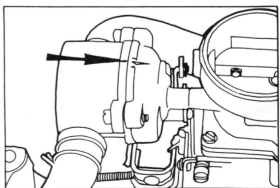

Fig. G:16 Position auto-choke housing so that marks are aligned - Motorcraft type

the distance from the body face to the bottom of the float. If the float travel is outside specification, adjust by bending the tab (Fig. G:8).

6. Refit the upper body while holding the manual choke lever in the closed position, and simultaneously connect the choke link to the fast idle cam. Position the choke cable bracket beneath the rear L.H. screw.

NOTE: Failure to hold the choke lever in the closed position will result in the choke lever being over-centred, and the choke will be rendered inoperative. If this occurs, do NOT force the lever back to its correct position. Release the cover retaining screw, move the lever to the closed position, and then retighten.

7. On models with automatic choke, position the fast idle cam and link rod on the lower body and secure with the shouldered pivot screw. Reconnect the fuel line. Where applicable, reconnect the automatic choke hoses, and top up the cooling system.

Choke Plate Pull-Down (Manual Choke)

1. Rotate the choke lever to its stop, and depress the choke plate (Fig. G:11).
2. Using a drill or gauge rod of appropriate diameter, check that the specified clearance exists between the lower edge of the choke plate and the wall of the air intake.
3. If adjustment is necessary, bend the tab on the choke spindle to obtain the correct setting.

Fast Idle (Manual Choke)

1. Connect a tachometer to the ignition and run the engine up to normal operating temperature.
2. With the engine running at its specified idling speed, hold the choke plate vertically, in the fully-open position, and rotate the choke lever until it is stopped by the choke linkage. Note the engine speed indicated on the tachometer (Fig. G:12).
3. If the revs are outside the specified fast idle speed, adjust the linkage by bending the tab connecting the fast idle cam.

Accelerator Pump Stroke

1. Unscrew the throttle stop screw several turns, until the throttle plate is fully closed. Note the number of turns on the screw.
2. Depress the diaphragm plunger on the accelerator pump, then, using a drill or gauge rod of appropriate diameter, check that the specified clearance exists between the plunger and the pump operating lever. If necessary, bend the goose-neck on the pump push-rod to adjust pump stoke (Fig. G:13).
3. Close the loop to lengthen the stroke, or expand it to shorten the stroke. Reset the throttle stop screw to its original position.

Choke Plate Pull-Down (Auto. Choke)

1. Remove the water housing and thermostatic spring from the automatic choke assembly.

2. Depress the vacuum piston until the vacuum port in the piston bore is revealed, then insert a length of 1.01 mm (0.040 in) diameter wire, suitably bent, into the port and raise the piston to trap the wire (Fig. G:14).
3. With the piston and wire held in this position, close the choke plate until its movement is stopped by the linkage. Partially open the throttle for the fast idle tab to clear the cam.
4. Using a drill or gauge rod of appropriate diameter, check that the specified gap exists between the lower edge of the choke plate and the wall of the air intake. If necessary, adjust by bending the extension of the choke thermostat lever (i.e. the part which abuts the piston operating lever).

De-Choke (Auto. Choke)

1. Close the choke plate, using the spring operated lever, then open the throttle fully and hold it against its stop.
2. Using a drill or gauge rod of appropriate diameter, check that the clearance between the lower edge of the choke plate and the wall of the air intake is as specified. Adjust, if necessary, by bending the projection on the fast idle cam.

Fast Idle (Auto. Choke)

1. With the choke plate pull-down correctly set, hold the choke plate in the pull-down position.
2. Check that the throttle lever fast idle tab is aligned with the 'V' mark or high speed step position on the fast idle cam (Fig. G:15).
3. If necessary, bend the fast idle rod at its existing bend to achieve this result.
4. Refit the thermostatic spring and water housing to the choke assembly, ensuring that the spring engages in the centre slot of the thermostatic lever.
5. Align the mating marks on the housing, then secure with the retaining screws. Reconnect the auto-choke housing water hoses, if disconnected, then refill the cooling system (Fig. G:16).
6. Connect a tachometer to the ignition and run the engine up to normal operating temperature. Position the throttle lever fast idle tab on the first step of the fast idle cam and check the engine speed. If outside the specified fast idle speed, adjust by bending the tab contacting the fast idle cam.

Idle Adjustment (Fig. G:17)

On earlier 'Pre-Emission' type carburettors, the engine idling speed or slow-running is effected by adjusting the throttle stop screw and the idling mixture volume control screw at the base of the carburettor as follows:

With the engine at normal operating temperature, adjust the throttle stop screw to obtain satisfactory idling speed. Unscrew the volume control screw until the engine begins to "hunt" (i.e. runs irregularly or lumpily), then screw it in again until the engine runs evenly. Re-adjust the throttle stop screw to obtain the correct engine idle speed. Repeat the operation if necessary, until a satisfac-

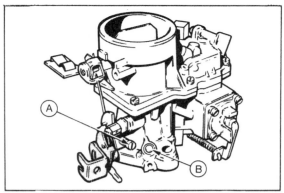

Fig. G:17 Idle adjustment screws on Motorcraft type carburettor

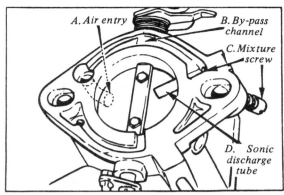

A. Air entry
B. By-pass channel
C. Mixture screw
D. Sonic discharge tube

Fig. G:18 Details of the 'Sonic' idle by-pass type carburettor on later models

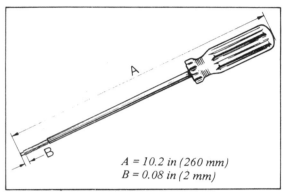

A = 10.2 in (260 mm)
B = 0.08 in (2 mm)

Fig. G:19 Dimensions for tool to remove plugs on later 'tamperproof' type carbs

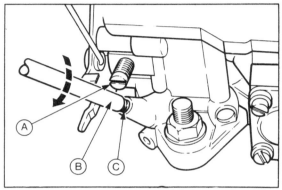

Fig. G:20 Screw remover tool (B) into plug (C) continue screwing until plug is withdrawn

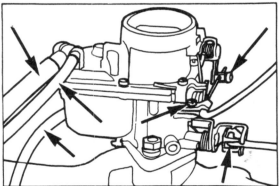

Fig. G:21 Items to be disconnected when removing Motorcraft type carburettor

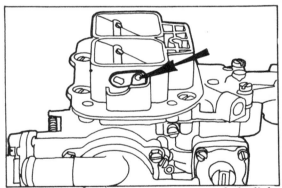

Fig. G:22 On Weber carb. disconnect choke link before lifting upper body

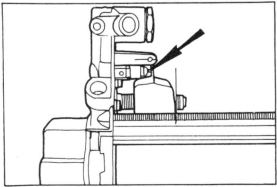

Fig. G:23 Check float level setting. Bend float tag (arrowed) to adjust - Weber type

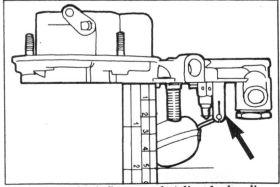

Fig. G:24 Check float travel. Adjust by bending tag (arrowed) - Weber type

tory idle is obtained.

NOTE: On vehicles with automatic transmission, select the 'P' or 'N' position and fully apply the handbrake when carrying out this adjustment.

Later 'Increased Severity Emission' type carburettors incorporate a 'By-pass' or Sonic idle system which allows steady idling to be obtained on much leaner fuel/air mixtures thus giving significant economy benefits. This idle system differs from the conventional system in that the majority of air flow and all of the fuel, at idle, is obtained through the By-pass system. Air is drawn into the By-pass system at a point above the throttle butterfly where it is mixed with the rich air-fuel mixture obtained via the mixture screw and the mixture is then discharged into the engine through the sonic discharge tube (Fig. G:18).

As stated at the beginning of this section, the idle mixture screw on this carburettor is fitted with a tamper-proof device in the form of a plastic seal during manufacture to prevent unauthorised interference with the setting. In service the mixture screw will not normally require adjustment and any idle adjustment should be confined to the idle speed screw. It is advised that no attempt be made to remove the sealing plug or alter the mixture screw setting.

The procedure for adjusting the mixture setting is included in this section, but this should only be required in the case of problem vehicles or when the carburettor has been overhauled. The use of a CO meter is essential when carrying out this adjustment to ensure the exhaust emission level is within the specified figure.

It should also be noted that replacement seals for the mixture screw are available to authorised workshops only.

The engine must be at normal operating temperature when carrying out the idle adjustment. Stabilise the engine by running it at fast idle (approx. 3.000 rev/min) for about half a minute to clear the inlet manifold of excess fuel.

On models with automatic transmission, select the 'P' or 'N' range and fully apply the handbrake when carrying out the idle adjustment.

Wait for the engine speed to stabilise then adjust the idle speed screw to achieve the specified idle speed of 800 ± 25 rev/min on 1300 engines and 750 ± 25 rev/min for the 1600 engine.

NOTE: On automatic transmission models, the idle speed should be 700 rpm with the selector in the 'D' position and the handbrake fully applied.

The location of the idle speed adjusting screw is shown in 'A' (Fig. G:20).

If a satisfactory idle condition is impossible to achieve, or the exhaust emission level, measured with a CO meter, is outside the specified figure, the following corrective procedure can be adopted. However, it must be stressed that the use of a CO meter is essential to carry out this adjustment satisfactorily.

1. A suitable tool to facilitate removal of the mixture screw sealing plug should be made up to the dimensions shown in Fig. G:19, using a thin blade screwdriver with a minimum overall length of 10.2 in (260 mm) and a screw such as that used to retain the lower trim panel brazed on the end.

2. On 1600 models remove the air cleaner assembly.

3. Using the plug remover tool, detach the plastic plug from the mixture screw. Then remove the centre knock-out section of the plug from the mixture screw housing using an electricians screwdriver (Fig. G:20).

4. On 1600 models, loosely refit the air cleaner assembly.

5. Stabilise the engine, as detailed above, then adjust the mixture screw and idle speed screw to give the specified CO reading at the correct idle speed.

The mixture CO % should be 1.5 ± 0.2 for the 1300 'Economy' engine, 1.6 ± 0.2 for the standard 1300, and 0.5 ± 0.1 on the 1600 OHC engine.

6. It should be noted that the adjustment above must be carried out within 10 to 30 seconds from the time the meters stabilise. If the time taken to carry out the adjustment is longer than 30 seconds, the engine must be run at fast idle for half a minute and the adjustment re-checked.

7. Re-check the idle speed and CO settings and re-adjust as necessary.

8. On 1600 models, remove the air cleaner assembly again.

9. Fit a new sealing plug to the mixture adjusting screw. Position the plug on the housing and tap it home. On some models a punch will be required to tap the plug fully into position, and in this case the load must be applied to the face of the plug and not on the centre section. The plug should finally be positioned flush with the carburettor housing.

10. On 1600 models refit the air cleaner assembly.

Carburettor Removal and Installation (Fig. G:21)

1. Remove the air cleaner. Disconnect the fuel supply and distributor vacuum pipes at the carburettor.

2. Release the spring clip and disconnect the throttle control shaft from the carburettor throttle shaft.

3. On auto-choke models, partially drain the cooling system, and disconnect the water hoses at the choke housing.

4. Remove the two retaining nuts and spring washers, and lift the carburettor and gasket off the inlet manifold. Discard the gasket.

Install carburettor in the reverse order of removal, with attention to the following points:

a) Ensure that the mating faces on the carburettor and inlet manifold are clean and free from old gasket material.

b) Use a new gasket between the carburettor and inlet manifold flange.

c) On manual choke models, ensure that there is sufficient free-play in the choke cable by pulling the control knob out approximately 0.25 in (6 mm) from the dash before reconnecting the cable.

d) On automatic choke models, top-up the cooling system after connecting the choke water hoses.

e) When installation is complete, set the slow running adjustment, as described previously.

WEBER CARBURETTOR . . . . [6]

Float Level Adjustment

1. Remove the air cleaner and disconnect the fuel line. Disconnect the choke plate operating rod (Fig. G:22).

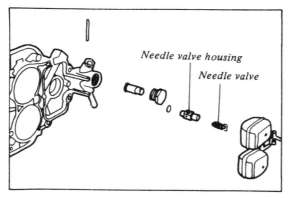

Fig. G:25 Components of the float needle valve assembly - Weber type

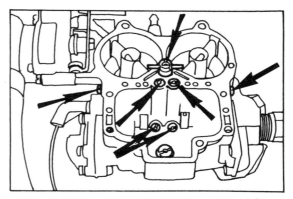

Fig. G:26 Locations of jets to be removed for cleaning - Weber type

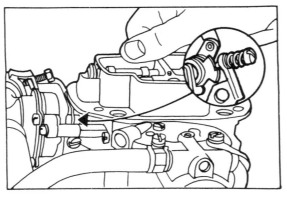

Fig. G:27 Position auto-choke fast idle cam and adjusting screw to check fast idle setting

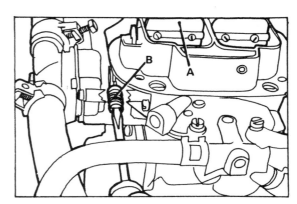

Fig. G:28 To adjust auto-choke fast idle, turn screw (B) with choke plates (A) fully open

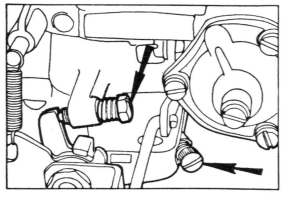

Fig. G:29 Idle adjustment screws on early Weber OHC models

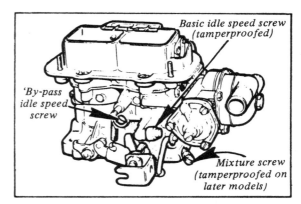

Fig. G:30 Idle adjustment screw on later Weber carb with by-pass idle system

Remove the retaining screws and lift off the upper body.

2. Hold the upper body in the vertical position with the float hanging down and measure the distance from the upper body face to the bottom of the float with a depth gauge or similar instrument. If the float level is outside specification, adjust by bending the tab resting against the needle valve (Fig. G:23).

3. Turn the body upside-down, and again measure the distance from the body face to the bottom of the float. If the float travel is outside specification, adjust by bending the tab resting against the needle valve housing (Fig. G:24).

4. Refit the upper body and reconnect the choke plate operating rod. Reconnect the fuel line.

Choke Plate Pull-Down - Manual type

1. With the choke fully closed, hold the choke lever against its stop.

2. Open the choke plates against the action of the toggle spring, and using a drill or gauge rod of appropriate diameter, check that the specified clearance exists between the lower edge of the choke plates and the wall of the air intakes.

3. If adjustment is necessary, remove the water and thermostatic spring housings, and adjust the screw under the blanking plug at the rear of the pull-down diaphragm. The phasing must be checked with the fast idle screw against the cam step.

Fast Idle Adjustment

1. Connect a tachometer to the engine, and run the engine until it reaches its normal operating temperature. Remove the air cleaner assembly. On automatic transmission models, place the selector lever the 'P' position.

2. On manual-choke carbs, with the engine running, hold the choke plates in the fully open, vertical position and rotate the choke operating lever until it is stopped by the choke linkage.

3. Check the fast idle speed, and adjust to the specified figure by bending the fast idle connecting rod using pliers. Replace the air cleaner assembly.

4. On auto-choke carburettors, run the engine until it reaches normal operating temperature and the choke plates are in the fully open, vertical position. (Note, if the choke plate will not reach the vertical position then either the engine has not reached full operating temperature or the auto-choke housing is faulty).

5. Switch off the engine, then turn the throttle linkage to open the throttle fully. Hold the throttle open and fully close the choke plates. Release the throttle, then allow the choke plate to return to the vertical position. The end of the fast idle screw should now be resting on the high part of the linkage cam. Do not touch the throttle linkage or accelerator pedal until the fast idle adjustment is completed (Fig. G:27).

6. Start the engine, without using the accelerator pedal, and check the engine speed on the tachometer. It should be 3000 rpm on pre-May 75 models and 2000 rpm after May 75 on carbs with a BA/BB, HA/HB suffix stamped on the carb body. If necessary, adjust the fast idle speed by

turning the fast idle screw (Fig. G:28).

7. When adjustment is complete, open the throttle to bring the engine to normal idling speed and replace the air cleaner assembly.

Idle Adjustment

On earlier Weber 'Pre-Emission' type carburettors the slow-running or idle adjustment should be carried out by adjusting the idle speed or throttle stop screw and the idling mixture control screw as follows (Fig. G:29).

With the engine at normal operating temperature, adjust the throttle stop screw to obtain satisfactory idling speed. Unscrew the volume control screw until the engine begins to "hunt" (i.e. runs irregularly or lumpily), then screw it in again until the engine runs evenly. Re-adjust the throttle stop screw to obtain the correct engine idle speed. Repeat the operation, if necessary, until a satisfactory idle is obtained.

NOTE: On vehicles with automatic transmission, select the 'P' or 'N' position and fully apply the handbrake when carrying out this adjustment.

On Later 'Increased severity emission' Weber carburettors, the idling should be adjusted as follows:

The engine must be at normal operating temperature when carrying out the idle adjustment. Stabilise the engine by running it at fast idle (approx. 3,000 rev/min) for about half a minute to clear the inlet manifold of excess fuel.

On models with automatic transmission, select the 'P' or 'N' range and fully apply the handbrake when carrying out the idle adjustment.

Wait for the engine to stabilise, then adjust the 'By-pass' idle speed screw to achieve the specified idle speed of 825 ± 25 rev/min.

The location of the 'By-pass' idle speed screw is shown in Fig. G:30.

If a satisfactory idle condition is impossible to achieve, or if the exhaust emission level, measured with a CO meter, is outside the specified figure, the following corrective procedure can be adopted. However, it must be stressed that the use of a CO meter is essential to carry out this adjustment satisfactorily.

1. A suitable tool to facilitate removal of the sealing plugs should be made up as detailed for the Motorcraft type carburettor previously.

2. Remove the air cleaner assembly. The cleaner body is secured to the carburettor by four screws and two mounting stays.

3. Using the plug remover tool, detach the plastic plug from the MIXTURE SCREW. Remove the centre knock-out section of the plug from the mixture screw housing, using an electrical screwdriver. DO NOT REMOVE THE SEALING PLUG FROM THE BASIC IDLE SPEED SCREW AT THIS STAGE.

4. Loosely refit the air cleaner assembly. It is not necessary to bolt the cleaner in position.

5. Stabilise the engine, as detailed above, then adjust the mixture screw and 'By-pass' idle speed screw to achieve the specified CO reading at the correct idle speed.

6. It should be noted that the adjustment above must be

carried out within 10 to 30 seconds from the time the meters stabilise. If the time taken to carry out the adjustment is longer than 30 seconds, the engine must be run at fast idle for half a minute again and the adjustment rechecked.

7. It should also be noted that on new engines the maximum idle speed may be up to 50 rev/min below specification, but this condition is only temporary and will disappear as the engine is run-in.

8. If it is still not possible to achieve the specified idle speed and CO settings, the 'Basic' idle speed setting should be adjusted as follows. However, this should only be required for porblem vehicles or when the carburettor has been overhauled. Before carrying out this adjustment, ensure that all engine adjustments are correct, e.g. dwell angle, ignition timing (see Tune-Up Section).

9. Remove the air cleaner assembly.

10. Fully screw in the 'By-pass' idle speed screw.

11. Using the plug removal tool, detach the sealing plug from the BASIC IDLE SPEED SCREW. When positioning the tool, the throttle will have to be partially opened to allow the tool to fit onto the plug. Remove the centre knock-out section of the plug from the speed screw housing.

12. Again stabilise the engine, then adjust both the mixture screw and the 'Basic' idle speed screw to achieve the specified % CO reading at an idle speed of 100 rev/min below specification.

13. Loosely refit the air cleaner assembly, stabilise the engine and re-adjust the 'By-pass' idle speed screw and the mixture screw to achieve the specified idle speed and % CO reading, as in operation '5' above.

14. Remove the air cleaner assembly again.

15. Fit a new sealing plug to the mixture adjusting screw. Position the plug on the housing and tap it home until it is a flush fit.

Service replacement plugs are blue in colour, as opposed to the original plugs which are white.

16. Fit a new sealing plug to the 'Basic' idle speed screw, if required. Position the plug on the housing, then use a pair of pliers to squeeze the plug fully into position.

17. Finally, refit the air cleaner assembly.

Carburettor Removal and Installation

1. Remove the air cleaner.
2. Disconnect the fuel supply and distributor vacuum pipes at the carburettor.
3. Release the spring clip and disconnect the throttle control shaft from the carburettor throttle shaft.
4. Partially drain the cooling system, and disconnect the water hoses at the automatic choke housing.
5. Remove the four retaining nuts and spring washers, and lift the carburettor and gasket off the inlet manifold. Discard the gasket.
6. Install the carburettor in the reverse order of removal, with special attention to the following points:-
7. Ensure that the mating faces on the carburettor and inlet manifold are clean and free from old gasket material.
8. Use a new gasket between the carburettor and inlet manifold flange.
9. Refill the cooling system, after connecting the choke water hose.
10. When installation is complete, set the slow running as described previously.

Technical Data

MOTORCRAFT (1300 OHV - MANUAL CHOKE) - Type suffix JA/KA/RA
Idling speed . . . . 780-820 rpm
Fast idle . . . . 1,400-1,600 rpm
Float-level . . . . 1.08 in (27.43 mm)
   travel . . . . 0.26 in (6.60 mm)
Choke plate pull-down . . . . 0.13 in (3.30 mm)
Accelerator pump stroke . . . . 0.10 in (2.54 mm)

MOTORCRAFT (1300 OHV - MANUAL CHOKE 'MAY 75 ON) - Type suffix KBA
Idling speed . . . . 775-825 rpm
Fast idle . . . . 1,300-1,500 rpm
Mixture % CO. . . . . 1.5% ± 0.2
Float level . . . . 1.11-1.17 in (28.25-29.25 mm)
Choke plate pull down . . . . 0.11-0.13 (2.75-3.25 mm)
Accelerator pump stroke. . . . . .0.10±0.005 in (2.6±0.13 mm)

MOTORCRAFT (1300 OHV - ECONOMY: FEB 76 ON) - Type suffix KTA
Idling speed . . . . 800 rpm
Fast idle . . . . 1,400 rpm
Mixture % CO. . . . . 1.5% ± 0.2
Float level . . . . 1.14 in (29 mm)
Choke plate pull down . . . . 0.12 in (3.0 mm)
Accelerator pump stroke. . . . . 0.08 in (2.0 mm)

MOTORCRAFT (1600 OHV - MANUAL CHOKE) - Type suffix BHA/VA/ANA
Idling speed . . . . 780-820 rpm
Fast idle . . . . 1,000 rpm
Float-level . . . . 1.10 in (27.93 mm)
   travel . . . . 0.26 in (6.60 mm)
Choke plate pull-down . . . . 0.14 in (3.55 mm)
Accelerator pump stroke . . . . 0.105 in (2.66 mm)

MOTORCRAFT (1600 OHV - AUTO-CHOKE) - Type suffix BNA/ZA

Idling speed . . . . 780-820 rpm
Fast idle . . . . 2,050-2,250 rpm
Float level . . . . 1.10 in (27.93 mm)
   travel . . . . 0.26 in (6.60 mm)
Choke plate pull-down . . . . 0.14 in (3.50 mm)
De-choke . . . . 0.30 in (7.62 mm)
Accelerator pump stroke . . . . 0.105 in (2.66 mm)
Vacuum piston link hole . . . . Outer
Thermostatic spring slot . . . . Centre
'V' mark setting . . . . 0.19 in (4.80 mm)

MOTORCRAFT (1600 OHC MAY 75 ON) - Type suffix KKA/KDA/KEA

Idling speed . . . . 775-825 rpm
Fast idle speed . . . . 1,000 rpm
Mixture % CO . . . . 0.5% ± 0.1
Float-level . . . . 1.11-1.17 in (28.25-29.75 mm)
Choke plate pull-down . . . . 0.12-0.14 in (3.0-3.5 mm)
De-choke . . . . 0.19-0.23 in (4.8-5.8 mm)
Accelerator pump stroke . . . . 0.11±0.005 in (2.77-3.03 mm)
Vacuum piston link hole . . . . Outer
Thermostatic spring slot . . . . Centre
'V' mark setting . . . . 0.2 in (5 mm) Man 0.18 in (4.5 mm) Auto.

WEBER (1600 GT - OHC AUTO-CHOKE) - Type suffix BA/CA

Idling speed . . . . 800 rpm
Fast idle speed . . . . 3,200 rpm on high cam
Fast idle setting . . . . 0.033 in (0.85 mm)
Float level:
   upper . . . . 1.38-1.39 in (35.00-35.50 mm)
   lower . . . . 1.97-2.02 in (50.5-52.0 mm)
Choke plate pull-down (min) . . . . 0.177 in (4.50 mm)

WEBER (2000 OHC - AUTO-CHOKE) - Type suffix DA/EA

Idling speed . . . . 675-725 rpm
Fast idle speed . . . . 3,000 rpm on high cam
Fast idle setting . . . . 0.039-0.043 in (1.00-1.10 mm)
Float level
   upper . . . . 1.522-1.545 in (38.75-39.25 mm)
   lower . . . . 1.97-2.02 in (50.0-51.5 mm)
Choke plate pull-down (min.) . . . . 0.159 in (4.00 mm)

WEBER (1600 GT OHC MAY 75 ON) - Type suffix GA/GB/HA/HB

Idling speed . . . . 780-820 rpm
Fast idle speed . . . . 1,900-2,100 rpm
Mixture & CO . . . . 1.5% ± 0.2
Float level
   Brass float . . . . 1.59-1.63 in (40.5-41.5 mm)
   Plastic float . . . . 1.37-1.41 in (34.8-35.8 mm)
Choke plate pull down . . . . 0.23-0.25 in (5.75-6.25 mm)
Choke phasing . . . . 0.08-0.10 in (2.15-2.55 mm)

WEBER (2000 OHC, MAY 75 ON) - Type suffix AA/AB/BA/BB

Idling speed . . . . 800-825 rpm
Fast idle speed . . . . 1,900-2,100 rpm
Mixture % CO . . . . 1% ± 0.2
Float level
   Brass float . . . . 1.59-1.63 in (40.5-41.5 mm)
   Plastic float . . . . 1.37-1.41 in (34.8-35.8 mm)
Choke plate pull down . . . . 0.27-0.29 in (6.75-7.25 mm)
Choke phasing . . . . 0.10-0.12 in (2.5-3.0 mm)

MOTORCRAFT (2000 OHC 'ECONOMY' FEB 76 ON) - Type prefix 76 HF, suffix KAA

Idling speed . . . . 800 rpm
Fast idle speed . . . . 2,000 rpm
Mixture % CO . . . . 1.5% ± 0.2
Float level . . . . 1.14 in (29 mm)
Vacuum pull down . . . . 0.16 in (4 mm)
De-choke . . . . 0.21 in (5.3 mm)
'V' mark setting . . . . 0.20 in (5.0 mm)
Accelerator pump stroke . . . . 0.11 in (2.8 mm)
Vacuum piston link hole . . . . Outer
Thermostatic spring slot . . . . Centre

FUEL
Trouble Shooter

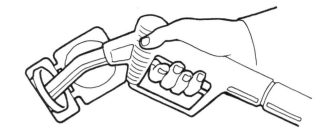

FAULT	CAUSE	CURE
Flooding	1. Improper seating or damaged float needle valve or seat 2. Incorrect float level 3. Fuel pump has excessive pressure	1. Check and replace parts as necessary. 2. Adjust float level. 3. Check fuel pump.
Excessive fuel consumption	1. Engine out of tune 2. Float level too high 3. Loose plug or jet 4. Defective gasket 5. Fuel leaks at pipes or connections 6. Choke valve operates improperly 7. Obstructed air bleed	1. Tune engine. 2. Adjust float level. 3. Tighten plug or jet. 4. Replace gaskets. 5. Trace leak and rectify. 6. Check choke valve. 7. Check and clear.
Stalling	1. Main jet obstructed 2. Incorrect throttle opening 3. Slow-running adjustment incorrect 4. Slow-running fuel jet blocked 5. Incorrect float level	1. Clean main jet. 2. Adjust throttle. 3. Adjust slow-running. 4. Clean jet. 5. Adjust float level.
Poor acceleration	1. Defective accelerator pump (if fitted) 2. Float level too low 3. Incorrect throttle opening 4. Defective accelerator linkage 5. Blocked pump jet	1. Overhaul pump. 2. Adjust float level. 3. Adjust throttle. 4. Adjust accelerator linkage. 5. Clean pump jet.
Spitting	1. Lean mixture 2. Dirty carburettor 3. Clogged fuel pipes 4. Manifold draws secondary air	1. Clean and adjust carburettor. 2. Clean carburettor. 3. Clean or replace pipes. 4. Tighten or replace gasket.
Insufficient fuel supply	1. Clogged carburettor 2. Clogged fuel pipe 3. Dirty fuel 4. Air in fuel system 5. Defective fuel pump 6. Clogged fuel filter	1. Dismantle and clean carburettor. 2. Clean fuel pipe. 3. Clean fuel tank. 4. Check connections and tighten. 5. Repair or replace fuel pump. 6. Clean or replace filter.
Loss of fuel delivery	1. Pump faulty (electric) 2. Slotted body screws loose 3. Diaphragm cracked 4. Loose fuel pipe connections 5. Defective valves 6. Cracked fuel pipes	1. Replace pump. 2. Tighten body screws. 3. Overhaul fuel pump. 4. Tighten fuel pipe connections. 5. Replace valves. 6. Replace fuel pipes.
Noisy pump	1. Loose pump mounting 2. Worn or defective rocker arm (if manual) 3. Broken rocker arm spring (if manual)	1. Tighten mounting bolts. 2. Replace rocker arm. 3. Replace spring.

Clutch & Gearbox

CLUTCH CABLE . . . .[1]

Replacement

Jack up the front of the car and support on stands. Working from under the car, slacken the clutch cable at its adjustment point on the clutch housing. Detach the release lever gaiter from the clutch housing, and disengage the ball end of the cable from the slotted hole in the release lever (Fig. H:2). Ensure the release bearing is not displaced from the release lever clevis during this operation. Slide the gaiter off the end of the clutch cable.

Inside the passenger compartment, remove the lower instrument panel insulator panel. Pull the clutch cable rearwards at the clutch pedal, withdraw the retaining pin from the bracket on the pedal and disengage the cable end from the slotted hole (Fig. H:3). Pull the cable through into the engine compartment and remove it from the car.

Pass the new cable through the tube in the bulkhead and pass the cable eye through the plastic bracket at the pedal. Fit the retaining pin and press firmly into the bracket. Refit the insulator panel.

Pass the lower end of the cable through the abutment in the clutch housing and fit the gaiter on to the cable. Connect the cable end to the release lever and refit the gaiter complete with spring to the clutch housing.

Finally, adjust the cable at the abutment on the clutch housing to obtain a free-play of approximately 1 - 1.25 in (23 - 31 mm) at the clutch pedal before it starts to operate the clutch mechanism. After tightening the adjuster locknut, press the pedal to the floor several times, then recheck the pedal free travel.

CLUTCH ASSEMBLY. . . . .[2]

Removal

The gearbox must first be removed from the car, as detailed under the appropriate heading in this section, before any work can be carried out on the clutch.

Before removing the clutch assembly from the flywheel, mark the position of the pressure plate cover relative to the flywheel to ensure correct alignment on reassembly.

Release the six clutch retaining bolts evenly, working diagonally across the pressure plate. This will avoid the possibility of distorting the pressure plate cover. Hold the pressure plate cover, remove the bolts and detach the pressure plate assembly and clutch disc from the flywheel. The pressure plate cover is located by three dowels on the flywheel.

To remove the release bearing, disengage the release arm from its fulcrum pin in the gearbox bell housing, then slide the release bearing assembly off the guide sleeve at the front of the gearbox and withdraw the release arm and bearing assembly from the clutch housing. Unhook the release bearing from the arm (Fig. H:5).

The release bearing can be separated from its hub by holding the bearing assembly with the bearing face downwards and tapping the shoulder of the hub sharply on a block of wood.

Clutch Disc - Inspection

Inspect the friction linings on the disc for wear, burning or contamination by oil or grease. If the linings are worn down to near the rivet heads, or if any other of the above conditions are apparent, the disc must be renewed.

If oil or grease contamination is found on the friction faces of the disc, the source must be determined and the fault rectified before fitting a new disc, otherwise the trouble may recur. This may be due to a defective gearbox input shaft seal or crankshaft rear oil seal.

If the disc is in good condition, check that the disc hub is a free sliding fit on the gearbox input shaft without excessive side play.

Pressure Plate - Inspection

Inspect the diaphragm spring fingers for wear where they contact the release bearing. Check the spring connections at both the pressure plate and cover for cracks and the rivets for tightness. If any rivets are damaged or loose, the assembly must be renewed.

Inspect the contact surface on the pressure plate for cracks and signs of burning or scoring, especially if the clutch disc linings were allowed to wear down to the rivets.

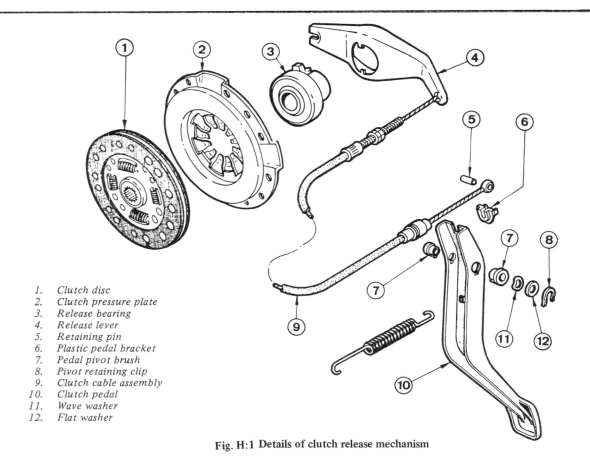

1. Clutch disc
2. Clutch pressure plate
3. Release bearing
4. Release lever
5. Retaining pin
6. Plastic pedal bracket
7. Pedal pivot brush
8. Pivot retaining clip
9. Clutch cable assembly
10. Clutch pedal
11. Wave washer
12. Flat washer

Fig. H:1 Details of clutch release mechanism

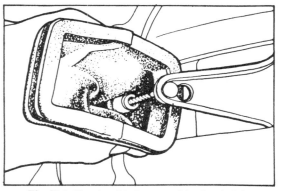

Fig. H:2 Clutch cable is secured by 'keyhole' in release lever

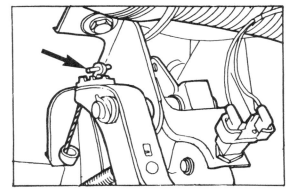

Fig. H:3 Retaining pin secures cable to pedal bracket

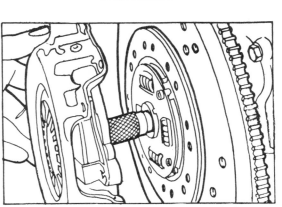

Fig. H:4 Use centring tool to align clutch disc with flywheel

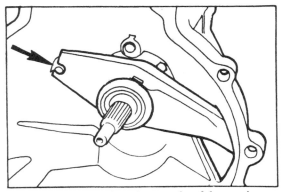

Fig. H:5 Release lever is secured to fulcrum pin by spring clip on lever

Check the plate for distortion using a straight-edge and feeler gauges. Renew the plate if necessary.

Flywheel - Inspection

Inspect the friction surface on the flywheel. Blueing or small cracks are of no particular importance, but if any deep scratches, scores, cracks or heat marks are present, the flywheel should be machined down or preferably replaced.

Release Bearing - Inspection

Inspect the bearing for wear, damage or looseness. Hold the bearing inner race and rotate the outer race while applying pressure to it. If the bearing rotation is rough or noisy, the bearing should be replaced. If obviously dry through lack of lubricant, the bearing must be renewed as it is a sealed unit. Do not wash the bearing in solvent as this will remove the lubricant contained in the assembly.

While checking the bearing, also check the guide sleeve on the gearbox. Check the outside surface of the guide sleeve for burrs or scoring. The hub should be able to slide freely on the sleeve without sticking.

Inspect the release arm for wear, damage and distortion. Renew if necessary.

Clutch Pilot Bearing

The clutch pilot bearing is located in the end of the crankshaft, and should be inspected for wear, damage or overheating. The needle bearing is a press fit in the crankshaft bore and should not be loose. If any of these conditions are apparent, the bearing must be replaced, as detailed in the appropriate ENGINE section.

Installation

A clutch centraliser tool, such as that shown in Fig.H: 4, is almost essential to ensure correct alignment of the clutch disc with the flywheel during reassembly. However, if great care is taken, it is possible to align the clutch by eye before finally tightening the pressure plate retaining bolts. If the disc is misaligned, difficulty will be encountered when attempting to refit the gearbox.

Ensure the friction surfaces on the flywheel and pressure plate are perfectly clean and free from oil or grease.

Place the clutch disc in position on the flywheel. The spring retaining plate side of the disc must face away from the flywheel. Normally, the flywheel side of the disc is appropriately marked near the centre. Align the disc with the centring tool, and locate the pressure plate on the flywheel face so that it engages the three dowels.

If the original pressure plate assembly is being refitted, align the marks made prior to removal. If a new assembly is being fitted, the balance marks on the clutch cover and flywheel must be placed opposite each other. The heavy side of the pressure plate is marked with a daub of paint, while the heavy side of the flywheel is marked with a drill point or daub of paint.

Fit the pressure plate retaining bolts and tighten evenly to 15 lb ft (2.0 kgm). Remove the centring tool.

Apply a light film of grease to the clutch release lever where it contacts the release bearing hub, and to the fulcrum pin pivot point, but do not use an excessive amount of grease. Also apply a light film of molybdenum disulphide grease to the outside surface of the guide sleeve on the gearbox.

Press the release bearing on to its hub, with the thrust face of the bearing away from the hub. This should require only light pressure. Ensure that the hub enters the bearing bore squarely and seats correctly against the bearing.

Smear molybdenum disulphide grease on the rear of the hub and bearing assembly, then engage the release arm in the slots in the bearing assembly. Slide the release bearing assembly on to the guide sleeve on the gearbox and engage the end of the release arm on the fulcrum pin (Fig.H: 5).

If required, a rubber band can be fitted around the release lever and the guide sleeve to hold the bearing assembly firmly in place against the lever. This will ensure that the bearing assembly is correctly located when the gearbox is assembled to the engine. There is no need to remove the rubber band as it will be destroyed in use.

Finally, refit the gearbox assembly as detailed under the appropriate heading and adjust the clutch cable freeplay.

GEARBOX REMOVAL & INSTALLATION . [3]

Removal

It will greatly facilitate removal of the gearbox if the car can be positioned over a pit or on a ramp. If neither of these is available, then the use of a pair of wheel ramps or chassis stands is essential for the job. Use these to raise the rear end of the car.
1. Disconnect the battery leads.
2. While your hands are still reasonably clean, working from inside the car, remove the gear lever. Lift up the gear lever gaiter and remove the small circlip holding the lever spring in compression. Bend back the lock washer tabs securing the plastic dome nut, and, using a suitably cranked spanner as shown in Fig. H:6, unscrew the nut securing the gear lever. Lift out the gear lever assembly.

On models with a centre console, the gear knob and console assembly must first be removed to allow access to the gear lever. Details of console removal are given in the BODY FITTINGS section later in the manual.
3. Working from underneath the car, disconnect the starter motor lead(s), remove the starter motor securing bolts (2 or 3, depending on the type of starter motor fitted) and withdraw the starter motor.
4. Slacken the clutch cable adjustment at the abutment on the clutch housing. Detach the release lever gaiter from the clutch housing, and disengage the cable end from the slotted hole in the release lever (Fig. H:2). Slide the gaiter off the clutch cable and disengage the cable from the clutch housing.

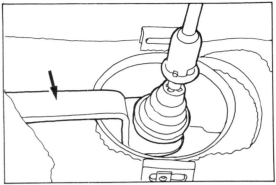

Fig. H:6 Plastic ball cap is easily unscrewed using cranked spanner. Gear lever can then be lifted out

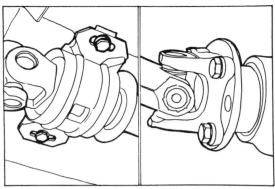

Fig. H:7 Where propshaft is of split type, centre bearing must be unbolted from floor pan as well as disconnecting rear flange from axle

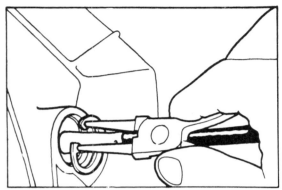

Fig. H:8 Speedo cable is secured in gearbox housing by circlip

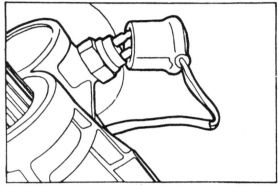

Fig. H:9 Wiring plug is a push-fit on reverse light switch

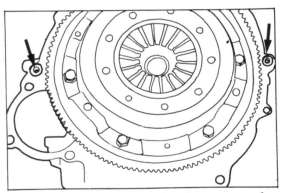

Fig. H:10 If engine locating dowels were removed with gearbox they must be transferred back to cylinder block

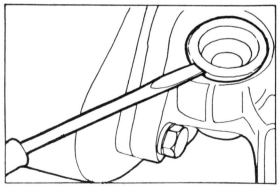

Fig. H:11 Speedo driven gear can be withdrawn from extension housing after first levering out drive cover

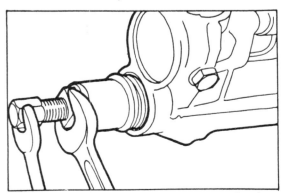

Fig. H:12 Withdrawing extension housing oil seal with Special Tool No. 16-006

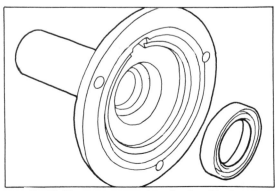

Fig. H:13 Install new seal in clutch guide sleeve, using a suitable tube to drive it into place

5. Remove the circlip securing the speedometer cable to the gearbox extension housing (Fig. H:8).

6. Pull back the sleeve at the reverse light switch on the rear of the extension housing and disconnect the leads from the switch terminals (Fig. H:9).

7. Unbolt the propshaft rear flange from the rear axle flange. On models with the split-type propshaft, also unbolt the centre bearing from the floor pan (Fig. H:7). Withdraw the propshaft from the gearbox extension housing. Fit a dummy shaft or dust cap to the extension housing to prevent loss of oil.

8. Support the weight of the gearbox with a jack and unbolt the gearbox support crossmember from the extension housing and floor pan. Detach the crossmember, and carefully lower the gearbox.

9. Remove the two bolts securing the lower plate to the front of the clutch housing and detach the plate.

10. Remove the six bolts securing the gearbox to the engine.

11. Withdraw the gearbox rearwards to disengage the input shaft splines from the clutch disc, then lower the gearbox and remove it from under the car.

On 1.6 and 2.0 litre models, to avoid disconnecting the exhaust pipe, turn the gearbox through 90° and pull it out over the exhaust pipe.

Installation

Installation is a simple reversal of the removal procedure, but special attention should be paid to the following points:

a) If the two engine locating dowels were removed with the gearbox, they must be refitted in their locations in the rear of the cylinder block as these help locate the engine adaptor plate while the gearbox is being installed (Fig. H: 10).

b) If required, a rubber band can be fitted around the clutch release lever and the guide sleeve on the gearbox to prevent the clutch release bearing sliding out. This will ensure that the bearing assembly is correctly located when the gearbox is installed. There is no need to remove the rubber band as it will be destroyed in use.

Alternatively, the release lever can be secured in the forward position by wiring it to the clutch housing. The wire can be released later.

c) Lightly grease the gearbox input shaft splines with molybdenum disulphide grease prior to installing the gearbox.

d) Once installed in position, secure the gearbox with two diametrically opposite bolts. Tighten these bolts first to pull the gearbox up to the engine, then fit and tighten the remaining bolts.

e) On models with the split-type propshaft, install the propshaft as detailed in the REAR AXLE section to avoid strain on the drive line.

f) Set the clutch cable adjustment to give a free-play of approximately 1 - 1.25 in (23 - 31 mm) at the clutch pedal before it starts to operate the clutch mechanism.

g) If drained, refill the gearbox with the recommended grade and quantity of oil through the gear lever aperture, before refitting the lever. Otherwise, merely check the oil level and top up as required.

h) Refit the gear lever so that the forked end engages correctly with the selector rail. When installation is complete, check that all gears are obtainable.

i) On models with a centre console, refit the console assembly as detailed in the BODY FITTINGS section.

Overhaul

In most cases of wear or damage to the components of the gearbox assembly it will probably be more convenient and economical to have the repair work carried out by a Transmission Specialist or Authorised Dealer who will have the specialised equipment and knowledge necessary to undertake work of this nature.

Another reasonable alternative would be to exchange the gearbox for a reconditioned or rebuilt unit in which all the necessary parts have already been inspected and renewed as required.

In this latter case, it will be necessary to remove the speedometer driven gear from the old unit before delivering it for exchange, as this gear is not normally supplied with a new unit. Lever the drive cover from the extension housing, using a screwdriver, and withdraw the gear from the housing (Fig. H:11). When installing the gear in the new unit, coat the drive cover with sealing compound before fitting.

Where the bell housing is of the detachable bolt-on type, this too should be removed for fitting to the new unit.

GEARBOX OIL SEALS . . . . [4]

Oil loss from the gearbox is invariably caused by leakage past the oil seals at the input and/or output shafts. Both of these oil seals are relatively easy to replace, but in the case of the input shaft seal the gearbox must first be removed from the car.

The proper remover and installer tools are shown in the illustrations refered to later, but if a bit of thought and care is used the seals can be replaced with equal success using any other suitable tools which are to hand, such as sockets, pieces of tubing, etc.. In this case, CARE is the keyword, as damage to the seal during installation will make replacement pointless.

Extension Housing Oil Seal

Replacement of this seal can be carried out while the gearbox is still installed in the car, but the propshaft must first be removed.

Position a drip tray underneath the gearbox extension housing. Extract the old seal, using the tool shown in Fig. H:12, or by carefully prising it out with a screwdriver or piece of hooked wire. Ensure the bore in the housing is clean and undamaged. Coat the new seal with multi-purpose grease and drive it into position in the extension housing. If a socket is being used to install the new seal, ensure it is of appropriate size so that it bears only on the outer diameter of the seal.

Coat the lip of the seal and the contact surface on the front end of the propshaft yoke with grease before refitting the propshaft. Take great care to avoid damaging the new seal when inserting the propshaft into the extension housing.

Input Shaft Seal

The gearbox input shaft seal is located in the clutch guide sleeve at the front of the gearbox. The gearbox must be removed from the car for the seal to be replaced.

Unbolt and detach the guide sleeve from the front face of the gearbox. Prise the old seal from the guide sleeve with a screwdriver. Clean all old gasket material from the mating faces on the guide sleeve and gearbox. Coat the new seal with multi-purpose grease and press it into position in the sleeve. The seal must be positioned so that the sealing lip will face towards the gearbox casing when fitted (Fig. H:13).

Cover the input shaft splines with masking tape to prevent damage to the oil seal as the guide sleeve is installed. Coat the lip of the seal with grease. Position a new gasket on the front face of the gearbox and fit the guide sleeve into place over the input shaft. Ensure that both the gasket and guide sleeve are correctly positioned with regard to the oil return hole in the front face of the gearbox casing. Coat the threads of the retaining bolts with sealing compound, then fit and tighten the bolts. Remove the masking tape.

Technical Data

CLUTCH

Type. . . . . Single dry plate, diaphragm spring pressure plate
Actuation . . . . .Cable
Clutch diameter:
   1.3 & 1.6 litre. . . . . .7.5 in (190 mm)
   2.0 litre . . . . .8.5 in (215 mm)
   2.3 litre . . . . .9.5 in (240 mm)
                                              9 in (230 mm)
Clutch pedal free travel. . . . . 1-1.25 in (23-31 mm)

GEARBOX

1.3 & 1.6 litre

Gear ratios:
   1st gear . . . . 3.58:1 . . . . 3.65:1
   2nd gear . . . . 2.01:1 . . . . 1.97:1
   3rd gear. . . . . 1.40:1 . . . . 1.37:1
   4th gear . . . . 1.00:1 . . . . 1.00:1
   Reverse . . . . 3.32:1 . . . . 3.66:1
Lubricant:
   Type. EP Gear Oil SAE 80 (to Ford Spec. SQ-M2C-9008-A)
   Capacity . . . . 1.6 pt (0.9 litre) . . . . 2.6 pt (1.5 litres)

CLUTCH
Trouble Shooter

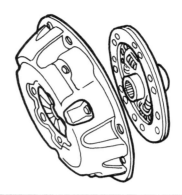

FAULT	CAUSE	CURE
Clutch slips	1. Clutch facing worn. 2. Clutch facing contaminated. 3. Warped clutch cover or pressure plate. 4. Incorrect adjustment (if adjustable).	1. Replace clutch assy. 2. Replace clutch assy. 3. Replace clutch assy. 4. Adjust clutch.
Clutch drags	1. Faulty clutch hydraulics (if hydraulic). 2. Faulty clutch adjustment (if adjustable). 3. Clutch disc warped. 4. Clutch hub splines worn or rusty. 5. Diaphragm worn or mal-adjusted.	1. Overhaul or replace clutch hydraulics. 2. Adjust clutch. 3. Replace clutch disc. 4. Replace or lubricate clutch. 5. Replace pressure plate.
Clutch chatter	1. Faulty pressure plate. 2. Faulty clutch disc. 3. Loose or worn engine mounting.	1. Replace pressure plate. 2. Replace clutch disc. 3. Replace mounting.
Clutch noise	1. Insufficient grease on bearing sleeve. 2. Clutch installed incorrectly.	1. Lubricate. 2. Check installation.
Clutch noise (pedal down)	1. Faulty release bearing.	1. Replace bearing.
Clutch noise (pedal on the way up)	1. Damaged or worn pilot bearing.	1. Fit new bearing.
Clutch grabs	1. Contaminated clutch lining. 2. Clutch worn or loose rivets. 3. Clutch splines worn or rusted. 4. Warped flywheel or pressure plate. 5. Loose mountings on engine or power unit	1. Replace clutch. 2. Replace clutch. 3. Clean or replace. 4. Repair or replace. 5. Tighten or replace.

Automatic Transmission

INTRODUCTION . . . .[1]

An automatic gearbox is probably the most complicated part of any car, and it is for this reason that DIY overhaul procedures have been deliberately omitted from this section as specialised knowledge and tools are needed to carry out any repairs satisfactorily.

If there is any malfunction with an automatic gearbox, the first step must always be to check the fluid level and then carry out a thorough fault diagnosis check to ascertain the cause of the trouble. This job should be done by a Ford dealer or a local auto transmission specialist with the gearbox in the car. It is pointless to remove the gearbox and dismantle it in the hope that the fault will be visible, for invariably it will not.

However, there are certain straightforward service, maintenance repairs and adjustments that can be done by the DIY owner and which may become necessary from time to time, and these are covered in detail in this section.

NOTE: Many drivers fail to realise how much the engine performance affects the correct operation of an automatic transmission. If the engine is in a bad state of tune or in need of an overhaul, then this will have a marked effect on the automatic gearchange pattern and which will appear to be a gearbox fault when, in fact, the cause is due to the engine. In all cases of apparent automatic gearbox troubles, always check the fluid level and the engine tune first.

TRANSMISSION IDENTIFICATION . . . .[2]

Three types of automatic transmission have been used on the Mk 3 Cortina. Early models, up to February 74 used the Borg Warner model 35 type. During February 74, build code PY, a limited number of 2000 cc Cortinas were fitted with the Ford C4 type transmission.

This was superseded by the Bordeaux built Type C3 in March 1974, and all subsequent models are fitted with this unit.

The three units can be identified by the type of con-

verter bell housing fitted. The BW 35 unit has a cast iron housing. The intermediate Ford C4 type has a bright alloy housing with a rectangular cooling vent on the LH side.

Later type C3 units also have an alloy housing but a transmission oil cooler is incorporated in the lower part of the engine radiator with oil pipes to the transmission to identify it.

NOTE: Some C4 type transmissions may also have a transmission oil cooler fitted which was offered as an optional kit when required.

FLUID LEVEL . . . .[3]

Full details of the procedure for checking the fluid level in the transmission are given in the ROUTINE MAINTENANCE section at the beginning of the manual.

ADJUSTMENTS - BW MODEL 35 . . . .[4]

Only the adjustments described below should be attempted. Any further adjustments (e.g. brake bands) should be entrusted to an Authorised Dealer or Transmission Specialist.

Selector Cable

1. Disconnect the selector cable from the operating arm on the transmission (Fig. I:1). Move the manual selector lever into the '1' position.
2. Pull the transmission operating arm into its rearmost position.
3. Slacken the adjuster nuts, and alter the position of the cable threaded sleeve in relation to the abutment bracket until the holes in the cable end and operating arm are aligned.
4. Reconnect the cable to the operating arm. The cable should be taut, but not stressed, when in position.
5. Secure the clevis pin with the spring clip. Tighten the adjuster nuts. Ensure that the spacers are in their correct positions. Check that all the selector positions can be engaged.

Downshift Cable

To check or adjust the downshift cable can only be done with the aid of a pressure gauge with adaptor and a reliable tachometer.

If these instruments cannot be hired locally, they can usually be bought quite cheaply second-hand otherwise the job should be left to a local Ford dealer or transmission specialist.

1. Before attempting to adjust the downshift linkage, ensure that the throttle valve opens fully, and is not impeded in its operation by the accelerator pedal stop.
2. Check the fluid level as described previously in this section.
3. The engine and transmission must be at normal operating temperature when performing this adjustment. With the engine stopped, remove the blanking plug from the pressure line take-off point in the rear face of the transmission case, and connect a transmission line pressure gauge
4. Connect an accurate tachometer to the engine.
5. Start the engine and set the idling speed to approx. 560 rev/min. Eliminate any free-play in the accelerator linkage..
6. Apply the foot and hand brake, move the selector lever into the 'D' position, then set the engine idling speed exactly to 500 rev/min.
7. Note the pressure gauge reading. This should be 3.52 - 4.57 atu (50 - 60 psi).
8. Increase the engine speed to 1,000 rev/min. and take a second pressure gauge reading. This should indicate a pressure rise of 1.05 - 1.41 atu. (15 - 20 psi) over the previous reading for 1600 cc and 2000 cc models, or an actual gauge reading of 5.62 - 7.03 atu. (80 - 100 psi) for 1600 GT models.
NOTE: Do NOT hold this increased engine speed for longer than 20 seconds.
9. If the indicated pressure or pressure rise is not within the specified range, slacken the adjuster nuts at the outer cable bracket on the engine compartment bulkhead and alter the position of the threaded sleeve in relation to the bracket (Fig. I:3).
10. Increase the effective length of the outer cable if the indicated pressure or pressure rise is low.
11. Conversely, if the pressure or pressure rise exceeds the specified limit, decrease the effective length of the outer cable.
12. Retest the line pressure after adjustment. When the correct setting is obtained retighten the cable adjuster nuts.
13. Reset the idle speed to specification. Stop the engine, disconnect the pressure gauge and refit the blanking plug to the take-off point. Take care not to over-tighten the plug in the aluminium threads of the transmission casing.
14. Remove the tachometer. Finally, road test the car and check the quality of the gear changes.

Starter Inhibitor Switch

1. When the starter inhibitor switch is functioning correctly the engine will only start with the selector lever in the 'P' or 'N' positions. If the engine will not start in the 'P' or 'N' selector positions, or if the starter motor operates in all selector positions, then the switch requires adjustment.

The reverse light should also operate only when the selector lever is in 'R'.
2. Before attempting to adjust the switch, check the adjustment of the selector cable, as described previously.
3. The combined starter inhibitor and reverse light switch is located on the L.H. side of the transmission case. The switch has four terminals; two large terminals for the reverse light switch, and two smaller terminals for the starter inhibitor switch (Fig. I:6).
4. Place the selector lever in the 'D' or '1' position. Suitably label the respective leads and disconnect them from the switch.
5. Slacken the switch locknut if fitted, then connect a small battery and test lamp across the reverse switch terminals.
6. Unscrew the switch fully from the transmission casing, then screw it in again until the test lamp just goes out. Mark the position of the switch.
7. Transfer the test lamp to the inhibitor switch terminal, then screw the switch in further until the test lamp just lights again. Mark this second position of the switch.
8. Unscrew the switch until it is midway between the two marked positions, and secure it with the locknut if fitted. Do NOT over-tighten the locknut; it need only be pinch tight. Reconnect the leads to the appropriate terminals on the switch.
9. Check that the switch functions as described above. If the switch still does not operate correctly, check the switch wiring and connections before replacing the switch.
NOTE: When replacing the switch unit or if there are signs of oil leakage past the switch threads, the switch should be removed and sealing compound applied to the threads before refitting.

Front Brake Band

To adjust the front brake band it will first be necessary to drain the transmission fluid from the plug on the sump, and then remove the sump from the transmission casing.
1. Slacken the front brake band servo adjustment locknut and move the servo lever outwards away from the servo body (Fig. I:4).
2. Place an accurate steel spacer block, 0.25 in (6.4 mm) thick between the adjusting screw and the servo piston pin.
3. Using a brake adjusting spanner and a spring balance as a simple torque wrench, tighten the adjusting screw to a torque of 10 lb in (1.15 kgm). Then tighten the locknut.

Note that if a spacer block is not available, the adjusting screw should be tightened to a torque of 10 lb in (1.15 kgm) as detailed earlier and then the adjusting screw slackened off exactly 4 turns. Then tighten the locknut.
4. When adjustment is complete, remove the spacer block - if fitted - then refit the sump pan together with a new gasket. Refill the transmission with fluid and check for oil leaks.

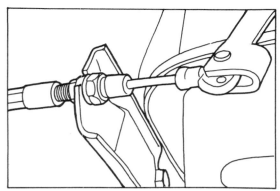

Fig. I:1 The selector cable connection at the transmission operating arm

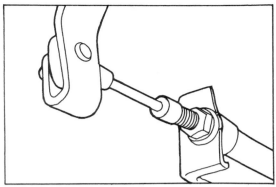

Fig. I:2 Selector cable connection at the base of the manual selector lever

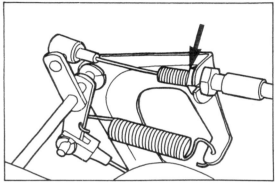

Fig. I:3 The downshift cable adjustment point at the throttle linkage

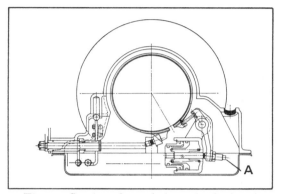

Fig. I:4 Section through front brake band showing adjuster screw (A)

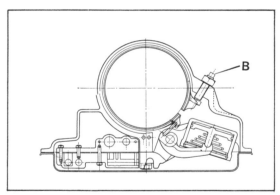

Fig. I:5 Section through rear brake band showing adjuster screw (B)

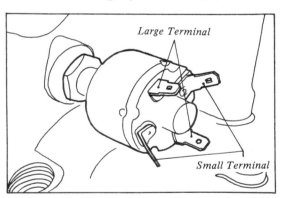

Fig. I:6 Note which wires go where on the BW35 transmission inhibitor switch

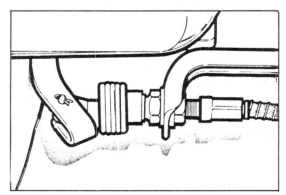

Fig. I:7 The manual selector lever and adjustment point - C4 transmission

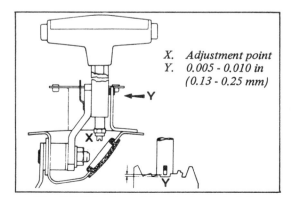

X. Adjustment point
Y. 0.005 - 0.010 in (0.13 - 0.25 mm)

Fig. I:8 Selector cable attachment at the transmission levers - C4 transmission

Rear Brake Band (Fig. I:5)

To adjust the rear brake band it will be necessary to lower the transmission unit first to gain access to the adjuster on the top of the casing.

1. Raise and support the front of the car, then place a jack under the transmission casing to support it.
2. Remove the four rear crossmember to floorpan bolts.
3. Remove the propshaft centre bearing support bolts - if fitted, then lower the shaft slightly and support it under the bearing housing.
4. Lower the gearbox on the jack until the engine sump is resting on the front suspension crossmember, then remove the rear crossmember from the transmission to give clearer access.
5. Slacken the rear brake band adjuster locknut, and then, using the brake adjusting spanner and spring balance as a simple torque wrench, tighten the adjusting screw to a torque of 10 lb ft (1.4 kg.m). Then slacken the adjusting screw by one complete turn and tighten the locknut.

NOTE: Position the spring balance attachment at a point, 6 inches (152 mm) from the centre of the spanner end as shown in Fig. I:10.

Make sure the spring balance is at right angles to the spanner when measuring the torque. Remember to double the figure on the spring balance ie; for a torque of 10 lb ft (1.4 kgm) a pull of 20 lbs (2.8 kgm) will be needed.

ADJUSTMENTS - FORD TYPE C4 . . . . [5]

Only the adjustments described below should be attempted. Any further adjustments or checks should be left to an Authorised Dealer or Transmission Specialist.

Selector Cable

Remove the retaining pin or clip and disconnect the cable end from the manual selector lever, see (Fig. I:7). Move the manual selector lever into the 'P' position, ensuring that it engages correctly. Move the lever on the transmission into the 'P' position (fully forward). The cable end should be adjusted to align exactly with the selector lever and the pin should be able to be inserted without any difficulty.

If adjustment is necessary, slacken the locknuts at the outer cable abutment bracket on the transmission and adjust the position of the outer sleeve to achieve this condition. Tighten the locknuts once the correct position has been obtained.

Reconnect the cable end to the selector lever, then check that the manual selector lever can be engaged in every selector position and that engagement can be felt. If necessary, re-adjust the cable to achieve this condition.

Down-Shift Cable

Before attempting to check the down-shift cable adjustment, check that the throttle plate is fully open when the accelerator pedal is fully depressed.

Turn the throttle operating shaft to the fully open throttle position and move the downshift lever on the transmission into the kickdown position. Check that a clearance of 0.004 - 0.010 in (0.1 - 0.25 mm), measured with a feeler gauge, is present between the full throttle stop and the throttle stop lever of the carburettor.

If adjustment is necessary, lengthen or shorten the cable by means of the adjustment nuts at the abutment bracket on the engine until the correct clearance is obtained. (Fig. I:9).

Selector Inhibitor Cable

The selector lever mechanism incorporates a pawl which engages in notches in the selector housing and thus inhibits movement of the lever between certain selector positions, unless the release button on the side of the selector 'T' handle is first depressed.

When the mechanism is functioning correctly it should not be possible to make the following changes without first depressing the button; P to R, R to P, D to 2,2 to 1, N to R.

If adjustment is necessary, first lift off the escutcheon at the selector lever and engage the lever in the 'D' position. Remove the rubber plug from the underside of the selector lever housing. Using a feeler gauge, adjust the pawl operating cable by means of the locknut, accessible through the aperture in the housing, to give the specified clearance of 0.005 - 0.10 in (0.13 - 0.25 mm) between the inhibitor stub and the notch in the housing (Fig. I: 8). When adjustment is complete, refit the plug and put back the escutcheon plate.

Front & Rear Brake Bands (Figs. I:11 and I:12)

Adjustment of the brake bands requires the use either of a pre-set torque wrench, Special Tool GAT-702, or a simple home-made torque wrench tool using a brake adjusting spanner and a spring balance to tighten the band adjusting screws to 10 lb ft (1.4 kg m).

NOTE: Position the spring balance attachment at a point, 6 inches (152 mm) from the centre of the spanner and as shown in (Fig. I:10).

Make sure the spring balance is at right angles to the spanner when measuring the torque. Remember to double the figure on the spring balance ie; for a torque of 10 lb ft (1.4 kg m) a pull of 20 lbs (2.8 kg m) will be needed.

Slacken the locknut on the band adjusting screw and slacken the screw by a few turns. Using the torque wrench, tighten the adjusting screw to 10 lb ft (1.4 kg m).

Slacken the front band adjuster screw by 1.75 turns and the rear screw by 3 turns, then secure them with the locknuts, holding the adjusting screw while doing so to prevent it turning. Ideally, new locknuts should be used.

ADJUSTMENTS - FORD TYPE C3 . . . . [6]

Only the adjustments described below should be attempted. Any further adjustments or checks should be left to an Authorised Dealer or Transmission Specialist.

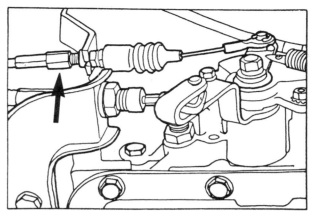

Fig. I:9 Downshift cable adjustment point
on C4 transmission

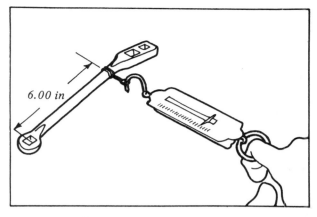

Fig. I:10 Simple home-made torque wrench
from brake adjuster spanner and spring balance

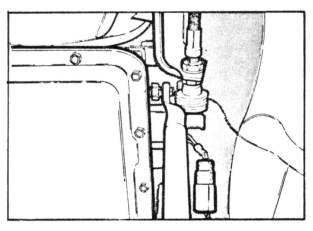

Fig. I:11 The front brake band adjustment
point - C4 transmission

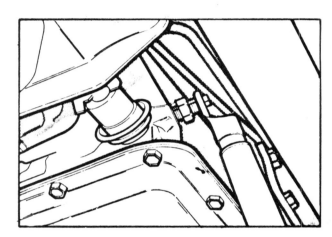

Fig. I:12 Adjusting the rear brake band screw -
C4 transmission

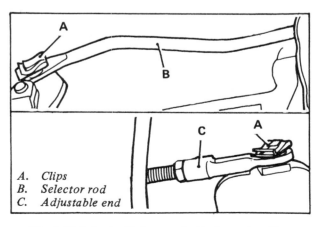

A. Clips
B. Selector rod
C. Adjustable end

Fig. I:13 Selector linkage rod attachment - adjust
at link end (C) - C3 transmission

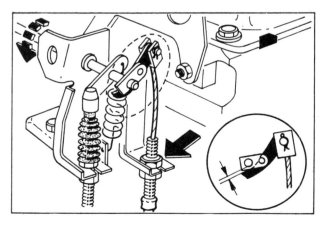

Fig. I:14 The adjustment point for the downshift
cable at throttle linkage

Selector Linkage Rod

Remove the retaining clip and disconnect the adjustable end of the linkage rod from the lower end of the manual selector lever (Fig. I:13). Move the gearshift lever at the transmission into the 'D' position (two notches back from the front stop). Engage the manual selector lever firmly in the 'D' selector position. The linkage rod should now fit easily onto the selector lever pin without strain.

If adjustment is necessary, slacken the locknut and lengthen or shorten the linkage rod at its adjustable end to achieve this condition. When tightening the locknut, make sure that the adjustable end of the rod remains vertical.

Reconnect the linkage rod to the selector arm. Check that the manual selector lever can be engaged in every selector position and that engagement can be felt. If necessary, re-adjust the linkage rod to achieve this condition.

Selector Inhibitor Cable

Check the selector inhibitor cable adjustment in a similar manner to that described for the C4 transmission previously.

Down-Shift Cable Adjustment

Before attempting to check the down-shift cable adjustment, check that the throttle plate is fully open when the accelerator pedal is fully depressed.

Depress the accelerator cable far enough to open the throttle plate fully. Press the down-shift cable connecting lever away from the throttle shaft lever, using a screwdriver, and check that a clearance of 0.020 - 0.050 in (0.5 - 1.3 mm) is present between the cable lever and the underside of the throttle shaft (Fig. I:14).

If adjustment is necessary, lengthen or shorten the cable by means of the adjustment nuts until the correct clearance is obtained.

Down Shift Cable Replacement

Disconnect the down-shift cable at the throttle linkage shaft by extracting the split pin or clip and withdrawing the clevis pin (Fig. I:15). Unscrew the adjusting nut and detach the cable threaded sleeve from the abutment bracket at the engine. Disengage the inner cable from the slot in the bracket.

At the transmission end of the cable, detach the cable outer sleeve from the abutment bracket by unscrewing the nut from the threaded sleeve and unhook the cable from the slot in the bracket. Disengage the inner cable end from the downshift lever and withdraw the cable from the transmission.

Fit the new cable in the reverse order of removal. At the abutment bracket on the engine, the lower adjusting nut must be screwed completely onto the threaded sleeve, and the upper nut only a few turns.

When adjustment is complete, adjust the cable as detailed above in 'ADJUSTMENT'.

Front Brake Band

Adjustment of the front brake band requires the use of a pre-set torque wrench, Special Tool 17-005, as the actual tightening torque figure for the band adjusting screw is not given by the manufacturer (Fig. I:16).

Disconnect the down-shift cable from the transmission down-shift lever on the left-hand side of the transmission. Slacken the locknut on the band adjusting screw and slacken the screw a few turns. Using the pre-set torque wrench, tighten the adjusting screw by 1.5 turns and secure it with the locknut, holding the adjusting screw while doing so to prevent it turning. Reconnect the down-shift cable to the transmission lever.

Starter Inhibitor Switch
C4 Transmission

The starter inhibitor switch is located on the lefthand side of the transmission case at the down-shift lever and selector lever spindle (Fig. I:17).

When the switch is functioning correctly, the engine will only start with the selector lever in the 'P' or 'N' position, and not in 'R', 'D', '2' or '1'. If the engine will not start in the 'P' or 'N' selector positions or if the starter motor operates in all selector positions, then the switch is either out of adjustment or defective.

The only adjustment of the switch is to reset its alignment with the transmission casing, and this should only be necessary if the switch has been incorrectly set in the first place, or the switch securing screws have worked loose. When correctly positioned, it should be possible to insert a 0.086 in (2.2 mm) setting pin or twist drill into the switch locking hole without any difficulty (Fig. I:17).

To replace the switch, first disconnect the down-shift lever return spring and allow it to hang down. Disconnect the downshift cable from the lever. Remove the nut from the end of the spindle and remove the downshift lever. Undo the two screws securing the inhibitor switch to the transmission casing and detach the switch. Disconnect the wiring connections.

Connect the wiring to the new switch and position the switch over the selector shaft, taking note of the guide slots. Refit the switch securing bolts together with the downshift cable abutment bracket, and tighten the bolts finger-tight. Refit the downshift lever and its return spring.

With the selector lever in the 'D' position, fit the setting pin mentioned above into the switch locking hole and tighten the switch securing screws. Remove the setting pin.

Reconnect the downshift cable to the lever on the transmission and adjust as detailed previously under 'ADJUSTMENTS'.

Finally, check that the new switch operates correctly as detailed above.

Starter Inhibitor Switch
C3 Transmission

The starter inhibitor switch is located on the lefthand side of the main transmission casing. The switch should function in the same way as that described for the C4

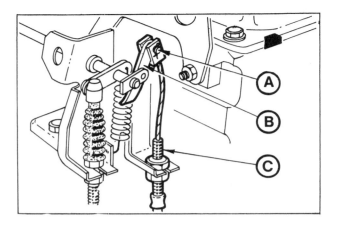

A. Clevis pin
B. Linkage connecting lever
C. Threaded sleeve

Fig. I:15 The downshift cable attachment point at the throttle linkage

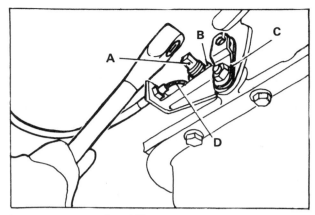

A. Adjustment screw
B. Locknut
C. Downshift lever
D. Downshift cable

Fig. I:16 A special torque wrench is needed to adjust brake bands - C3 type

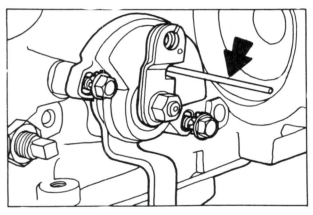

Fig. I:17 Aligning starter inhibitor switch with setting pin during installation - C4 type

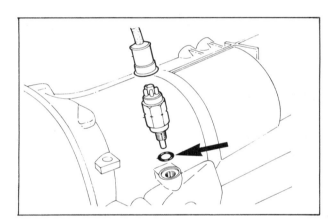

Fig. I:18 Starter inhibitor switch installation - C3 type. Use new 'O' ring when refitting switch

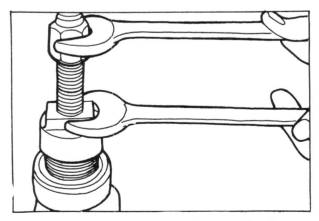

Fig. I:19 Lever out extension housing oil seal or use special extractor tool as shown

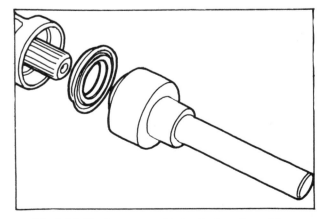

Fig. I:20 Fit the new seal into the housing with seal lip facing inwards, using drift or special tool

transmission above. If the switch is defective it must be replaced as it is non-adjustable (Fig. I:18).

To remove the switch, simply disconnect the wiring plug and unscrew the switch from the casing. A new 'O' ring must be used when refitting the switch. Ensure that the switch is tightened to its specified torque setting of 14 lb ft (2.0 kg m) - this is most important.

TRANSMISSION REPLACEMENT . . . . [7]

Removal

1. Position the vehicle over a pit, or drive it up onto ramps.
2. As a safety precaution, disconnect the battery leads.
3. Disconnect the engine telescopic damper from the mounting brackets on the engine and body panel, where fitted
4. Disconnect the exhaust pipes at the manifolds and detach them from the front mounting bracket. The degree to which the exhaust system will have to be removed will depend on the individual model and the type of exhaust system fitted. Pull the system clear of the gearbox and secure it out of the way with wire or string.
5. Disconnect the starter motor leads. Remove the securing bolts and withdraw the starter motor.
6. On models with BW35 or C4 type transmissions disconnect the selector cable from the selector lever and the abutment bracket on the transmission (Fig. I:2).
7. On models with C3 transmission, disconnect the selector linkage rod from the manual selector lever and the gearshift lever on the transmission (Fig. I:13).
8. Disconnect the down-shift cable from the transmission down-shift lever at the abutment bracket shown in Fig. I:9.
9. On BW35 transmissions, remove the upper bolts securing the converter housing to the engine.
10. Disconnect the vacuum pipe from the vacuum diaphragm on the side of transmission casing - if fitted.
11. Remove the bolt or circlip securing the speedometer cable retainer to the transmission casing and disconnect the speedo cable.
12. Disconnect the wiring from the starter inhibitor switch, noting where each wire goes.
13. Disconnect the oil cooler pipes from the transmission - if fitted. Plug the pipe ends to prevent the ingress of dirt.
14. Unbolt the propshaft rear flange from the rear axle flange. The flanges should be marked before removal to ensure correct alignment on reassembly. On models with the split-type propshaft, also unbolt the centre bearing from the floor pan (Fig. H: 7). Withdraw the propshaft from the transmission extension housing. Fit a plastic bag tightly over the end of the extension housing to prevent oil loss.
15. Detach the lower cover plate from the front of the converter housing.
16. Remove the bolts securing the torque converter to the engine drive plate. These are accessible, one at a time, through the starter motor aperture
17. Support the weight of the transmission with jack and unbolt the transmission rear support crossmember from the floor pan.
18. Carefully lower the jack until the engine sump touches the front suspension crossmember with the transmission at an angle.
19. With the transmission still supported on the jack, remove the bolts securing the transmission to the engine, and withdraw the transmission filler tube (Fig. I: 20). On the C4 type transmission, the filler tube must be disconnected from the oil pan. Plug the oil filler opening in the transmission to prevent dirt entering.
21. Carefully withdraw the transmission assembly. Note that the torque converter will still be full of oil, so, as the transmission is moved, press the converter firmly against the transmission to prevent it being displaced.

Installation

Installation is a simple reversal of the removal procedure, but special attention should be paid to the following points:-
a) Ensure that the engine adaptor plate is correctly located on the guide bushes on the rear face of the cylinder block. If the two guide bushes were removed with the transmission, they must be transferred to their correct locations in the rear of the block.
b) Before assembling the transmission unit to the engine, check that the torque converter hub is fully engaged in the pump gear at the front of the transmission. With the C3 transmission, when correctly engaged, the distance between the flange of the converter housing and the centering stub face on the converter body should be at least 0.4 in (10 mm). On BW 35 transmission, ensure that the drive tags on the rear of the converter and the slots in the front pump are correctly aligned when installing the torque converter in its housing. Rotate the converter so that the drive tags will be in the 9 o'clock and 3 o'clock positions. The slots in the pump driving gear are then rotated to a similar position, with the aid of a screwdriver or similar tool. Take care to ensure that the sealing ring is not damaged when sliding the converter assembly onto the transmission input shaft.
c) When installing the transmission, ensure that the converter drain plug is positioned in line with the opening in the engine drive plate, if fitted.
d) With the converter assembly flush with the cylinder block, it should rotate easily. Only after this has been achieved should the engine-to-transmission bolts be fitted and tightened.
e) Set the down-shift cable adjustment as detailed under 'ADJUSTMENTS' previously.
f) When reconnecting the selector linkage, both the manual selector lever and the transmission selector lever should be set in the 'D' position. The rod or cable end should fit easily without strain. If necessary, adjust the cable or rod length to achieve this condition (Figs. I:9 or I:13).
g) Install the propshaft as detailed in the REAR AXLE section to avoid strain on the drive shaft.
h) If drained, refill the transmission with the recommended grade and quantity of Automatic Transmission Fluid. Otherwise, merely check the fluid level and top up as required.

EXTENSION HOUSING OIL SEAL.......[8]

Replacement

Replacement of this seal can be carried out while the transmission is still installed in the car, but the propshaft must first be removed.

Position a drip tray under the transmission extension housing. Extract the old oil seal, using the special tool shown in Fig. I:19, or by carefully prising it out with a screwdriver or hooked piece of wire.

Ensure the bore in the housing is clean and undamaged. Press the new seal into position in the housing, with the sealing lip facing inwards (Fig. I:20). If a socket or similar make-shift tool is being used to install the new seal, ensure that it is an appropriate size so that it bears only on the outer diameter of the seal.

Take great care to avoid damaging the new seal when inserting the propshaft into the extension housing.

SELECTOR MECHANISM..............[9]

Removal

On models with a centre console, the console must first be removed to gain access to the selector mechanism.

Unclip the escutcheon from the selector housing and lift it clear of the selector mechanism. Slide the quadrant illumination lamp out of the base of the selector lever.

Remove the securing clip and detach the selector linkage rod or cable from the lower end of the manual selector lever. Where a cable linkage is used, the cable outer sleeve must also be detached from the abutment bracket on the selector housing.

Undo the four bolts securing the selector lever housing to the transmission tunnel and lift out the selector mechanism assembly

Installation

Install the selector mechanism in the reverse order of removal. Pay special attention to the position of the gasket when fitting the housing to the transmission tunnel.

When reconnecting the selector linkage, set both the transmission selector lever and the manual selector lever in the 'D' position. The rod or cable end should fit on the selector lever pin without strain. If necessary, adjust the rod or cable length to achieve this condition.

Technical Data

Make.	Borg Warner
Type.	BW 35
Selector positions	P - R - N - D - 2 - 1
Fluid type	Automatic transmission fluid (Ford Spec M-2C33F)
Fluid capacity.	11.25 pints (6.4 litres)
Make.	Ford
Type.	C4
Selector positions	P - R - N - D - 2 - 1
Fluid type	Automatic transmission fluid (Ford Spec M-2C33F or SQM-9007-AA)
Fluid capacity (inc oil cooler)	12.3 pints (7.0 litres)
Make.	Ford - Bordeaux
Type.	C3
Selector positions	P - R - N - D - 2 - 1
Fluid type	Automatic transmission fluid (Ford Spec SQM-2C-9007-AA)
Fluid capacity (inc oil cooler)	11.4 pints (6.5 litres)

Rear Axle/Propshaft

PROPSHAFT . . . .[1]

Two types of propshaft are used on the Mk 3 Cortina, one-piece or a two-piece, or split-type as it is commonly known. (Fig. J:1).

The split-type propshaft has a centre support bearing and an additional Universal joint or in some cases a Constant Velocity joint. On some models a rubber 'Guibo' type coupling replaces the front universal joint.

In all cases the universal joints are not serviceable, as they are secured in position by peening over the opening in the yoke instead of by circlips. This will necessitate replacement of the complete shaft assembly if one or more joints show signs of wear or damage. There are some Specialist Engineering Firms who will machine out the yokes to accept replacement circlip-type joints, and if one can be found this will provide a great saving over total replacement.

However, the bearing in the centre support bearing can be replaced, and is normally supplied as a kit along with all the relevant components required for overhaul of the assembly. Details of the bearing overhaul are given overleaf.

Removal

1. Raise and support the rear of the car, then, with the handbrake applied, remove the four bolts, with their spring washers, securing the propshaft rear flange to the rear axle flange (Fig. J:2).
2. With the split-type propshaft, remove the two bolts securing the centre bearing to the brackets on the floor panel. If spacers are fitted between the centre bearing housing and the mounting brackets their locations should be noted for reassembly, as otherwise the front and rear sections of the shaft will be at the wrong angle to one another (Fig. J:3).
3. Lower the rear end of the shaft and withdraw the front slip yoke from the transmission extension housing. Fit a suitable plug or tie a plastic bag over the rear end of the transmission to prevent loss of oil.

Installation

4. Lubricate the front sleeve of the propshaft with gearbox oil or automatic transmission fluid to prevent damage to the gearbox or transmission rear oil seal. Remove the plug or bag from the rear of the transmission and carefully insert the propshaft onto the shaft splines.
5. With the one-piece propshaft, connect the shaft to the rear axle flange and secure with the four bolts and new spring washers. Tighten the bolts to 45 lb ft (6.5 kg m).
6. On the two piece propshaft with three universal joints or with the rubber front coupling, install the shaft as follows:
a) Fit the centre-bearing to the floor panel, but leave the bolts loose at this stage. Ensure that any spacers removed previously are refitted between the bearing housing and the body brackets (Fig. J:3).
b) Place a 5/32 in (0.15 in/4 mm) thick spacer between the propshaft rear flange and the rear axle flange, and secure with the four flange bolts (Fig. J:4).
c) With the car resting on its rear axle or wheels, locate the centre bearing parallel to the drive shaft and free of stress, then tighten the two retaining bolts to 15 lb ft (2.3 kg m).
d) Loosen the bolts at the propshaft rear flange and remove the spacer. Refit the bolts with new spring washers and tighten to 45 lb ft (6.5 kg m).
7. In the case of the two piece propshaft with the C/V joint at the centre, install the propshaft as follows:
a) Bolt the centre bearing in place on the body mounting brackets, not forgetting any spacers removed previously, but leave the bolts loose at this stage.
b) Connect the rear end of the shaft to the axle flange and secure with the four bolts and new spring washers. Tighten the bolts to 45 lb ft (6.5 kg m).
c) Jack up the rear of the car and support so that the rear axle hangs down freely to its fullest extent.
d) Pull the front section of the propshaft, together with the centre bearing, forwards in the direction of the transmission until the C/V joint is felt to bear against the rear of the centre bearing.
e) With the propshaft and C/V joint held in this position, tighten the two centre bearing retaining bolts, taking care that the bearing housing is located squarely to the propshaft. Tighten the bolts to 15 lb ft (2.3 kg m).
f) Lower the car to the ground.
8. Finally, in all cases, check the oil level in the transmission and top up as necessary.

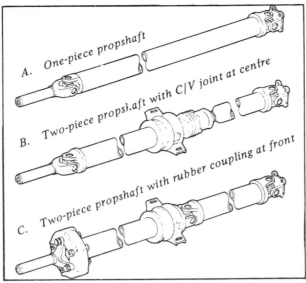

Fig. J:1 Three different types of propshaft may be found on Cortina variants

A. One-piece propshaft

B. Two-piece propshaft with C/V joint at centre

C. Two-piece propshaft with rubber coupling at front

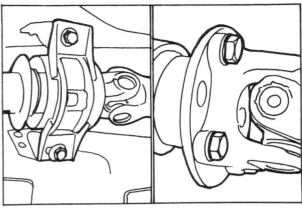

Fig. J:2 On two-piece propshafts, undo flange bolts (right) and centre bearing bolts (left)

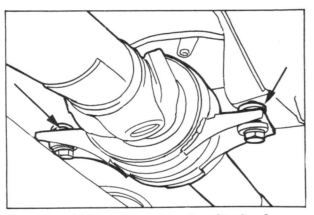

Fig. J:3 Note any spacer washers fitted under housing flange and remember to refit them

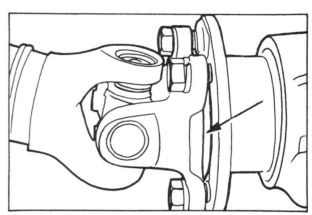

Fig. J:4 On rubber coupling type shafts, a spacer must be fitted to align centre bearing - see text

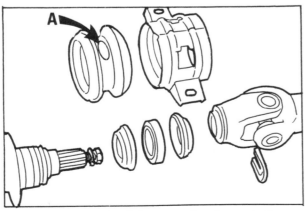

Fig. J:5 Details of the centre bearing, note the position of the boss (A) when refitting

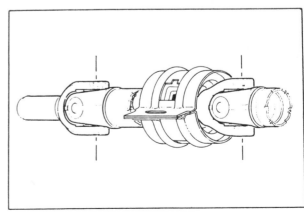

Fig. J:6 To avoid imbalance, mark the two shafts to reassemble in original position

Overhauling the Centre Bearing

1. Mark the two sections of the propshaft to ensure correct alignment on reassembly. This is important. (Fig. J:6).

2. Bend back the lock washer tab and slacken the bolt at the centre joint yoke. On propshafts with a C/V joint, the front flange has to be unbolted from the joint housing to gain access to the centre-bolt.

3. Withdraw the U-shaped retainer to the side and separate the two sections of the shaft (Fig. J:7).

4. Slide the bearing housing and rubber insulator off the front section of the shaft.

5. Using a two-legged puller, remove the ball bearing and protective caps from the front section of the shaft (Fig. J:8).

6. Bend back the six tabs on the bearing carrier and separate the rubber insulator from the carrier.

7 Fill the space between the new bearing and the protective caps with lithium based grease, then press the bearing, together with the caps, onto the front section of the shaft, using a tube of suitable diameter.

8. Bend the six metal tabs on the carrier slightly outwards and insert the new rubber insulator with the boss uppermost (A, Fig. J: 5) into the carrier. Secure the insulator in position by bending the six tabs rearwards over the beaded edge of the insulator (Fig. J:9).

9. Slide the carrier assembly over the ball race at the end of the shaft.

10. Screw the centre-bolt, with a new lock washer, into the end of the shaft, leaving just sufficient space for the U-shaped retainer to be inserted.

11. Align the location marks made previously and assemble the two sections of the shaft. The two shaft halves should be positioned as shown in Fig. J: 6, with the master spline aligned.

12. Fit the U-shaped retainer plate with the raised boss side towards the centre bearing, and tighten the centre bolt securely. Secure the bolt by bending up the lock washer tab.

13. On propshafts with the C/V joint, secure the joint front flange to the front shaft with the centre bolt, then assemble the flange to the joint housing, aligning the sections of the shaft as above.

AXLE SHAFTS . . . . [2]

Removal

1. Slacken the wheel nuts. Jack up the rear of the car and support on stands. Remove the road wheel.

2. Ensure the handbrake is fully released, then remove the brake drum.

3. Remove the four bolts securing the bearing retainer plate (and brake backplate) to the axle casing; these are accessible, two at a time, through the holes provided in the axle shaft flange (Fig. J:10).

4. Withdraw the axle shaft, complete with bearing and retainer plate (Fig. J:11).

If difficulty is encountered in removing the shaft, due to the bearing being tight in the housing, it can be pushed out of the casing by screwing two suitable bolts into the axle casing flange from behind at two diametrically opposite points so that they bear on the rear of the axle shaft flange. If even this does not move the shaft, the only alternative is to use a slide hammer which attaches to the wheel studs.

5. Once the axle shaft is removed, temporarily refit one of the flange bolts to hold the brake backplate in position.

Installation

6. Ensure that the outer surface of the bearing race and the location in the axle housing are clean and free from corrosion. Smear both lightly with grease to facilitate subsequent removal.

7. Insert the axle shaft into the axle tube. Line up the retainer plate holes with those in the axle casing, then engage the shaft splines in the differential side gear and gently tap the shaft fully home.

8. Fit the retainer plate bolts and tighten evenly to 22 lb ft (3.2 kg m).

9. Refit the brake drum and road wheel, then lower the car onto its wheels.

10. Finally, check the oil level in the rear axle and top up if necessary.

Bearing Replacement

The axle shaft bearing is a press fit on the axle shaft and is held in position by a steel retaining collar. The collar may be cut off the shaft with a cold chisel, after drilling it through with a 0.3 in (8 mm) diameter bit, or pressed off with the bearing. However, since a pressure in excess of 1,200 lb (544 kg) is required to press the new bearing onto the shaft, and a pressure in excess of 2,400 lb (1088 kg) to fit the retaining collar, it is recommended that this operation be left to a Specialist Machine Shop or Authorised Dealer with suitable equipment.

The axle shaft oil seal is integral with the axle shaft bearing by the way.

REAR AXLE ASSEMBLY . . . . [3]

Removal

1. Slacken the wheel nuts. Jack up the rear of the car and support on stands. Remove both road wheels.

2. Disconnect the propshaft from the axle pinion flange. It is not necessary to completely remove the propshaft, merely lower the rear end and move it to one side.

3. Disconnect the handbrake equaliser from the bottom of the handbrake lever, by removing the retaining clip and clevis pin. Detach the handbrake cable from the two mounting brackets on the under body; on the righthand side unscrew the adjuster locknut to release the cable, on the left-hand side pull out the U-shaped spring retainer.

4. Place a clamp on the flexible brake hose at the axle casing to prevent fluid loss, then disconnect the hose from the bracket on the axle casing. Plug the pipe and hose ends to prevent the ingress of dirt.

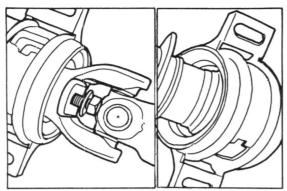

Fig. J:7 Undo centre bolt and withdraw 'U' shaped retainer, then detach bearing housing

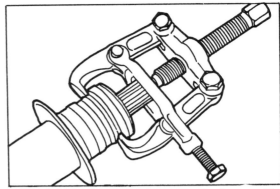

Fig. J:8 The bearing and caps can be drawn off shaft with a suitable puller

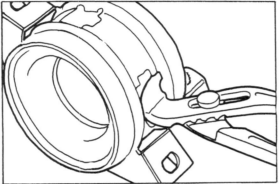

Fig. J:9 Secure the rubber insulator in the retainer by bending over six metal tabs

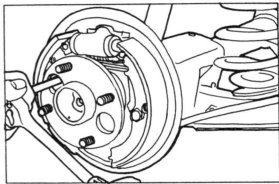

Fig. J:10 The axle shaft retaining bolts are accessible through holes in axle shaft flange

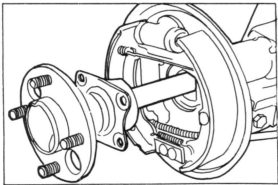

Fig. J:11 Withdraw the axle shaft, complete with bearing and retainer plate, from axle unit

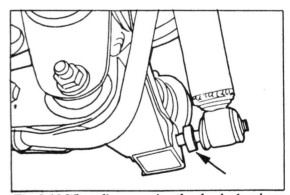

Fig. J:12 When disconnecting the shock absorbers note the spacer washer (arrowed)

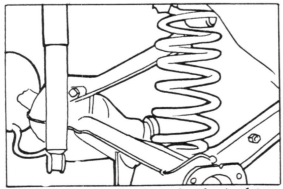

Fig. J:13 Detach coil spring and rubber insulator, make sure insulator is in good condition

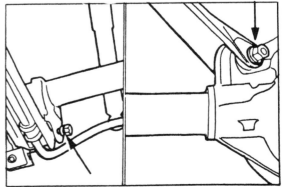

Fig. J:14 The radius arm attachment points (arrowed) on the axle unit housing

5. If the axle is being removed for overhaul, drain out the oil by detaching the rear cover plate from the centre of the axle. Refit the cover plate once the oil has been drained.

6. Slightly raise the rear axle and detach the lower ends of both shock absorbers from their mountings on the axle brackets (1 bolt and nut at each mounting). Retain the spacer washer fitted between the shock absorber and bracket at each mounting (Fig. J:12).

7. Lower the axle sufficiently to allow the coil spring to be removed, together with their rubber insulators (Fig. J:13).

8. Remove the bolt, nut and washer attaching each of the upper and lower radius arms to the axle (Fig. J:14).

9. Detach the radius arms from the axle mountings, and lift out the axle assembly.

Installation

Installation is a reversal of the removal procedure, with special attention to the following points:

a) With the axle raised into position, fit the radius arms to the axle and insert the mounting bolts from the outside, but do not fully tighten the nuts at this stage (Fig. J:00).

b) Insert the shock absorber mounting bolts into the axle brackets from the front. Ensure that the spacer washers are fitted between the brackets and the shock absorbers (Fig. J:12). Tighten the mounting bolts to 45 lb ft (6.5 kg m).

c) Use new spring washers at the propshaft flange bolts. Tighten the bolts to 45 lb ft (6.5 kg m).

d) After reconnecting the handbrake cable, adjust the handbrake linkage as detailed in the ROUTINE MAINTENANCE section previously.

e) After reconnecting the brake hose to the brake pipe, bleed the braking system as detailed in the BRAKES section.

f) Once the weight of the car is back on its wheels, adjust the pinion nose angle - if adjustable - then tighten the radius arm attachment bolts to 45 lb ft (6.5 kg m).

g) Finally, when installation is complete, refill the axle with the specified grade of oil or top up the oil level as required.

Axle Overhaul

Overhaul of the differential is not a practical proposition due to the number of special tools and variety of shims required to rebuild the unit. This should therefore be left to an Authorised Dealer or Transmission Specialist.

The differential assembly is built-in to the axle casing, and therefore the complete axle assembly must be delivered for overhaul or repair. The axle shafts and brake assemblies, including the back plates should be removed from the axle.

Technical Data

PROPSHAFT

Type
1300 cc OHV	One-piece
1600 cc OHV/OHC Domestic early models	One-piece
1600 cc OHC	Split-type
2000 cc OHC	Split-type

REAR AXLE

Type	Salisbury, integral differential

Axle ratio:
1.3 L/HC Saloon	4.11:1 Standard
1.3 L/HC Estate	4.11:1 Standard
1.3 HC Saloon/Estate later models - 74 on	4.44:1 Standard
1.3 Economy - 76 on	4.11:1 Standard, 4.44:1 Optional
1.6 OHV/OHC Saloon	3.89:1 Standard, 4.11:1 Optional
1.6 OHV/OHC Estate	4.11:1 Standard
2000 OHC Saloon	3.75:1 Standard, 3.89:1 Optional

OIL CAPACITY

Type 'A' axles	1.76 pints (1 litre)
Type 'B' axles	1.94 pints (1.1 litres)
Oil grade	Ford M2C-28BA

Rear Suspension

INTRODUCTION......................[1]

The rear suspension is of the coil spring and four link type. The two trailing lower links and two diagonal upper links combine to absorb cornering forces and control axle movement. The coil springs are mounted between the lower links and underbody and on earlier models are attached to the lower links by a retaining plate and bolt. Later models from autumn 1973 incorporate a raised spring locating spigot on the lower arm and the need for a retaining plate is obviated. On both early and late models the coil springs are held to the upper body by the compression action of the car weight, and the travel limit of the shock absorbers and control arms. Also from Autumn 1973 an anti-roll bar (stabiliser bar) was fitted to the suspension lower link arms

Two direct acting telescopic shock absorbers are mounted at an angle between the axle body and car underframe to provide control stability.

From January 1972 all Cortinas were fitted with a modified lower link arm and axle case mounting, which enables the pinion drive line angle to be adjusted for quieter running. Identification is by serrated plates (which are used in conjunction with nuts and bolts) on the lower link arms attachment to the rear axle casing. Whenever the axle or lower link arm has been removed or the bushes replaced, the pinion nose angle should be checked and adjusted if required. This will ensure correct alignment of the drive line.

SHOCK ABSORBERS ....[2]

Checking

The condition of the shock absorber can be checked by visually inspecting the unit body for evidence of fluid leakage. Very slight traces of fluid are to be expected, but excessive loss of fluid will result in breakdown of the pull or pressure stroke.

Check the unit piston rod for signs of scoring, as this will eventually damage the fluid sealing.

Check the basic operation of the shock absorber, i.e.

whether its operation is extra stiff or notchy or spongy. Under normal driving conditions, defective shock absorbers make rumbling and knocking noises.

If any of these checks reveal evidence of excessive wear or faulty operation, the shock absorber should be replaced.

Once removed from the car, the condition of the unit can be more accurately checked, as detailed under 'TESTING'.

Replacement (Fig. K:1)

1. Jack up the rear of the car and support on stands under the axle.
2. Disconnect the lower end of the shock absorber from its mounting on the axle bracket (1 bolt and nut). Retain the spacer washer fitted between the shock absorber and bracket (Fig. K:2).
3. Disconnect the upper end of the shock absorber from its mounting bracket on the underbody (1 bolt and nut).
4. If new bushes are being fitted to the shock absorbers, first install the rubber bush in the shock absorber eye and then press the metal spacer tube into position in the bush (Fig. K:3).
5. Install the new unit on the car and secure it to the body mounting bracket. Note that the mounting bolt is fitted from the front.
6. Similarly, attach the lower mounting to the axle bracket. Again the bolt is fitted from the front. Ensure that the spacer washer is fitted between the shock absorber and the bracket (Fig. K:2).
7. Tighten the upper mounting bolt to 32 lb ft (4.5 kgm), and the lower mounting bolt to 45 lb ft (6.5 kgm).
8. Finally, lower the car back on to its wheels.

Testing

Once removed from the car, the shock absorber can be tested as follows:

With the unit clamped vertically in a vice, operate the piston rod to its full extent several times by hand. Draw the unit out to its full length, then compress it. The resistance felt should be even and jerk free throughout the upward and downward strokes. Any variation or sudden loss of resistance indicates the presence of air in the system, loss of fluid, or a faulty valve.

If a lack of resistance or a springy 'feel' is felt at the beginning of each stroke, this usually indicates the presence of air. In this case, leave the unit in the vertical position for a few minutes to allow the bubbles of air to collect at the top of the pressure chamber, then give the piston rod a few short strokes from the fully compressed position, followed by a few slow full strokes to remove all air from the chamber. Repeat the test.

It is normal that shock absorbers which have been stored over a long period may require bleeding in this manner.

It should be noted that the 'bleed' setting within the unit will only be partially operated by the slow speed action when working the unit by hand, and this should be taken into account when trying to form an opinion of the operational condition of the unit.

It should also be noted that gas-filled dampers are used on 'S' and 'Ghia' variants, instead of the hydraulic type used on other models.

REAR STABILISER BAR . . . . [3]

The rear stabiliser bar is attached to the lower radius arms on each side of the vehicle, and is easily disconnected after removing the two bolts, washers and nuts which secure its mounting brackets to each of the radius arms (Fig. K:4).

The rubber bushes at the bar mounting brackets are easily replaced after removing the brackets from the bar ends. The end-most bracket is retained on the bar by a self-locking nut, and it should be noted that a washer is fitted both in front of and behind the bracket bush (Fig. K:5). This bush also has a spacer tube inserted into its bore.

Once removed, the bush can be pressed out of the bracket eye. It may simplify removal if the bush flange is first cut off with a sharp knife. Coat the new bush with Vaseline or other suitable lubricant to make fitting easier. Fit the spacer tube once the bush is in position in the eye.

Rub suitable lubricant into the bores of the bushes, and slide the bushes on to the bar ends. Fit a washer on each side of the end bush and secure with the self-locking nut.

Fit the stabiliser bar to the radius arms and insert the mounting bolts from the inside outwards. Fit the self-locking nuts and tighten to 33 lb ft (5.0 kgm).

COIL SPRINGS. . . . . [4]

1. Slacken the wheel nuts. Jack up the rear of the car and support on stands. Remove the appropriate road wheel.
2. Slightly raise the rear axle with a jack and detach the lower ends of both shock absorbers from their mountings on the axle brackets (1 bolt and nut at each mounting). Retain the spacer washer fitted between the shock absor-

ber and bracket at each mounting (Fig. K:2).
3. Lower the axle sufficiently to allow the appropriate coil spring to be removed, together with its rubber insulator (Fig. K:6). When lowering the axle, take care to avoid straining the brake hose.

Installation

1. If a replacement coil spring is being fitted, ensure it is of the same rating as the one removed. The rating is identified by the colour code on the spring, which should be the same.
2. Fit the rubber insulator to the top of the coil spring. Note that the lower coils of the spring are thicker in section than the upper ones due to the variable rate characteristics of the spring. Ensure that the spring is fitted the correct way up (Fig. K:7).
3. Position the spring on the seat on the radius arm, ensuring it is correctly located, then raise the axle to its normal ride height.
4. Reconnect the shock absorbers to the axle, ensuring that the spacer washers are fitted between the brackets and the shock absorbers (Fig. K: 2). Tighten the mounting bolts to 45 lb ft (6.5 kgm).
5. Refit the road wheel and lower the car to the ground. Tighten the wheel nuts.

UPPER RADIUS ARMS . . . . [5]

Removal

1. Remove the appropriate coil spring from between the lower radius arm and the body, as detailed previously.
2. After the spring has been removed, again raise the axle far enough for the upper radius arm mounting bolts to be relieved of load and to be removed.
3. Remove the bolt, nut and washer securing the respective ends of the upper arm to the axle casing and the body mounting bracket (Fig. K: 8). Detach the arm from the mountings and remove it.

Installation

Installation is simply a reversal of the removal procedure. Insert both the radius arm mounting bolts from the outside. Do not fully tighten the arm mounting bolts until the axle is in its normal ride position, or the weight of the car is on its wheels. The tightening torque is 45 lb ft (6.5 kgm) for both bolts.

Bush Replacement

The arm front mounting bush is located in the forward end of the arm, and the rear bush in the mounting lug on the axle casing. Both bushes are easily replaced once the arm has been removed.

To replace the front bush, clamp the arm with a suitable size of socket and piece of tube in a vice, as shown in Fig. K: 9, and press out the old bush. Coat the new bush with suitable lubricant, such as petroleum jelly, and press

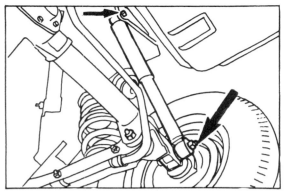

Fig. K:1 The shock absorber mounting to the body and the rear axle casing

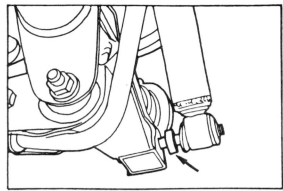

Fig. K:2 Ensure that the spacer washer (arrowed) is fitted between bracket and shock absorber

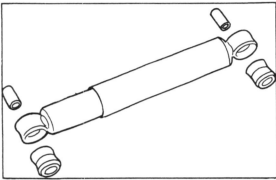

Fig. K:3 Worn shock absorber bushes should be replaced. Lubricate bushes to fit them easily

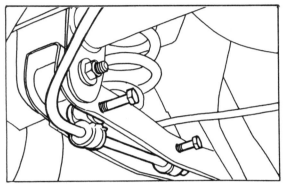

Fig. K:4 Details of the rear stabiliser bar attachment to the lower suspension arms

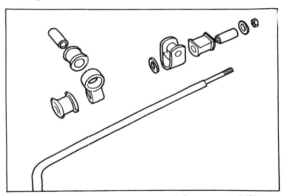

Fig. K:5 The components of the rear stabiliser bar mountings

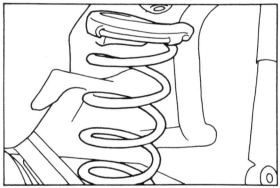

Fig. K:6 When the axle has been lowered, the coil springs can be removed

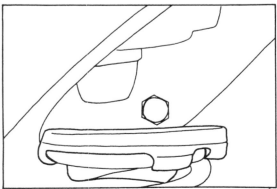

Fig. K:7 Ensure spring is correct way up, then fit rubber insulator to the top of the spring

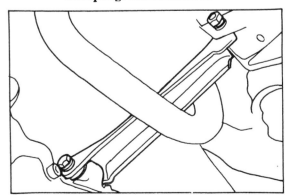

Fig. K:8 The upper radius arm attachment to the body and rear axle casing

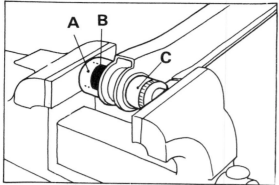

Fig. K:9 Press bush (B) out of the radius arm using piece of tubing (A) and socket (C)

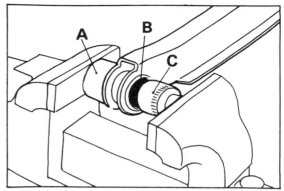

Fig. K:10 Press in the new bush using the same tools as for removing

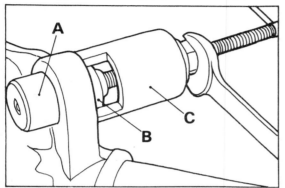

Fig. K:11 To remove axle casing bush, either drift it out, or use special tool as shown

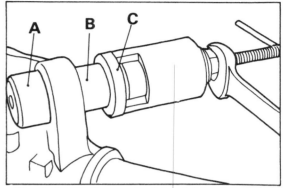

Fig. K:12 Fit the new bush by driving it in using a socket, or use special installer tool

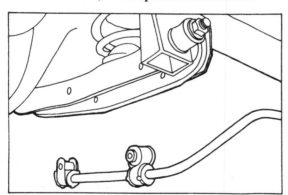

Fig. K:13 Disconnect the stabiliser bar mounting and tilt the bar to one side when removing arm

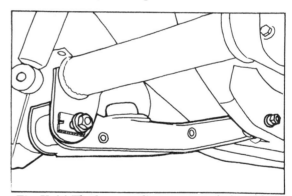

Fig. K:14 The lower radius arm installation. Note that the mounting bolts are fitted from the outside

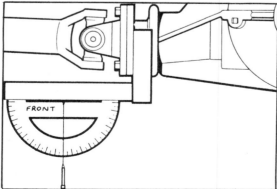

Fig. K:15 Using a protractor to measure the angle of the propshaft rear flange

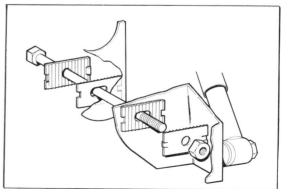

Fig. K:16 Details of the radius arm attachment showing serrated adjustment plates

Rear Suspension

it into position in the arm eye as shown in Fig. K:10.

The rear bush is replaced either by drifting it out with a suitable size socket or tube, or using a suitable Bush Remover/Installer Tool, as shown in Figs. K:11 and K:12.

NOTE: The rear bushes are of the voided type and must be fitted with the solid rubber part in the vertical position so that the voids are parallel with the radius arm. The new bush will be marked 'TOP' or 'OBEN' to ensure correct positioning.

LOWER RADIUS ARMS . . . . [6]

Removal

1. Remove the appropriate coil spring from between the radius arm and body, as detailed above, having first disconnected the stabiliser bar from the underside of the arm. Tilt the stabiliser bar to one side out of the way (Fig. K:13).
2. Detach the handbrake cable from the clip on the radius arm.
3. Remove the bolt, nut and washer securing the respective ends of the lower arm to the axle bracket and body mounting (Fig. K:14). Detach the arm from the mountings and remove it.

Installation

Installation is a simple reversal of the removal procedure. Insert both the radius arm mounting bolts from the outside. Do not fully tighten the arm mounting bolts until the axle is in its normal ride position, or the weight of the car is on its wheels, so that the spring is loaded. The tightening torque is 45 lb ft (6.5 kgm) for both mounting bolts, and 33 lb ft (5.0 kgm) for the stabiliser bar attachment bolts.

Bush Replacement

Both the arm mounting bushes are located in the arm itself, and are replaced in a similar manner to that described above for the front bush in the upper radius arm. Note that the rear bush on each arm is of the Voided type and must be fitted so that the solid rubber part is in the vertical position, with the voids parallel to the radius arm.

The bushes are marked 'TOP' or 'OBEN' to ensure correct positioning.

PINION NOSE ANGLE. . . . . [7]

To accurately measure the pinion nose angle requires the use of a suitable protractor with the car positioned unladen and dead level over an inspection pit or raised and supported.
1. Attach the protractor mid-way along the longitudinal member of the chassis and jack up the front or rear axle until the car body is dead level.
2. With the car level, measure the angle of the propshaft flange (Fig. K:15).The angle should be as follows:
a) Single piece propshaft 2° to $3^{\circ}30'$ inclined forwards.
b) Split propshaft 0° to $1^{\circ}30'$ inclined forwards.
3. If the angles are not correct adjust the pinion nose angle as follows:
4. Slacken the lower suspension arm nuts and bolts at both axle ends so that the serrated plates are separated from each other (Fig. K:16).
5. Position a jack under the differential unit in such a position that the protractor can be placed behind the rear flange (Fig. K:15).
6. Raise or lower the differential carrier until the correct angle is obtained.
7. Carefully push the loose serrated plates on the bolts onto the axle bracket plates so that they engage. Make certain that the plates on each suspension arm are engaged by an equal amount on either side, and not offset in relation to each other then finger tighten the nuts.
8. Check that the lower link attachment bolts are at right angles to the vehicle centre line before tightening the retaining bolts and nuts.
9. With the drive angle adjusted and car on the ground, check the clearance between the propshaft and the underside of the floor pan. The minimum distance should be as follows:
a) Single piece propshaft (rear end) 4.17 in (106 mm).
b) Split piece propshaft (from drive flange) 5.12 in (130 mm).

Technical Data

REAR SUSPENSION

Type. . . . . Four-link, trailing arms with coil springs
and double-acting telescopic shock absorbers.
Adjustable drive line angle on models after
January 1972.
Anti-roll bar fitted on all models after october 1973

Front Suspension

FRONT WHEEL ALIGNMENT . . . .[1]

Ideally, the front wheel alignment should be checked after any overhaul operation in which a suspension component has been removed, or its location altered.

Apart from the castor angle which is adjusted by altering the effecive length of the lower suspension arm tie-rods (Fig. L:2), and the toe-setting of the front wheels, detailed in the following STEERING chapter, the remainder of the suspension settings are not adjustable.

Optical equipment is required to check the settings accurately, and it is therefore recommended that this operation be left to an Authorised Dealer or other specialist such as a Tyre Centre who will have the necessary equipment.

FRONT HUBS . . . .[2]

Bearing Adjustment

To check the adjustment of the front wheel bearings, raise each wheel in turn, clear of the ground. Grasp the wheel on its outer edge at two diametrically opposite points and rock the wheel on the stub axle. If excessive movement is present, the bearings should be adjusted as follows:

1. Remove the centre cap from the road wheel and lever the dust cap from the hub. On vehicle fitted with alloy wheels, it will be necessary to remove the road wheel first.
2. Extract the split pin, remove the nut retainer and slacken the hub nut several turns.
3. Rock the wheel and hub assembly in and out a few times to push the brake pads away from the disc.
4. Tighten the hub nut to 27 lb ft (3.7 kg m) using a torque wrench, or until a heavy drag can be felt, while rotating the wheel in its normal direction of rotation to seat the bearings, then slacken the nut back about quarter of turn or two castellation slots of the retainer. There should now be end-float of approximately 0.003 in (0.07 mm) when the hub is pushed backwards and forwards along the axis of the stub axle.
5. Refit the slotted retainer on the hub nut so that one set of slots are in line with the hole in the spindle, and secure with a new split pin (Fig. L:3).
6. Check that the wheel rotates freely without roughness, noise or drag. If not, the bearings should be cleaned and inspected as described below.

7. If satisfactory, tap the grease cap into place and refit the hub cap. On models with alloy wheels, refit the road wheel.
8. Finally, pump the brake pedal several times to bring the brake pads back into their correct operating clearance with the disc and restore normal brake pedal travel before driving the car.

Hub Removal

1. Jack up the front of the car and support on stands. Remove the road wheel.
2. Bend back the lock tabs and remove the two bolts securing the caliper to the suspension upright. Slide the caliper off the brake disc and hang it from a suitable point on the suspension or underbody.
4. Lever the dust cap from the hub, extract the split pin and remove the hub nut retainer.
5. Unscrew the hub nut, remove the thrust washer and the outer bearing cone and roller assembly from the hub, then withdraw the hub and disc assembly off the stub axle (Fig. L:4).

Hub Installation

1. Prior to installing the hub assembly, inspect the grease seat at the inner end of the hub bore and renew if worn or damaged. It is good practice to renew the seal each time the hub is removed. Prise out the old seal, using a screwdriver, but take care not to damage the hub bore. Lubricate the outside surface of the new seal with grease to facilitate installation, then press the seal into position in the hub bore, with the sealing lip towards the bearing.
2. Apply a smear of grease to the lips of the seal, then, keeping the hub centred on the stub axle to avoid damaging the hub seal, install the hub assembly on the stub axle.
3. Install the outer bearing cone and roller assembly in the hub, then fit the thrust washer and screw on the hub nut.
4. Set the bearing adjustment as detailed above.
5. Refit the brake caliper over the brake disc and secure with the two mounting bolts, using a new locking plate. Tighten the caliper bolts to 50 lb ft (7.0 kg m) and secure with the locking plate tabs.
6. When installation is complete, refit the road wheel and lower the car back onto its wheels.

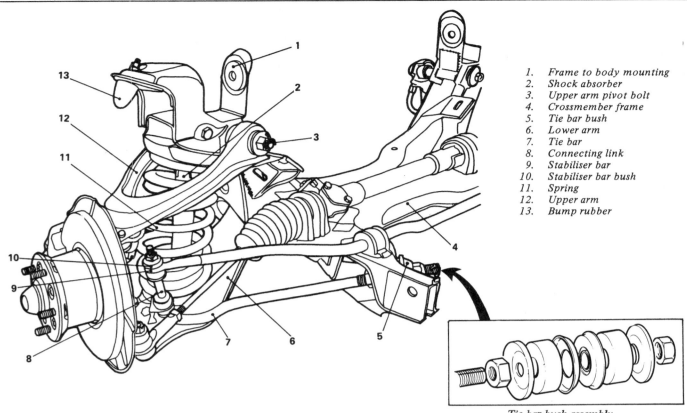

1. Frame to body mounting
2. Shock absorber
3. Upper arm pivot bolt
4. Crossmember frame
5. Tie bar bush
6. Lower arm
7. Tie bar
8. Connecting link
9. Stabiliser bar
10. Stabiliser bar bush
11. Spring
12. Upper arm
13. Bump rubber

Tie-bar bush assembly
- later type

Fig. L:1 Details of front axle and suspension
assembly

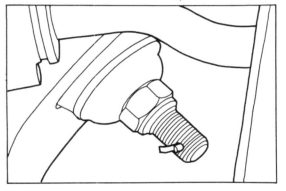

Fig. L:2 Castor angle adjustment point, at tie-bar
front mounting

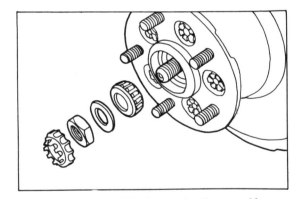

Fig. L:3 Details of hub outer bearing assembly

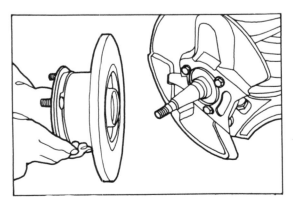

Fig. L:4 Removing hub and brake disc assembly

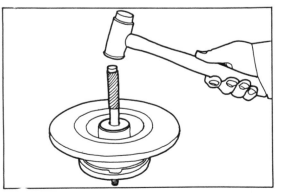

Fig. L:5 Install new bearing cups, using a suitable
driver tool

Bearing Replacement

When either the cup or cone and roller assembly of one bearing requires replacement, both bearing assemblies should be replaced. Always fit new bearing cups when replacing the bearing cones.

1. Remove the hub assembly as described above, then lever the grease seal from the rear of the hub and lift out the inner bearing cone and roller assembly.
2. Wash out the bore of the hub with petrol to remove all old grease, etc. Take care to avoid getting grease or solvent on the friction surfaces of the brake disc.
3. Remove both bearing cups from the hub. Use a punch and hammer to tap alternately at diametrically opposite points on the cup from inside the hub. Do not allow the cup to tilt in the hub. Take great care to avoid damaging the hub bore during the removal operation, as this could prevent the new cups seating properly.
4. Install the new bearing cups, tapered face outwards, using a suitable driver tool or drift (Fig. L:5). Ensure that both cups seat properly in the hub bore.
5. Pack the new cone and roller assemblies with fresh lithium-based grease, working as much lubricant as possible between the rollers and cages. Smear grease around both bearing cups, but leave an empty space in the hub between the cups to allow for expansion of the grease when warm.
6. Fit the inner bearing cone and roller assembly in the rear of the hub. Install the grease seal, with the lip to the bearing. Ensure the seal is correctly located in the bore.
7. Refit the hub assembly on the stub axle and set the bearing adjustment as detailed above.

SHOCK ABSORBERS. . . . . [3]

The condition of the shock absorbers can be checked while still on the car, and their operation tested once removed, as detailed in the REAR SUSPENSION & AXLE section previously.

Replacement

1. Jack up the front of the car and support on stands. Remove the appropriate road wheel.
2. Place a bottle jack under the hub or lower suspension arm and slightly compress the arm and spring (Fig. L:6).
3. Remove the nut and bolt securing the shock absorber top mount to the upper suspension arm (Fig. L:7).
4. Remove the two nuts securing the lower mounting to the lower arm and withdraw the shock absorber downwards through the aperture in the lower arm (Fig. L:8).
5. Position the new unit on the car and secure the upper mounting with the nut and bolt. The bolt must be fitted with its head towards the front of the car (Fig. L:7).
6. Secure the lower mounting bracket to the suspension arm with the two nuts.
7. Relieve the pressure on the lower arm and withdraw the bottle jack. Refit the road wheel and lower the car to the ground.

STUB AXLE ASSEMBLIES . . . . [4]

Removal

1. Remove the front hub assembly as detailed previously.

2. If required, detach the brake disc splash shield after bending back the lock tabs and removing the retaining bolts.
3. Remove the split pin and nut securing the track rod to the steering arm and separate the joint, using a suitable joint breaker tool (Fig. L:9).
4. Remove the split pin and castellated nut securing each of the suspension arm swivel joints to the stub axle housing, and separate the joint tapers using a joint separator tool, such as that shown in Fig. L:10.
5. Disengage the sub axle assembly from the arm ball pins and remove it from the car.

Installation

Refit the stub axle assembly on the car in the reverse order of removing. Use new split pins to secure the ball joint nuts. Also use a new lock plate to secure the splash shield bolts, if removed.

Finally, refit the front hub assembly and set the bearing adjustment as detailed previously.

FRONT SUSPENSION BALL JOINTS. . . . . . [5]

The swivel joints at the outer ends of the suspension arms can be easily replaced if worn or damaged. The appropriate arm must first be disconnected from the stub axle housing, or the stub axle housing removed as detailed above.

The joint housing is rivetted to the arm and is removed by drilling out the rivet heads. Tap the remains of the rivets out of the holes in the arm. Fit the new joint in position and secure to the arm using the bolts and nuts supplied in the joint kit.

Reassemble the removed or disconnected components as detailed under the heading previously.

It should be noted that some makes of replacement ball joints are of the "sealed-for-life" type, and where these are fitted periodic lubrication is neither required nor possible as the grease point is omitted.

COIL SPRINGS. . . . . [6]

If a replacement spring is being fitted, ensure it is of the same rating as the one removed, as a variety of different springs are available to suit the various applications, and several changes in specification have been made during the course of production. The rating is identified by the paint colour code on the spring.

SUSPENSION LOWER ARMS . . . . [7]

Removal

1. Jack up the front of the car, support on axle stands and remove the appropriate road wheel. Ensure there is sufficient clearance below the car to lower and remove the suspension arm and spring.
2. Remove the two nuts and bolts securing the tie-bar and stabiliser bar to the lower arm (Fig. L:11).
3. Release the lock washer tabs and unscrew the nuts

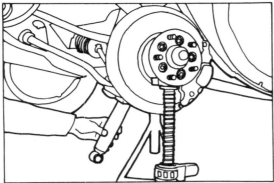
Fig. L:6 Compress coil spring with jack placed under hub or when removing shock absorber

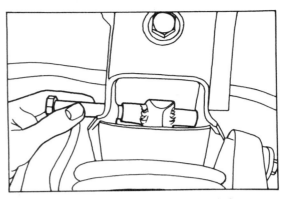
Fig. L:7 Shock absorber top mounting bolt must be fitted with head towards front of car

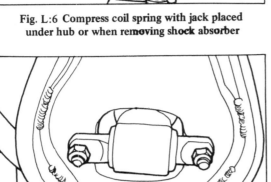
Fig. L:8 Shock absorber lower mounting on underside of suspension arm

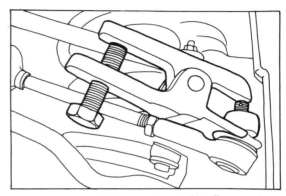
Fig. L:9 Use joint separator tool to disconnect track rod end from steering arm

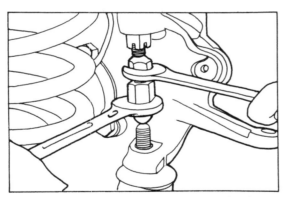
Fig. L:10 Free ball joint tapers from stub axle locations using ball joint separator tool

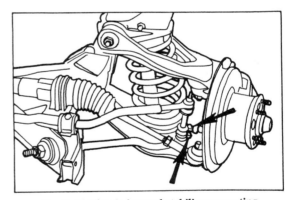
Fig. L:11 The tie bar and stabiliser mounting to the lower arm sub-frame

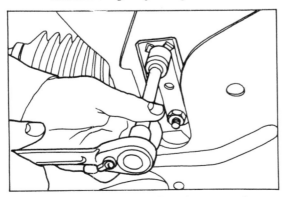
Fig. L:12 Release lock tabs and remove nuts from steering rack U-clamps

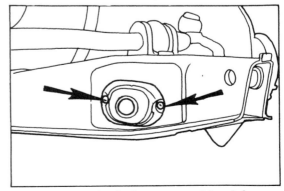
Fig. L:13 Tie bar bushes are secured to sub-frame with pop rivets

securing the rack U-clamps to the sub-frame (Fig. L:12). This is necessary to allow removal of the lower arm pivot bolt later.

4. Place a bottle jack under the hub assembly and raise the arm to slightly compress the coil spring (Fig. L:6). Detach the shock absorber from its upper and lower mountings and withdraw the shock absorber downwards through the aperture in the lower arm. Carefully lower the jack until the lower arm abuts the frame, then remove the jack.

5. The coil spring can be compressed using either the proper Ford coil spring compressor tool which is fitted inside the spring, or a pair of external spring compressors of the type available from most motor accessory shops. In the latter case, great care must be taken to ensure the compressors are correctly engaged on the spring coils at two diametrically opposite points.

6. With the coil spring compressed, remove the split pin and nut securing the lower arm ball joint to the stub axle housing, then separate the joint using a suitable joint separator tool (Fig. L:9). It may be necessary to disconnect the track rod from the steering arm to gain access to the lower arm ball joint.

7. Remove the nut from the lower arm pivot bolt and drift the bolt out of the arm and frame location, raising the steering rack as necessary to avoid the bolt head damaging the rack gaiter. Lever the arm away from its mounting point on the sub-frame.

8. Where clamp type spring compressors were used, remove the lower arm and the coil-spring, complete with the compressors, from the car. The compressors should be left in position on the spring unless a new spring is to be fitted.

9. Where the Ford spring compressor tool was used, unscrew the tool centre-bolt to release the spring tension. Withdraw the bolt securing the tool to the shock absorber top mount and remove the tool, spring and lower arm from the car. Unbolt the tool lower plate from the arm.

Installation

10. Position the spring on the lower arm with the feathered edge of the spring uppermost.

11. If the clamp type compressors are being used, raise the spring (compressed) and arm into position on the car and engage the lower arm ball joint in the stub axle housing. Tighten the ball joint securing nut only hand-tight at this stage.

12. If the Ford tool is being used, locate the compressor through the arm and spring, ensuring that the spring plate is correctly positoned on the underside of the arm. Locate the spring, arm and tool assembly on the sub-frame and

secure the tool to the shock absorber top mount with the through-bolt as before. Compress the spring to the approximate kerb height position and engage the lower arm ball joint in the stub axle housing. Tighten the ball joint securing nut only hand-tight at this stage.

13. Lubricate the ends of the mounting bush in the lower arm with glycerine to facilitate installation. Locate the arm in the sub-frame and fit the pivot bolt and nut. The bolt must be positioned with its head towards the front of the car. Do not fully tighten the nut at this stage.

14. Tighten the lower arm ball joint nut and secure with a new split pin.

15. If disconnected, reconnect the track rod to the steering arm and secure with the castellated nut and a new split pin.

16. Reposition the jack under the lower arm and remove the spring compressor(s).

17. Refit the shock absorber. The upper mounting bolt must be fitted with its head towards the front of the car (Fig. L:7).

18. Reconnect the tie-bar and stabiliser bar to the lower arm and secure with the two bolts and nuts.

19. Once the car has been lowered onto its wheels, finally tighten the lower arm pivot bolt and nut to its specified torque of 55 lb ft (7.5 kg m).

TIE BARS............................[8]

The location of the tie bars at the front sub-frame affects the front wheel castor angle (Fig. L:2). It is most important, therefore, that the front wheel alignment be checked after carrying out any work which involves disconnecting the tie-bars from the sub-frame.

STABILISER BAR....................[9]

Removal & Installation

Remove the bolt securing each of the two mounting clamps to the front subframe and detach the clamps (Fig. L:11).

Disconnect the ends of the stabiliser bar from the mounting lugs at the lower suspension arm by removing the retaining nut at the upper end of the connecting link. It will be necessary to hold the link bolt with a second spanner at the lower end while undoing the nut. Collect the dished washer fitted on either side of the bar insulating bushes. Remove the stabiliser bar from the car.

Install the stabiliser bar in the reverse order of removal, using new mounting bushes if necessary. Ensure the spacer tube is fitted on the connecting link bolt, and dished washers are fitted on either side of the insulators at the bar ends.

Technical Data

FRONT WHEEL ALIGNMENT

Toe setting

    Pre-74 models................................. 0.14 in (3.5 mm) Toe-in

  Post 74 models (all Cortinas from

    August 1973, build code NG) ....0.04 in (1 mm) Toe-in

WHEEL BEARINGS

Adjustment .... 27 lb ft (3.7 kg m), then back off

          ¼ turn or 2 castellation slots

Steering

TOE SETTING . . . .[1]

The toe setting of the front wheels is the amount by which the wheels point in or out at the front, in relation to the vehicle centre-line, and may be given as a dimension measured at the wheel rim or as an angular measurement. When the wheels point inwards they are said to have toe-in or negative toe, and toe-out or positive toe when they point outwards.

The toe setting in this case should be 0.16 in (4.0 mm) toe-in with maximum and minimum checking limits of 0 to 0.25 in (0 to 6.3 mm).

Specialist equipment, preferably that of the optical measuring type, is necessary to accurately check the wheel alignment. It is therefore recommended that this operation be entrusted to an Authorised Dealer or other specialist such as a Tyre Centre who will have the necessary equipment.

Adjustment of the toe setting is achieved by altering the effective length of the track rods. Each track rod should be adjusted by an equal amount to preserve the steering wheel spokes in the straight-ahead position. Both track rods should be approximately the same length after adjustment as, if they are appreciably different, the wheel angles (toe on turns) will be adversely affected (Fig. M:1).

TRACK ROD ENDS. . . . .[2]

Replacement

Wear in the track rod end ball joints cannot be compensated for by adjustment, and thus renewal of the complete track rod end is necessary.
1. Jack up the front of the car and support on stands. Remove both road wheels.
2. Slacken the locknut adjacent to the track rod end.
3. Extract the split pin and remove the castellated nut securing the track rod ball stud to the steering arm.
4. Disconnect the ball stud from the steering arm, using a suitable ball joint separator (Fig. M:2). Do not knock out the ball stud as this is liable to damage the steering arm or rack. If a proper tool is not available it may be pos-

sible to shock the ball stud free by striking both sides of the steering arm simultaneously using two hammers. In this case, take great care to avoid distorting the arm.
5. Unscrew the track rod end, noting the number of turns required to free it from the track rod.
6. Apply a smear of grease to the track rod threads and screw on the new track rod end, using the same number of turns required to remove the old end.
7. Connect the joint stud to the steering arm, fit and tighten the castellated nut and secure with a new split pin. Tighten the locknut at the track rod end.
8. Repeat for the track rod end at the other side of the car.
9. Refit the road wheels and lower the car to the ground.
10. Finally, have the front wheel toe setting checked as detailed previously.

STEERING RACK GAITER. . . . .[3]

Replacement

It is important that no tears exist in the rubber gaiters which protect the steering rack as this would allow the lubricant to escape and dirt to enter the unit. If damaged, the gaiters can easily be renewed as follows:
1. Remove the track rod end and locknut from the track rod, as detailed above, noting the number of turns required to unscrew the track rod end.
2. Slacken the small and large clip securing the gaiter to the track rod and steering gear housing respectively. In production a wire retaining clip may be used to secure the gaiter to the rack housing and this is not intended for re-use (Fig. M:3). It should therefore be discarded and replaced with a new screwed-type clamp on reassembly.
3. Place a drip tray under the steering gear to catch any oil which will be released when the gaiter is removed.
4. Detach the gaiter from the rack housing and slide it down and off the track rod.
5. Drain the oil from the steering rack. It is important to drain as much oil as possible to prevent overfilling when refilling the steering gear.
6. Apply a light smear of grease to the inside surface of

the new gaiter where it will contact the track rod.

7. Position the securing clips on the gaiter so that the screw heads will face forwards once fitted.

8. Slide the gaiter up the track rod and into position on the rack housing. Ensure that the smaller end of the gaiter locates correctly in the groove in the track rod.

9. Ensure that the gaiter is not twisted or strained, then tighten the securing clips.

10. Assemble the locknut and track rod end to the track rod using the same number of turns required to remove it. Connect the track rod to the steering arm and secure with the castellated nut and split pin. Tighten the rod end locknut.

11. Unscrew the two bolts securing the rack slipper cover plate to the rack housing and remove the cover plate, shim pack, spring and slipper (Fig. M:4). Inject 0.37 pints (0.21 litres) of SAE 90 Hypoid Gear Oil in through the slipper aperture. Traverse the rack to assist the flow of lubricant. Do not overfill. Refit the slipper, spring, shim pack, gasket (where fitted) and cover plate.

12. Refit the road wheel and lower the car to the ground.

13. Finally, have the front wheel toe setting checked as detailed previously.

STEERING RACK . . . . [4]
Replacement

1. Jack up the front of the car and support on stands. Remove both front road wheels.

2. Set the steering in the straight-ahead position.

3. Disconnect the lower steering shaft from the steering column and the steering unit pinion shaft, as detailed under the appropriate heading later in this section. Remove the shaft assembly.

4. At each track rod end, remove the split pin and castellated nut and disconnect the track rod end ball pin from the steering arm (Fig. M:2).

5. From underneath the crossmember, bend back the lock tabs and remove the nuts securing the two U-clamps (Fig. M:5). Detach the tab washers, clamp plates and U-clamps. On OHV engines, it will be necessary to remove the oil filter cartridge to carry out this operation.

6. Withdraw the steering rack from its location on the crossmember and remove it from the car (Fig. M:6).

7. If the steering rack is being replaced by another unit, the mounting rubbers and track rod ends should be removed for fitment to the new assembly.

8. Installation is a reversal of the removal procedure, with special attention to the following points:

a) Check the condition of the mounting rubbers and renew if necessary before installing the steering gear.

b) Ensure that both the steering wheel and road wheels are in the straight-ahead position before installing the unit on the car.

c) Use new locking plates under the U-clamp nuts. Bend up the lock tabs to secure.

d) Refit the lower steering shaft as described under the appropriate heading later in this section.

e) When installation is complete, have the front wheel toe setting checked as detailed previously.

f) Finally, check that the steering wheel is in its correct

symmetrical position when the front wheels are in the straight-ahead position.

Adjustment

Two adjustments of the steering gear are possible; the rack slipper bearing clearance adjustment, and the pinion bearing pre-load adjustment. Both these adjustments are effected by varying the thickness of a shim pack under a cover plate. The steering gear is best removed from the car to carry out either of these adjustments.

As accurate measurement is essential to ensure correct adjustment of the unit, it is therefore recommended that this be left to a local Ford dealer or a specialist as the adjustment can have great bearing on the life and efficiency of the unit.

Overhaul

In most cases of wear or damage to the steering unit, it will probably be more economical and convenient to exchange the complete assembly for a new or reconditioned unit rather than attempt to repair it.

The most common points of wear are at the rack support bush, the gear teeth on the rack and pinion, the pinion shaft bearings and the track rod ball joints at the ends of the rack. Wear at the rack bush, at the opposite end of the rack housing from the pinion, will allow excessive radial movement of the rack at that end. Damage or worn gear teeth on the rack or pinion will make the steering excessively slack in use. Excessive side movement at the pinion shaft indicates worn bearings. If either of the track rods fail to stay in any set position, this is a sure sign that the rack end ball joints are worn. If the track rods are difficult to move or are sloppy when moved, this indicates damage caused through lack of lubricant in the rack.

STEERING COLUMN. . . . . [5]
Replacement - Pre Sept 73

1. Remove the retainer screw in the underside of the steering wheel, and detach the steering wheel embellishment, where fitted (Fig. M:7).

2. Remove the steering wheel retaining nut, and pull the wheel off the splined steering shaft. Remove the choke control knob if fitted (Fig. M:8).

3. Remove the screws and detach the two halves of the steering column shroud. Remove the choke control from its attachment bracket if fitted (Fig. M:9).

4. Disconnect the ignition switch and direction indicator assembly wiring looms. Remove the direction indicator switch, then slide the indicator cancelling cam and spring off the top of the steering shaft (Fig. M:10).

5. Disconnect the brake pedal return spring. Bend back the lock tabs, remove the two retaining bolts, and remove the clamp plate securing the universal joint to the lower end of the steering column shaft (Fig. M:15).

6. Remove the column assembly mounting bolts, and withdraw the assembly from the car (Fig. M:11).

Install the column in the reverse order of removal, with special attention to the following points.

1. Ensure that the grommet at the bottom of the column locates correctly in the dash panel. When fitting the indicator cancelling cam, the ear on the cam must be

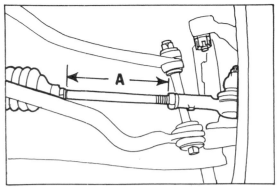

Fig. M:1 When adjusting the toe setting, each track rod must be equal in length (A)

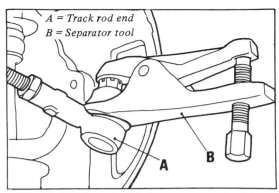

Fig. M:2 Using a ball joint separator tool to disconnect the track rod end from steering arm

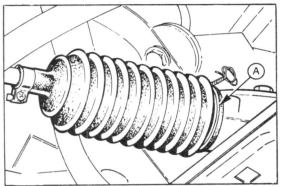

Fig. M:3 Undo both clips securing the rack gaiter and slide it off the track rod

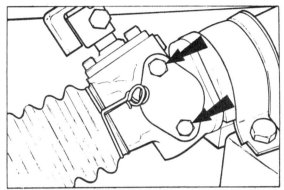

Fig. M:4 Refill the rack with oil through the slipper aperture after removing cover plate

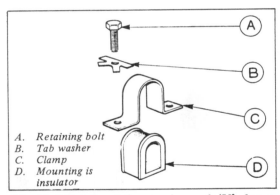

A. Retaining bolt
B. Tab washer
C. Clamp
D. Mounting is insulator

Fig. M:5 Details of the steering rack 'U'-clamp mounting to the suspension sub-frame

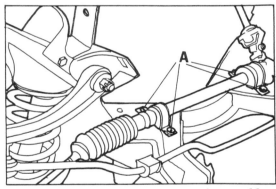

Fig. M:6 Withdraw the steering rack assembly - drawing shows suspension removed for clarity

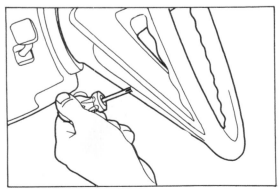

Fig. M:7 Removing the screws securing the steering wheel embellishment - early type

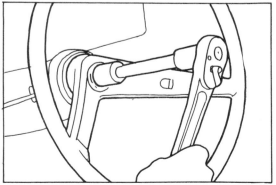

Fig. M:8 Remove steering wheel securing nut and pull the wheel off the column splines

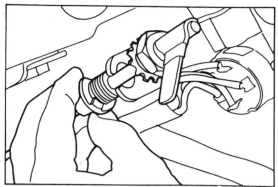

Fig. M:9 Undo the locknut and detach the choke control from the steering column bracket

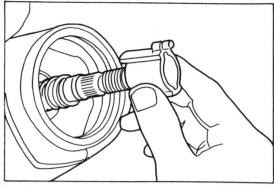

Fig. M:10 Removing the indicator cam and spring from the top of the steering column

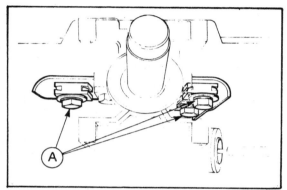

Fig. M:11 The steering column mounting is secured to the bulkhead by three bolts

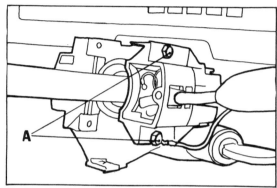

Fig. M:12 Undo the bolts securing the indicators, wipers and light switches and remove the switches

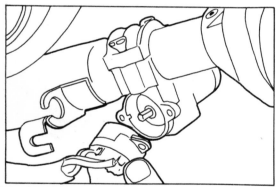

Fig. M:13 Removing the ignition switch assembly from the end of the steering column lock

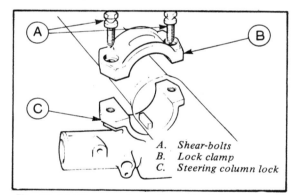

A. Shear-bolts
B. Lock clamp
C. Steering column lock

Fig. M:14 The steering column lock is secured to the column by two shear-bolts

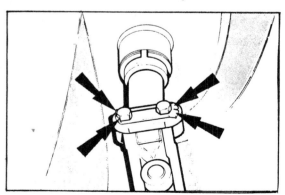

Fig. M:15 Undo bolts and swing plate to one side to disconnect shaft from column

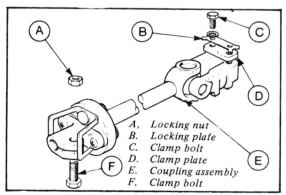

A. Locking nut
B. Locking plate
C. Clamp bolt
D. Clamp plate
E. Coupling assembly
F. Clamp bolt

Fig. M:16 Details of the lower steering shaft assembly. Coupling parts not replaceable

adjacent to the cancelling lever on the indicator switch when the road wheels are in the straight ahead position (Fig. M:10).

2. Set the front wheels in the straight ahead position and align the steering wheel before engaging it with the splines on the steering shaft and the lug on the cancelling cam. Check that the indicators cancel correctly before tightening the steering wheel nut.

Removal - Sept 73 on

1. Disconnect the battery.
2. From inside the engine compartment, bend back the lock tabs on the steering shaft clamp plate and slacken both bolts (Fig.M:15). Remove one of the bolts and swing the clamp plate to one side.
3. If required, the steering wheel can be removed at this point. Prise out the insert from the centre of the wheel and remove the wheel retaining nut. Withdraw the steering wheel from the steering shaft.
4. Unclip the steering column upper shroud. Remove the three cross-head screws and detach the steering column lower shroud.
5. Unscrew the lower dash insulation panel, and allow the panel to hang down in the wheel well
6. Remove the bolts securing the wiper and dip/indicator switches to the steering column (Fig.M:12). Detach the loom strap from the column and allow the switches to hang free (Fig.M:13).
7. Pull off the section of air duct which passes under the steering column.
8. Disconnect the ignition switch multi-plug connector.
9. Remove the three bolts securing the steering column bracket to the fascia rail and pedal box (Fig. M:11).
10. Remove the steering column assembly from the car.

Installation

Install the steering column in the reverse order of removal. Pay special attention to the following points:

a) When positioning the column assembly in the car, ensure that the seal at the bulkhead is correctly fitted. It will facilitate installation of the seal if it is lubricated with soap solution.
b) Before fully tightening the column bolts, ensure there is sufficient clearance for the upper shroud. The column must also be positioned centrally in the depression on the lower edge of the fascia rail. Tighten the column bolts to 22 lb ft (3.0 kg m).
c) Before fully tightening the column shroud securing screws, set the shroud so that there is a 0.080 in (2 mm)

gap between the shroud and the steering wheel central boss.
d) When reconnecting the flexible coupling shaft to the steering shaft, adjust the position of the clamp on the shaft to ensure the flexible coupling is in the nominally flat position, then tighten the clamp plate bolts. A new lock plate should be used, and the bolts tightened to 15 lb ft (2.0 kgm). Bend up all four corners of the lock plate to secure the bolts (Fig. M:15).

Replacing the Steering Column Lock

On Cortina models up to October 1973 the steering column lock can be replaced with the steering column in-situ. Later models - October 73 on- the steering column assembly must be removed from the car to enable the steering lock to be replaced.

The lock clamp is secured to the steering column by two shear-bolts which must be removed by dot punching and drilling them out. It may also be possible to remove the bolts by tapping them round with a centre punch then unscrewing them.

Position the new steering lock housing on the steering column, ensuring that the lock spigot is engaged in the hole in the steering column tube (Fig. M:14). Fit the lock clamp and secure with the two shear-bolts, but tighten them only finger-tight at this stage. Check the operation of the lock. If satisfactory, tighten the shear-bolts until their heads shear off.

LOWER STEERING SHAFT . . . . [6]
Replacement

1. Place the steering wheel in the straight-ahead position, then bend back the lock tabs on the coupling clamp plate and slacken both of the bolts (Fig.M:15). Remove one of the bolts and swing the clamp plate to one side.
2. Remove the clamp bolt and nut securing the flexible coupling to the steering unit pinion shaft (Fig. M:16).
3. Disengage the lower end of the coupling from the pinion shaft and remove the coupling assembly.
4. Engage the new coupling assembly on the pinion shaft, aligning the master splines, and install the clamp bolt and nut.
5. Reassemble the coupling clamp to the lower end of the steering shaft, using a new lock plate. Ensure the flexible coupling is in the nominally flat position before tightening the bolts to 15 lb ft (2.0 kg m). Bend up all four corners of the lock plate to secure the bolts (Fig. M:15).
6. Fully tighten the coupling to pinion shaft clamp bolt to 15 lb ft (2.0 kg m).

Technical Data

STEERING GEAR

Type. . . . . .Rack and pinion
Ratio 18.7
Turns, lock to lock 3.7

WHEEL ALIGNMENT

Pre-74 models. . . . . 0.14 in (3.5 mm) Toe-in
Post 74 models (all Cortinas from August 73,
    build code NG). . . . . .0.04 in (1 mm) Toe-in

STEERING

Trouble Shooter

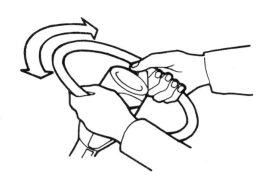

FAULT	CAUSE	CURE
Steering feels stiff	1. Low tyre pressures 2. Incorrect wheel alignment 3. Stiff track rod ends 4. Steering box/rack needs adjustment	1. Correct tyre pressures. 2. Correct wheel alignment. 3. Check and replace if necessary. 4. Adjust if necessary.
Steering wheel shake	1. Wheels and tyres need balancing 2. Tyre pressures incorrect 3. Incorrect wheel alignment 4. Wheel hub nut loose 5. Wheel bearings damaged 6. Front suspension distorted 7. Steering box/rack needs adjustment 8. Shock absorbers faulty	1. Balance as necessary. 2. Correct. 3. Correct alignment. 4. Adjust wheel bearings. 5. Replace wheel bearings. 6. Check, repair or replace. 7. Adjust as necessary. 8. Check and rectify.
Steering pulls to one side	1. Uneven tyre pressure 2. Wheel alignment incorrect 3. Wheel bearings worn or damaged 4. Brakes improperly adjusted 5. Shock absorbers faulty 6. Suspension distorted 7. Steering box/rack worn	1. Correct. 2. Correct. 3. Replace and adjust. 4. Adjust brakes. 5. Check and rectify. 6. Check and rectify. 7. Adjust or replace.
Wheel tramp	1. Over-inflated tyres 2. Unbalanced tyre and wheel 3. Defective shock absorber 4. Defective tyre	1. Correct pressure. 2. Check and balance if necessary. 3. Check and rectify. 4. Repair or replace.
Abnormal tyre wear	1. Incorrect tyre pressure 2. Incorrect wheel alignment 3. Excessive wheel bearing play 4. Improper driving	1. Check pressures. 2. Check wheel alignment. 3. Adjust wheel bearings. 4. Avoid sharp turning at high speeds, rapid starting and braking, etc.
Tyre noises	1. Improper tyre inflation 2. Incorrect wheel alignment	1. Correct tyre pressures. 2. Correct wheel alignment.

Brakes

HYDRAULIC SYSTEM OVERHAUL. . . . . . [1]

Any components of the braking system which show signs of fluid leakage should be overhauled or replaced immediately. Only units which appear satisfactory after careful examination of the components should be re-assembled using new seals. Any unit which has damaged bores or pistons must be discarded and replaced by a new unit. If in any doubt, renew the unit.

Overhaul of any components of the hydraulic system should be carried out under conditions of scrupulous cleanliness. Clean all dirt and grease from the exterior of components before removal or dismantling.

Wash all components in commercial alcohol, methylated spirit or clean brake fluid. Do not use mineral-based oils, such as petrol, paraffin or carbon tetrachloride. Blow out all internal passages with compressed air.

Inspect the piston and cylinder bore surfaces for score ridges or corrosion ptis. The unit must be discarded if any of these conditions are present.

Only new seals should be used when reassembling. These are generally available in the form of a repair kit containing all the necessary parts required for the overhaul of a particular unit.

All seals, even though new, should be inspected carefully before fitting. Check that the sealing lips are perfectly formed, concentric with the bore of the seal, and free from 'knife-edges', surface blemishes, or marks. Any seal which does not appear perfect, no matter how minute the blemish may appear to be, should be discarded.

BRAKE ADJUSTMENT . . . . [2]

Both the front disc brakes and the rear drum brakes are self-adjusting and consequently do not require periodic adjustment.

The operation of the self-adjust mechanism in the rear brakes should be checked when the shoes are being examined to ensure mechanism is operating correctly.

Handbrake adjustment will not normally be required as this should be taken up automatically by the rear shoe adjuster mechanism.

FRONT BRAKE PADS. . . . . [3]

Replacement

The brake pads should be renewed if they are worn below the minimum safe thickness of 1/8 in (3 mm), or if they are the cause of braking problems.

Whenever one or more pads require replacement, both pads at both front brakes should be replaced to maintain braking balance.

NOTE: If for any reason the existing brake pads are to be refitted instead of being renewed, they must be suitably marked with their respective position when removing. It is not permissible to interchange brake pads as this can lead to uneven braking.

1. With the road wheel removed, extract the spring clips from the inboard end of the pad retaining pins and withdraw the two pins from the caliper (Fig. N:2). If difficulty is encountered in removing the pins, they can be tapped out of their locations using a suitable pin drift, but care should be taken to avoid damaging the caliper.
2. Withdraw the brake pads, complete with shims and wire anti-rattle clips, using long nosed pliers, if necessary (Fig. N:3). Detach the wire clips and separate the shims from the brake pads.
3. Brush or blow any dust or dirt out of the caliper recess.
4. Inspect the rubber dust cover fitted to each piston, and replace if punctured, split, or otherwise unserviceable.
5. Press each of the caliper pistons back into their cylinder bores, using a tyre lever or other flat piece of iron (Fig. N:4). Lever against the hub of the brake disc during this operation, not the outside edge of the disc.
6. The fluid level in the master cylinder reservoir will rise when the pistons are pressed back, and it may be

necessary to syphon off excess fluid to prevent it over-flowing.

7. Check that the friction surfaces on the brake disc are clean and free of grease, oil or brake fluid.

8. Check that the replacement pads are of the correct type for the car - this is very important.

9. Assemble the shims and anti-rattle springs to the new pads and install the pad assemblies in the caliper. Ensure that both the pads and shims are correctly fitted. The arrow incorporated in the shims must point in the direction of wheel forward rotation.

10. Check that the pads are free to move easily in the caliper recess. Fit the pad retaining pins from the outboard side and secure them in position with the spring clips (Fig. N:2). The pins must not be forced into their locations.

11. Depress the brake pedal several times to bring the brake pads into their correct working clearance with the disc.

12. Finally, when the operation has been completed at both front brakes, lower the car and check the fluid level in the master cylinder reservoir.

FRONT BRAKE CALIPER. . . . . [4]

Removal

With the front of the car jacked up and supported on stands, remove the road wheel.

Remove the brake pads from the caliper as described above. If it is intended to overhaul the caliper assembly, depress the brake pedal to move the caliper pistons outwards from their cylinders and thus facilitate removal of the pistons later.

Disconnect the flexible brake hose from the caliper locking plate, after first cleaning all dirt from the surrounding area. Fit suitable plugs in the pipe and hose end to prevent loss of fluid and the ingress of dirt.

Bend back the locking plate tabs and remove the two bolts securing the brake caliper to the suspension upright (Fig. N:6). Lift the caliper off the brake disc.

Installation

Installation is a simple reversal of the removal procedure, with special attention to the following points:-

a) Use a new locking plate at the caliper mounting bolts. Tighten the bolts to 50 lb.ft (7.0 kgm) and secure with the locking plate tabs.

b) When reconnecting the flexible brake hose to the caliper locking plate, hold the brake hose with a second spanner while tightening the hose locknut to avoid twisting the hose.

Ensure that the hose is positioned so that it will not foul the body or suspension components during steering and suspension movement.

c) Refit the brake pads as detailed previously, pushing the pistons back into their cylinder if need be.

d) When installation is complete, bleed the braking system as detailed later in this section.

Seal Replacement

Partially withdraw one piston from its bore in the caliper body. Remove the spring retaining ring securing the rubber dust cover to the top of the cylinder, and detach the dust cover from its locating groove in the piston skirt. Completely remove the piston from its cylinder; removal can be facilitated by injecting compressed air into the fluid connection.

Remove the piston sealing ring from its groove in the cylinder bore, using a suitable blunt instrument, such as a plastic needle. Take great care to avoid scratching the cylinder bore during this operation.

Repeat the process for the other cylinder.

Clean and inspect the components of the caliper as detailed under 'HYDRAULIC SYSTEM OVERHAUL' at the beginning of this section.

NOTE: Under no circumstances must any attempt be made to separate the two halves of the caliper body which are bolted together.

If the pistons and cylinder bores are in good condition, reassembly the caliper as follows:

Lubricate the pistons, piston sealing rings and cylinder bores with clean brake fluid.

Fit a new piston seal to the annular groove in one of the cylinder bores. Fit the dust cover to the piston, with the inner edge located in the groove in the piston skirt. Insert the piston, crown first, into the cylinder bore and push it fully home (Fig. N:8).

Locate the outer edge of the dust cover on the caliper body at the top of the bore (Fig. N:9). Check that the cover is properly located, then secure it to the caliper with the spring retainer ring.

Assemble the other piston to the caliper in a similar manner.

FRONT DISC BRAKE . . . . [5]

Replacement

Remove the caliper and the front hub and brake assembly as detailed in the FRONT SUSPENSION section.

Bend back the locking plate tabs and unscrew the four securing bolts from the rear face of the disc (Fig. N: 10). Discard the locking plates.

If the disc is heavily scored or grooved, or has excessive corrosion build-up at the hub or outside edge, it may be trued up by grinding down to within the minimum permissible thickness of 0.45 in (11.4 mm), but replacement is preferable.

Before reassembling the disc to the hub, ensure that the mating faces on both the hub and disc are perfectly clean. Use new locking plates and tighten the four retaining bolts to 32 lb.ft (4.5 kgm). Secure with the locking plate tabs.

Refit the hub assembly on the stub axle and set the wheel bearing adjustment as detailed in the FRONT SUSPENSION section.

After installation, the disc run-out, relative to the axis

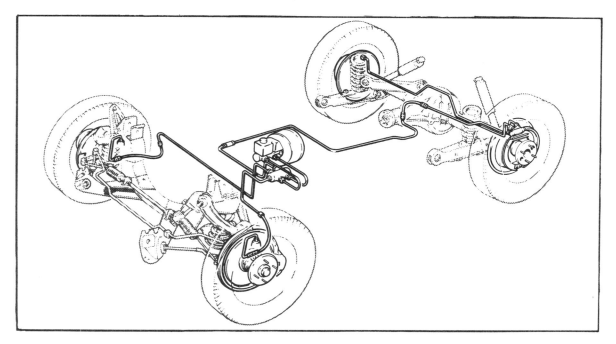

Fig. N:1 Layout of braking system components

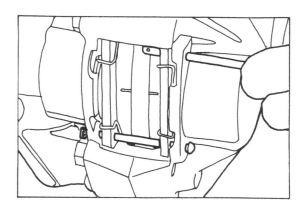

Fig. N:2 Pad retaining pins can be withdrawn
after removing securing clips

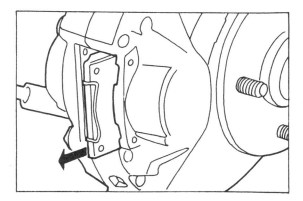

Fig. N:3 Remove pads complete with shims and
anti-rattle clips

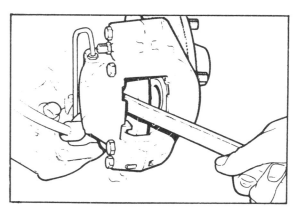

Fig. N:4 Caliper pistons must be pressed back into cylinder bore to allow new pads to be fitted

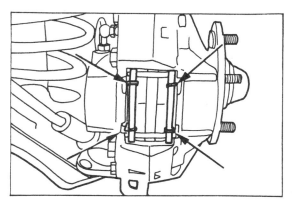

Fig. N:5 Ensure wire anti-rattle clips are located
as shown before fitting pad retaining pins

of the spindle body, should be checked using a dial indicator, as shown in Fig. N:11. If the run-out exceeds 0.0035 in (0.09 mm) total indicator reading the cause must be established and eliminated. It is often possible to reduce the run-out by repositioning the brake disc on the hub.

REAR BRAKE SHOES (Bendix) ....[6]

Replacement

The brake shoes should be renewed if the lining material has worn down to the minimum safe thickness of 1/16 in (1.5 mm) with these bonded-type shoes, or if they are the cause of braking problems.

The shoes should be replaced in sets of four. On no account should only one pair of shoes be replaced as this can lead to uneven braking.

1. Raise the rear of the car, support on stands and remove the road wheels.
2. Ensure the handbrake is fully released, then withdraw the brake drums.
3. Detach both brake shoe return springs from the shoes. This is best done using a piece of hooked wire, as shown in Fig. N:13.
4. Remove the hold-down spring at each shoe (Fig. N:14). A simple tool to carry out this operation can be made-up from an old screwdriver, as shown in the illustration. The tool is used to press the spring towards the back plate and then to lever the spring hook away from the retainer bracket. If required, the retainer bracket may be removed from the backplate by aligning it with the two notches in the locating hole.
5. Remove the front shoe first. Pull the bottom end of the shoe forwards as this will operate the self-adjust mechanism to the point where the two ratchet levers will come out of engagement (Fig. N:15). The shoe can then be removed by twisting it to release it from the adjuster spacer strut.
6. Pull the rear shoe downwards away from the backplate and disconnect the handbrake cable from the handbrake operating lever on the shoe (Fig. N:16).
7. Fit a rubber band over the wheel cylinder to retain the pistons in position.
8. Inspect the backplate and drum for evidence of oil, grease, or brake fluid contamination. If any of these are present, the cause must be established and dealt with before fitting the new shoes. Grease or oil can be cleaned off with petrol or paraffin; brake fluid should be removed using methylated spirit or commercial alcohol. Finally, wash all parts - especially the brake drum - with a solution of soap and hot water, then dry thoroughly.
9. Renew the shoe return springs if they are damaged or stretched, or if there is any evidence of overheating, indicated by discolouring, which will have affected the temper of the springs. When fitting new springs, ensure that the correct replacements are obtained.
10. Transfer the handbrake operating lever and spacer strut to the new rear brake shoe as follows:
a) Detach the handbrake lever from the old rear shoe

by removing the spring clip and tapping out the lever pivot pin (Fig. N:17). The lever can then be slid along the shoe web and out of the slot in the spacer strut.
b) Lever the spacer strut upwards, as shown in Fig. N:18, to release it from the shoe web and the return spring.
c) Fit the pivot pin into the handbrake lever, assemble the lever to the new shoe and fit the spring clip onto the pivot pin.
d) Engage the handbrake lever return spring in the hole in the shoe web, hook the spacer strut onto the spring and lever it into position on the shoe (Fig. N:19).
11. Transfer the ratchet levers from the front brake shoe as follows:
a) Remove the spring clip and detach the longer ratchet lever from the old shoe (Fig. N:20).
b) Lever the spring retainer washer up off the pivot pin on the shoe web and remove the smaller ratchet lever and spring from the pivot pin (Fig. N:20). Discard the spring retainer.
c) Assemble the smaller ratchet lever and spring on the new front shoe. Slide two 0.008 in (0.2 mm) feeler gauges between the brake shoe and the underside of the lever, then fit a new spring retainer washer (Fig. N:21). Ensure that the retainer is positioned with the tabs uppermost. Remove the feeler gauges and check that the lever rotates easily on the pivot pin and returns freely with the spring pressure.
d) Fit the longer ratchet lever to the brake shoe and secure with the spring clip. Ensure that no clearance exists between the lever and the shoe.
e) Position the two ratchet levers so that 4 to 5 teeth are overlapping, as shown in Fig. N:22.
12. It should be noted that this type of brake assembly must not have any form of lubrication applied to it during assembly, unlike the Girling product brakes fitted to other variants.
13. Remove the rubber band from the wheel cylinder.
14. Engage the handbrake cable in the lever on the rear shoe and locate the shoe in position against the wheel cylinder and lower pivot point. Check that the handbrake lever is resting on the head of the adjustment plunger at the backplate.
15. Slide the front shoe into position in the slot of the spacer strut, then locate the shoe against the wheel cylinder and pivot point (Fig. N:23).
16. Pull the smaller ratchet lever downwards against its spring, using a piece of hooked wire, and push the upper ratchet lever forwards to the minimum adjustment position (Fig. N:24).
17. Secure each shoe in position with its hold-down spring, using the same tool as for removal. Ensure that the hook of the spring engages correctly in the retainer bracket.
18. Fit the brake shoe return springs, again using the hooked piece of wire. The larger spring is fitted at the top, adjacent to the wheel cylinder (Fig. N:25).
19. Ensure that the brake shoes are central, then refit the brake drum.
20. Finally, depress the brake pedal several times to adjust up the self-adjust mechanism. The operation of the brakes should checked on road test.

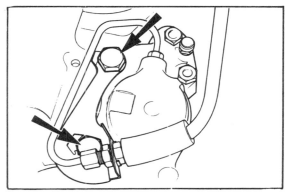

Fig. N:6 Caliper retaining bolts. Hose must be disconnected to gain access to lower bolt

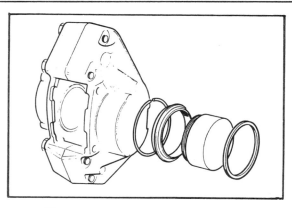

Fig. N:7 Details of caliper piston assembly

Fig. N:8 With dust cover located in groove in piston skirt, press piston squarely into bore

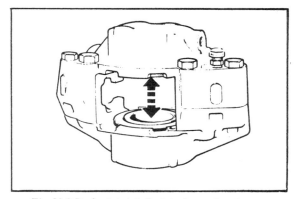

Fig. N:9 Push piston fully into bore, then locate dust cover at top of cylinder

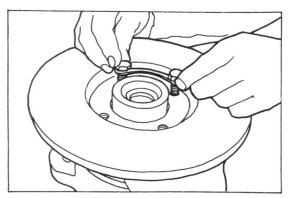

Fig. N:10 Use new locking plates when assembling brake disc to wheel hub

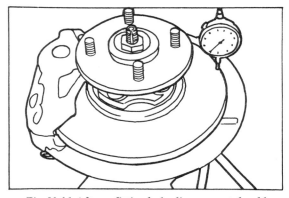

Fig. N:11 After refitting hub, disc run-out should be checked with dial gauge

A. Shoe hold-down springs
B. Brake shoe (rear)
C. Shoe return springs
D. Wheel cylinder
E. Pivot pin retaining clips
F. Spacer strut
G. Brake shoe (front)
H. Large ratchet
J. Small ratchet
K. Carrier plate

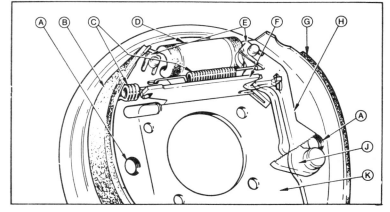

Fig. N:12 Details of self-adjust mechanism on Bendix rear brakes

Girling Brakes

Replacement

The brake shoes should be renewed if the lining material has worn down to the minimum safe thickness of 1/16 in (1.5 mm) with these bonded-type shoes. Shoes should be replaced only in sets of four to maintain braking balance.

1. Raise the rear of the car, support on stands and remove the road wheels.
2. Ensure the handbrake is fully released, then withdraw the brake drums.
3. Remove the hold-down pin from the front shoe by depressing the retaining washer, turning it a quarter of a turn to release it from the end of the hold-down pin, and pulling off the dished washer and spring (Fig. N:26). This is best done with a pair of pliers. Withdraw the hold-down pin from the rear of the backplate.
4. Disengage the lower return spring from the front shoe and remove it from the rear shoe (Fig. N:26). Unhook the upper return spring from the retaining bracket on the rear shoe, then withdraw the front shoe, complete with the upper spring and adjuster strut (Fig. N:27).
5. Remove the hold-down pin from the rear shoe in the same manner as described above for the front shoe.
6. Release the shoe retaining bracket from the handbrake lever pivot at the rear shoe and separate the shoe from the handbrake lever (Fig. N:26).
7. Fit a rubber band over the wheel cylinder to retain the pistons in position.
8. Inspect the brake backplate and drum for contamination, and clean off, if present, as described for the Bendix Rear Brakes previously. Similarly, inspect the shoe return springs and renew if necessary.
9. Before installing the new shoes, check that the handbrake lever stop assembly on the backplate is undamaged and free to move in its housing (Fig. N:29). If necessary, renew the stop by withdrawing it from the backplate.
10. Apply a light smear of lithium based grease to the shoe contact pads on the backplate, the handbrake lever pivot pin and the adjuster strut ends and threads, as shown in Fig. N:30.
11. Fit the near rear shoe onto the handbrake lever pivot pin and secure in position with the shoe retaining bracket. Locate the shoe against the wheel cylinder piston and the lower pivot point (Fig. N:31). Check that the handbrake lever is positioned over the stop assembly on the backplate.
12. Secure the shoe in position with the hold-down pin, spring and dished washer. Compress the spring and turn the dished washer a quarter of a turn to lock it in position.
13. Engage the adjuster strut over the rear shoe and handbrake operating lever, with the longer leg of the fork against the brake shoe (Fig. N:32).
14. Position the front shoe in the adjuster strut fork and against the wheel cylinder. Fit the lower shoe return spring to the rear shoe and then the front shoe. Pull the front shoe into position on the lower pivot point. Fit the hold-down pin in the same manner as for the rear shoe.

15. Fit the upper return spring to the front shoe, locate the hook in the oval hole and then engage it on the rear shoe retaining bracket (Fig. N:33). Ensure that the tag on the retaining bracket is located in the cut-out in the shoe.
16. Turn the ratchet wheel to expand the adjuster strut and remove all slack movement. This should bring the adjuster arm on the rear shoe into its correct operating position at the ratchet wheel (Fig. N:34).
17. Ensure that the brake shoes are central, the refit the brake drum.
18. Depress the brake pedal several times to adjust up the self-adjust mechanism. Pedal movement will reduce as the adjustment is made. Correct adjustment is indicated when the pedal movement is constant for several consecutive applications.
19. Finally, after refitting the road wheel and lowering the car to the ground, check the operation of the brakes on road test.

REAR WHEEL CYLINDERS . . . . [7]

Seal Replacement (Fig. N:35).

The wheel cylinder need not be removed from the brake backplate to inspect or overhaul it. Removal is only necessary when the cylinder must be replaced due to wear or damage.

To overhaul the cylinder, first remove the brake drum and detach the brake shoes, as already described.

Clean all dirt, grease and oil from the exterior of the cylinder and the surrounding area.

Detach the rubber dust cover and retaining spring from each end of the cylinder, and withdraw the piston assemblies and centre spring from the cylinder bore. Remove the rubber seal from each piston.

Clean and inspect the components as described in 'HYDRAULIC SYSTEM OVERHAUL' at the beginning of this section.

If the pistons and cylinder bores are in good condition, reassemble the cylinder as follows:

Lubricate the pistons, piston seals and cylinder bore with clean hydraulic fluid.

Fit a new seal to each of the pistons. Slide one of the pistons, seal end first, into the cylinder bore, taking great care to avoid damaging the seal lip during insertion. From the other end, insert the centre spring and the second piston. Fit the rubber dust covers on each end of the cylinder and secure in place with the retainer springs.

Refit the brake shoes and brake drum, then bleed the brakes as detailed under the appropriate heading later in this section.

Replacement

Remove the brake drum and detach the brake shoes as detailed previously.

Disconnect the brake pipe (two pipes at the left-hand brake assembly) from the rear of the wheel cylinder. Fit a suitable blanking plug in the pipe end(s) to prevent loss of

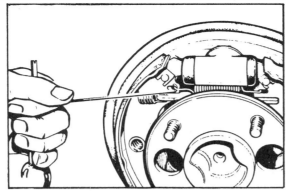

Fig. N:13 Use piece of hooked wire to detach shoe return springs (Bendix)

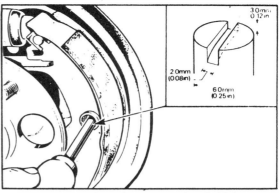

Fig. N:14 Simple tool to remove shoe hold-down springs can be made up as shown

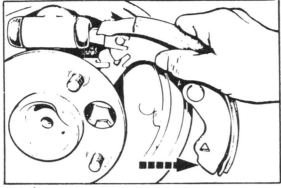

Fig. N:15 Pull lower end of shoe outwards to move adjustment ratchets out of engagement

Fig. N:16 Disconnect handbrake cable from operating lever on rear shoe (Bendix)

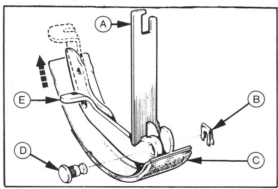

A   Spacer strut
B   Spring clip
C   Rear brake shoe
D   Pivot pin
E   Handbrake lever

Fig. N:17 Handbrake operating lever must be detached from rear shoe as shown (Bendix)

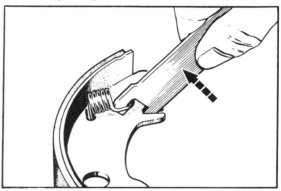

Fig. N:18 Disengage spacer strut from rear shoe as shown (Bendix)

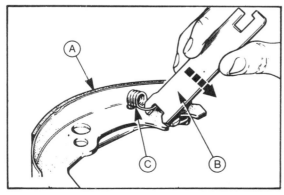

A   Rear shoe   B   Spacer strut   C   Return spring

Fig. N:19 Assemble spacer strut to new shoe as shown

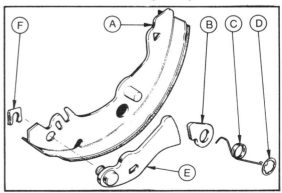

A   Front brake shoe
B   Short ratchet
C   Spring
D   Spring retainer
E   Long ratchet
F   Spring clip

Fig. N:20 Detach adjustment ratchets from front shoe as shown (Bendix)

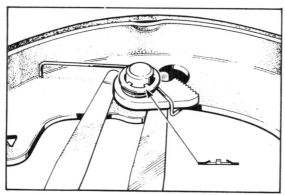

Fig. N:21 Fit two 0.008 in (0.2 mm) feeler
gauges between ratchet lever and brake shoe

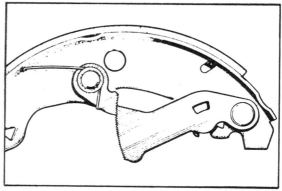

Fig. N:22 Position ratchets so that 4 to 5 teeth
are overlapping (Bendix)

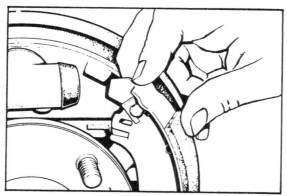

Fig. N:23 Ensure front shoe engages correctly in
slot of spacer strut before locating shoe

Fig. N:24 Set ratchets in minimum adjustment
position by pulling down small ratchet

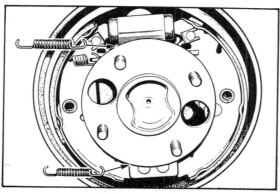

Fig. N:25 Use wire hook again to refit shoe return
springs. Larger spring is fitted at top

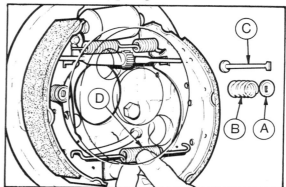

Fig. N:26 Detach hold-down pin and lower return
spring from front shoe as shown (Girling)

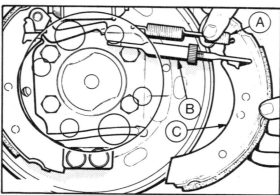

Fig. N:27 Unhook upper spring and withdraw
front shoe, with adjuster strut and spring

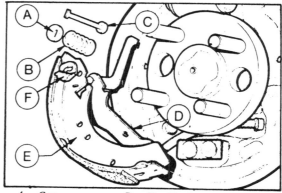

A   Cup   D   Handbrake operating lever
B   Spring   E   Rear brake shoe
C   Hold-down pin   F   Shoe retaining bracket

Fig. N:28 Remove hold-down pin and shoe retainer bracket and detach rear shoe

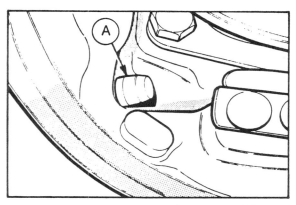

Fig. N:29 Check that handbrake lever stop is free to move in backplate before reassembly

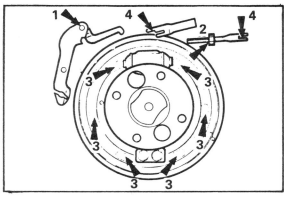

1. Handbrake lever pivot pin
2. Adjuster strut threads
3. Shoe contract pads
4. Adjuster strut ends

Fig. N:30 Apply a light smear of lithium based grease at points shown - Girling

A   Wheel cylinder piston
B   Handbrake stop assembly
C   Lower pivot
D   Hold-down pin

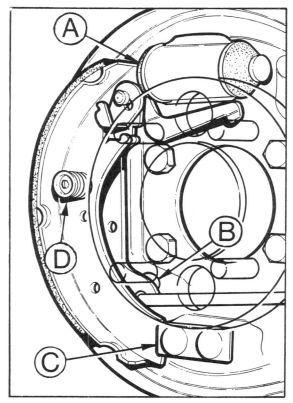

Fig. N:31 Ensure handbrake lever on rear shoe is positioned over stop assembly (B)

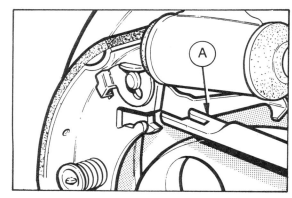

Fig. N:32 Install adjuster strut (A) with longer leg of fork against rear brake shoe - (Girling)

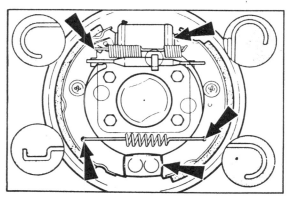

Fig. N:33 Locate shoe return springs as shown. Fit lower spring first

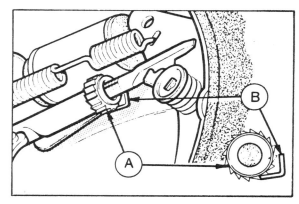

A = Ratchet wheel
B = Adjuster arm

Fig. N:34 Expand adjuster strut to take up slack and bring adjuster arm into correct position

fluid and the ingress of dirt. In the case of the right-hand brake assembly, unscrew the bleed valve.

Remove the two bolts securing the wheel cylinder to the backplate and detach the cylinder.

On the Girling rear brake assemblies, when installing the new wheel cylinder, ensure that the sealing ring is correctly located on the cylinder spigot before positioning the cylinder on the backplate.

Reconnection of the brake pipe(s) will be facilitated if the brake pipe union(s) is (are) started in the threads of the cylinder connection(s) before installing the cylinder attaching bolts. Once secured to the backplate, the pipe connection(s) can then be fully tightened.

Otherwise, installation is a simple reversal of the removal procedure. Finally, bleed the brakes as described later in this section.

MASTER CYLINDER . . . . [8]

Removal

Block the vent hole in the reservoir filler cap with a small piece of plasticine or adhesive tape, as shown in Fig. N:36, to minimise fluid loss while disconnecting the brake pipes.

Disconnect the fluid pipes from the master cylinder outlets, noting their respective positions for reassembly, and fit suitable plugs in the outlet ports.

Remove the two nuts and spring washers securing the master cylinder to the servo unit and lift the unit clear.

If the master cylinder is to be overhauled, remove the reservoir cap and drain out the hydraulic fluid.

It should be noted that hydraulic fluid will damage paint work if allowed to come into contact with it. Any spilt fluid must be wiped (or washed with cold water) from the affected area immediately.

Installation

Install the master cylinder in the reverse order of removal. If a replacement cylinder is being fitted, ensure it is of the correct type, as otherwise the pedal effort will be affected.

When installation is complete, top up or fill the fluid reservoir with fresh hydraulic fluid, and bleed the braking system as detailed elsewhere in this section.

Seal Replacement (Fig. N:40)

Carefully prise the fluid reservoir from the top of the master cylinder. Remove the two rubbers seals from the fluid inlet ports.

With the cylinder body secured in a vice with soft jaws, depress the operating rod the relieve the pressure on the piston stop pin and withdraw the stop pin from the secondary inlet port.

Extract the circlip from the end of the cylinder bore, using circlip pliers (Fig. N:37). Withdraw the primary piston assembly (Fig. N:38). By gently tapping the master cylinder against a soft surface, such as a block of wood,

remove the secondary piston assembly from the bore (Fig. N:39).

Dismantle the primary piston assembly by removing the screw from the end of the assembly and detaching the sleeve, spring, spring retainer and seal (Fig. N:38). Carefully prise the other seal from the end of the piston.

Detach the spring, spring retainer and seal from the rear end of the secondary piston (Fig. N:39). Remove the other seal from the opposite end of the piston.

Clean and inspect the components of the master cylinder as detailed in 'HYDRAULIC SYSTEM OVERHAUL' at the beginning of this section.

If the pistons and cylinder bore are in good condition, reassemble the master cylinder as follows:

Lubricate the pistons, piston seals and cylinder bore with clean hydraulic fluid.

Fit a new seal in the groove at the front end of the primary piston (Fig. N:38). Assemble the second seal, spring retainer, spring and sleeve to the other end of the piston and secure in position with the screw.

Fit a new seal to the groove at the front end of the secondary piston (Fig. N:39). Assemble the second seal, retainer and spring to the opposite end of the piston. Lubricate the piston assembly thoroughly with clean brake fluid and insert it into the cylinder bore with the spring leading.

Similarly lubricate the primary piston assembly and insert it into the cylinder bore, again with the spring leading. Secure the piston in the cylinder bore with the circlip, ensuring it is correctly located in its groove.

Depress the operating rod and insert the piston stop pin into its location in the secondary inlet port.

Fit new seals to the fluid inlet ports and refit the fluid reservoir to the cylinder body.

BRAKE SERVO UNIT . . . . [9]

The brake servo unit is serviced only as an assembly, and therefore, if damaged or defective, the complete unit must be replaced.

Testing

With the engine stopped, the transmission in neutral, and the handbrake applied, depress the brake pedal several times to exhaust the vacuum in the system. Depress the pedal, hold it in this position, and start the engine. If the servo is operating correctly, the pedal will tend to fall away under foot pressure, and less pressure will be required to hold the pedal in the applied position. If no difference is felt, the system is not functioning. Check the vacuum hose and connections for leaks or blockage before replacing the unit.

Check Valve

The check valve at the vacuum connection on the servo unit can be easily replaced if defective or suspect.

Before removing the check valve, note the position of the outlet nozzle for reassembly.

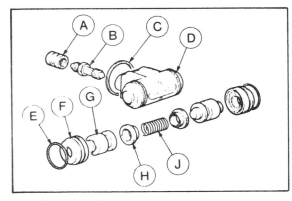

A. Dust cap (where applicable)
B. Bleed nipple (where applicable)
C. Sealer ring (girling only)
D. Wheel cylinder
E. Boot retainer spring
F. Boot
G. Piston
H. Piston seal
J. Centre spring

Fig. N:35 Exploded view of rear wheel cylinder
assembly

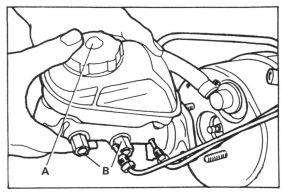

A = Plasticine
B = Plugs

Fig. N:36 Plug vent hole in filler cap with plasticine to minimise fluid loss

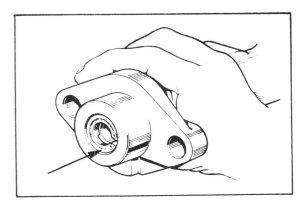

Fig. N:37 Remove circlip from cylinder bore to
release piston assemblies

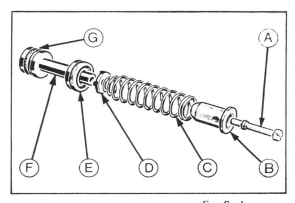

A. Screw
B. Sleeve
C. Spring
D. Retainer
E. Seal
F. Piston
G. Seal

Fig. N:38 Details of primary piston assembly

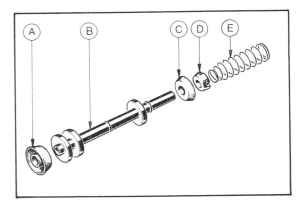

A. Seal
B. Piston
C. Seal
D. Retainer
E. Spring

Fig. N:39 Details of secondary piston assembly

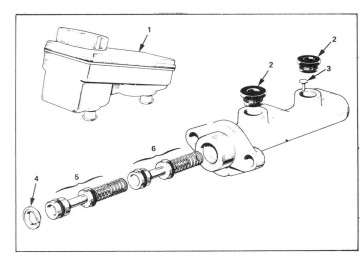

1. Fluid reservoir
2. Rubber seals
3. Piston stop pin
4. Circlip
5. Primary piston assembly
6. Secondary piston assembly

Fig. N:40 Exploded view of master cylinder
assembly

Disconnect the vacuum hose and prise the check valve out of the rubber grommet in the front face of the servo housing (Fig. N:41). Fit the new check valve, ensuring that the outlet is at the same angle as the original. Reconnect the vacuum hose.

Removal

It will be necessary to remove the instrument panel lower insulation pad from inside the car to gain access to the brake pedal bracket.

At the brake pedal, withdraw the spring retaining clip and push out the clevis pin securing the servo unit push rod to the brake pedal. Remove the clevis pin bushes from their locations in the pedal and allow the push rod to fall free from the pedal. Disconnect the pedal return spring.

Remove the master cylinder from the servo unit, as detailed previously.

Disconnect the vacuum hose from the servo unit. Remove the four nuts and washers securing the rear end of the servo unit mounting bracket to the bulkhead, and lift out the servo unit and mounting bracket complete.

To separate the servo unit from its mounting bracket, simply remove this securing nuts and washers and detach the servo unit.

Installation

Installation is a simple reversal of the removal procedure, with special attention to the following points:
a)   When refitting the master cylinder on the servo unit, ensure the seal is correctly located.
b)   Grease the push rod clevis pin and bushes before installing them at the brake pedal.
c)   If necessary, adjust the stop light switch at the brake pedal bracket so that the stop lights operate after 0.20 - 0.60 in (5 - 15 mm) travel, measured at the centre of the pedal pad, from the fully retracted position.
d)   Bleeding the braking system as detailed later in this section.
e)   Finally, check the operation of the servo unit, as described above.

PRESSURE DIFFERENTIAL VALVE.....[10]

Removal

Disconnect the battery. Disconnect the wiring plug from the warning light switch on the differential valve.

Block the vent hole in the master cylinder filler cap with a small piece of plasticine or adhesive tape, as shown in Fig. N:36, to minimise fluid loss while the fluid pipes are disconnected from the valve.

Disconnect the five fluid pipes from the valve assembly, noting their respective positions for reassembly, and fit suitable blanking plugs to the ends of the two pipes from the master cylinder (Fig. N:43).

The pipes serving the front braking circuit are fitted with 13 mm unions, whereas the pipes serving the rear circuit are fitted with 11 mm unions. This ensures that the

pipes cannot be assembled incorrectly.

Remove the single bolt and nut securing the valve assembly in position and lift out the valve.

Any hydraulic fluid which is spilled during the removal operation must be cleaned off immediately using cold water, to prevent damage to the paintwork.

Installation

Installation is a simple reversal of the removal procedure. Ensure that the five fluid pipes are reconnected to their correct positions on the valve assembly (Fig. N:43).

When installation is complete, bleed the braking system as detailed late in this section.

Seal Replacement

Unscrew and remove the warning light switch from the valve body. Remove the blanking plug from the end the valve and, using a small electrical screwdriver inserted into the fluid connection at the opposite end of the assembly, gently push out the piston, two sleeves and the rubber seals from the cylinder bore (Fig. N:44). Remove the two rubber seals from the piston and slide off the sleeves.

Clean and inspect the components of the valve assembly as detailed in 'HYDRAULIC SYSTEM OVERHAUL' earlier in this section.

If the condition of the piston and bore are satisfactory, reassemble the valve as follows:

Ensure the two circlips on the piston are not defective in any way: replace if necessary.

Slide the two sleeves onto the piston and hold in position using the rubber seals. Lubricate the piston assembly and cylinder bore with clean hydraulic fluid. Slide the piston and sleeve assembly into the cylinder, then refit the blanking plug to the end of the cylinder, using a new sealing washer. Screw the warning light switch into its location in the valve body.

BLEEDING THE BRAKES............[11]

The fluid level in the both halves of the master cylinder reservoir must be maintained at a reasonable level throughout the bleeding operation as, if the level is allowed to drop excessively, air may be drawn into the system. Use only fresh hydraulic fluid for topping-up. Never re-use fluid which has already been passed through the system.
1.   Remove the filler cap from the master cylinder reservoir, and top-up the fluid level as required.
2.   Remove the rubber dust cover (if fitted) from the bleed valve at the right-hand front brake. Attach one end of a bleed tube to the bleed valve and immerse the free end in a small quantity of hydraulic fluid in a glass jar (Fig. N:45).
3.   Open the bleed valve about half a turn. Depress the brake pedal through its full travel and then allow it to return to the fully released position. Hydraulic fluid should have been pumped into the jar; if not, open the bleed

Fig. N:41 Note position of outlet pipe on check valve before removing

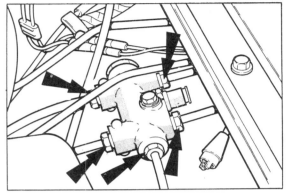

Fig. N:43 Note positions of pipes at differential valve before disconnecting

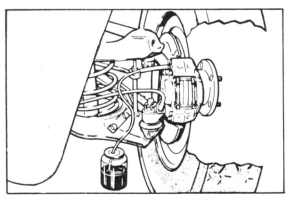

Fig. N:45 Continue bleeding brakes until fluid entering jar is free from air bubbles

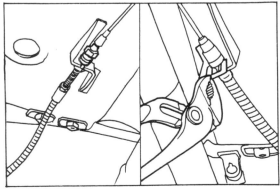

Fig. N:47 Disconnect cable from abutment brackets on underbody

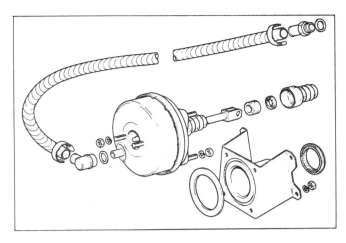

Fig. N:42 Details of servo unit installation

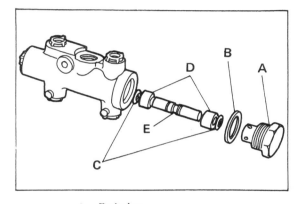

A   End plug
B   Sealing ring   D   Sleeves
C   Piston seals   E   Piston

Fig. N:44 Details of pressure differential valve assembly

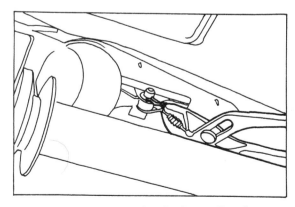

Fig. N:46 Disconnect handbrake equaliser from handbrake lever by removing clip and clevis

valve further.

4. Continue depressing the brake pedal, pausing briefly (about three seconds) after each stroke, until the fluid coming from the bleed tube is completely free from air bubbles.

5. Finally, with the brake pedal in the fully depressed position, close the bleed valve. Take care not to over-tighten the valve; tighten it only sufficiently to seal. Remove the bleed tube and refit the dust cover on the valve.

6. Repeat the complete process for the other front brake, then the rear brakes

7. Finally, re-bleed the right-hand front brake to check that air has not been drawn in through the master cylinder.

8. Top up the fluid reservoir to the level indicated on the side, then refit the filler cap, after checking that the vent hole is clear.

In some instances, where only one of the hydraulic circuits, i.e. front or rear circuit, has been opened in the course of repair work, it may suffice to bleed only the relevant circuit.

HANDBRAKE . . . . [12]

Cable Replacement

1. Jack up the rear of the car and support on stands. Re-move both rear road wheels.

2. Fully release the handbrake. Working from beneath the car, remove the spring clip and withdraw the clevis pin and wave washer securing the handbrake equaliser bracket to the lower end of the handbrake lever (Fig. N:46).

3. Disconnect the two runs of the cable from the abutment brackets on the vehicle underbody (Fig. N:47). The cable is retained by the adjuster locknuts at the right-hand bracket, and a spring retainer clip at the left-hand bracket. Also release the cables from the clips on the rear suspension radius arms.

4. Remove the rear brake drums and disconnect the end of the handbrake cable from the handbrake operating lever at each brake backplate assembly. Withdraw the cable from the backplates and remove it from under the car.

5. Lubricate the new cable thoroughly with suitable grease at the equaliser bracket and where the cable enters the outer sleeve.

6. Pass the cable through the backplates and connect it to the operating levers. Refit the brake drums.

7. Secure the cable to the abutment brackets and to the clips on the radius arms. Ensure the adjuster assembly is correctly located at the right-hand abutment bracket (Fig. N·47).

8. Reconnect the equaliser bracket to the handbrake lever with the clevis pin, wave washer and spring clip.

9. Refit the road wheels, then set the cable adjustment as detailed in the ROUTINE MAINTENANCE section.

Technical Data

FRONT BRAKES

Type.	Disc, fixed caliper, twin opposed pistons, self-adjusting
Disc diameter	9.74 in (247.5 mm)
Disc run-out (inc. hub).	0.002 in (0.05 mm)

REAR BRAKES (8.0 in Diam.)

Application	1.3/1.6 litre Saloon & Estate car models
Type.	Bendix, drum, leading & trailing shoe, single double-acting wheel cylinder, self-adjusting
Drum diameter	8.0 in (203.2 mm)
Shoe width.	1.5 in (38.1 mm)
Wheel cylinder diameter	0.75 in (19.05 mm)

REAR BRAKES (9.0 in Diam.)

Application	1.6 litre Heavy Duty Estate car & 2.0 litre models
Type.	Girling, drum, leading & trailing shoe, single double-acting wheel cylinder, self-adjusting
Drum diameter	9.0 in 9228.6 mm)

HYDRAULIC SYSTEM

Type.	Dual line, split front and rear, with pressure differential warning switch
Brake fluid.	Disc brake fluid, to Ford Specification ESEA-M6C-1001-A (green), or SAM-6C-9101-A or C (Amber)

BRAKES
Trouble Shooter

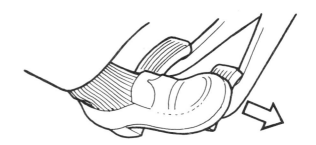

FAULT	CAUSE	CURE
Excessive brake pedal travel	1. Brakes need adjusting or replacement. 2. Air in system. 3. Leaking or contaminated fluid. 4. Faulty master cylinder.	1. Adjust or renew brake shoes. 2/3. Bleed hydraulic system. 4. Fit new master cylinder.
Brake fade	1. Incorrect pad or lining material. 2. Old or contaminated fluid. 3. Excessive use of brakes or car overloaded.	1. Fit new pads or shoes. 2. Renew brake fluid. 3. Check vehicle load.
Spongy brake pedal	1. Air in hydraulic system. 2. Shoes badly lined or distorted. 3. Faulty hydraulic cylinder.	1. Bleed system. 2. Fit new pads or shoes. 3. Check hydraulic circuit.
Brake pedal too hard	1. Seized wheel cylinder or caliper piston. 2. Glazed friction material.	1. Replace seized component. 2. Fit new shoes/pads.
Brake pedal requires pumping or loss of pedal	1. Brakes wrongly adjusted. 2. Air in hydraulic system. 3. Fluid leak from component or brake pipe. 4. Loss of fluid from master cylinder.	1. Adjust brakes. 2. Bleed system. 3/4. Check hydraulic circuit and replace parts as necessary.
Brakes grab when applied	1. Contaminated friction material. 2. Wrong linings fitted. 3. Scored drums or discs.	1/2. Replace (don't clean) pads or shoes. 3. Fit new drum or disc.
Brake squeal	1. Worn retaining pins (disc). 2. Faulty damping shims or shoe retaining clips. 3. Dust in drum. 4. Loose backplate or caliper.	1. Fit new pins. 2. Fit new shims or clips. 3. Remove dust from drums and shoe. 4. Tighten caliper or backplate.
Brake judder	1. No clearance at master cylinder operating rod. 2. Shoe tension springs either broken or weak. 3. Wheel cylinder or caliper piston seizing. 4. Faulty self-adjusting mechanism. 5. Seized handbrake mechanism.	1. Adjust rod if possible. 2. Replace tension springs. 3. Fit new caliper or cylinder. 4. Check mechanism. 5. Check handbrake operation.

Cont'd over

FAULT	CAUSE	CURE
Brake pull to one side only	1. Contaminated friction material on one side (grease, oil or brake fluid). 2. Loose backplate. 3. Seized cylinder. 4. Faulty suspension or steering.	1. Replace shoes/pads all round. 2. Tighten backplate. 3. Replace seized cylinder. 4. Check suspension and steering.
Handbrake ineffective	1. Worn rear shoes or pads. 2. Brakes require adjusting. 3. Faulty handbrake linkage. 4. Cable or rod requires adjustment.	1. Fit new pads/shoes. 2. Adjust brakes. 3. Check linkage and operating mechanism. 4. Adjust cable or rod.
Servo (where fitted) late in operation	1. Blocked filter. 2. Bad vacuum sealing or restricted air inlet.	1. Clean or replace filter. 2. Tighten vacuum hose connections and check hoses.
Loss of servo action when braking heavily	1. Air leak in servo - vacuum low.	1. Either overhaul servo or replace.
Loss of fluid (Servo only)	1. Seal failure. 2. Scored servo bores. 3. Damaged or corroded fluid pipes.	1/2. Replace or overhaul servo. 3. Inspect and fit new pipes.

General Electrics

HEADLAMP ASSEMBLIES . . . . [1]

Early Cortina, Base, L and XL models were fitted with two round, sealed-beam or semi-sealed beam headlights. GT and GXL models had a four-headlight system with round semi-sealed units and Halogen-type bulbs.

Later, XL, GT and 'E' models after October 1973 had two large rectangular headlight units with Halogen-type bulbs. Other Cortina models retained the two round headlights of either sealed or semi-sealed type.

Round Headlights-Sealed-Beam Type (Fig. O:1)

The headlight filament is sealed inside a single glass unit incorporating the lens and reflector. In the event of one or more filaments 'blowing' the complete unit must be replaced as follows:

(Early type). Remove the radiator grill first, by undoing the nine securing screws. Undo the three screws securing the lamp bezel to the back-plate then detach the lamp unit from the bezel. Disconnect the wiring connector from the rear of the light. Note that the connector also carries the side light bulb. Replacement is a straight reversal of the removal procedure.

(Later type) Undo the four screws attaching the headlight surround to the body front panel. Undo a further three screws securing the light bezel to the back-plate, then detach the light unit from the bezel. Disconnect the wiring connector from the rear of the light. Note that the connector also carries the side light bulb.

Replacement is a reversal of the removal procedure.

Round Headlights - Semi-Sealed Type (Fig. O:2)

To replace the bulb, disconnect the wiring plug from the rear of the headlight, then remove the protective rubber cap by turning it anti-clockwise. Twist off the spring washer and withdraw the bulb from the headlight reflector. If the bulb is of the Halogen type, it must not be touched with the fingers, as the grease will cause premature failure of the bulb. If it has been touched accidentally, the glass should be cleaned carefully with methylated spirits and dried with a soft, dust-free cloth.

Replacement is a reversal of the removal procedure.

Rectangular Headlights - Bulb Replacement

These headlights are of the semi-sealed type and the bulb can be replaced from within the engine compartment without having to remove the light unit (Fig. O:3).

Release the bulb retaining clip, then disconnect the wiring plug and sealing cap from the rear of the light unit.

Press the bulb retaining ring against its spring and turn it in a clockwise direction and then withdraw the bulb from the reflector. Remove the bulb from the holder.

The glass envelope of the bulb must not be touched with the fingers, as the grease will cause premature failure of the bulb. If it has been touched accidentally, the glass should be washed carefully in methylated spirits and dried with a soft, dust-free cloth.

Fit the bulb carefully, ensuring that it is properly seated in the light reflector and that the three bulb terminals protrude through their alloted holes in the rubber cover before reconnecting the wiring plug.

Rectangular Headlight Unit Replacement

The headlight assembly is secured to the front panel by a single retaining screw and is easily removed to replace the headlight unit (Fig. O:4).

Remove the radiator grill - secured by nine screws, then remove the single screw attaching the headlight to the body.

Pull the headlight unit forward and detach the bulb and holder from the rear of the light. Take care not to touch the bulb envelope with the hands or fingers - use only a soft clean cloth.

Disengage the light assembly from the two lower location lugs. Fit the headlight assembly in the reverse order of removal, then have the headlight alignment checked afterwards (Fig. O:5).

Note that if the bulb has been touched accidentally with the fingers during removal or assembly, it should be cleaned carefully with methylated spirits and dried with a soft, dust-free cloth.

Sidelight Bulbs

The sidelight bulb is located at the rear of the headlight unit reflector and can easily be reached from inside the engine compartment. On cars with sealed-beam headlights, the sidelight bulb is mounted on the connecting plug at the rear. To replace the bulb, simply detach the connecting plug and detach the sidelight bulb from its holder.

Models with semi-sealed headlights have the sidelight bulb inserted into the rear of the reflector. To replace the sidelight bulb, remove the bulb holder from the reflector and then detach the bulb from the reflector.

FRONT INDICATOR LIGHT.............[2]

Bulb Replacement

The indicator light bulb can be replaced after removing the indicator lens, which is retained by two screws. The bulb is a bayonet fitting type. When refitting the lens, ensure the gasket is seated properly (Fig. O:6).

Light Unit Replacement

The front indicator lamp is secured in position on the front wing by a nut and washer at the rear of the lamp, which is reached from under the wing panel. It may be necessary to scrape away any underbody sealant to enable the spanner to fit onto the nut. The indicator lamp wire must be disconnected from inside the engine compartment and pushed through the grommet in the inner wing panel before the light unit can be removed. Install the new light in the reverse order of removal.

Flasher Unit Replacement

The flasher unit is clipped to the rear of the instrument panel and can easily be removed. Unclip the unit and disconnect the wires from the terminals. Connect the wires to the new unit and refit behind the instrument panel (Fig. O:7).

REAR LIGHT ASSEMBLY..............[3]

The rear light assembly incorporates the stop/tail lights, direction indicator and reverse light, grouped together in one unit.

Bulb Replacement

Access to the bulbs is gained by undoing the four crosshead screws and detaching the lens from the light unit body. All the bulbs are of the bayonet fitting type and are removed by pressing and turning them anti-clockwise (Fig. O:8).

Make sure the bulb is firmly located when refitting.

Light Unit Replacement

On Estate cars only, remove the relevant trim rear side panel to gain access to the rear of the light unit.

On all models, remove the bulb holders from the light unit, then undo the nuts and washers securing the unit to the car body. Detach the light unit assembly from the body.

Refit the unit in the reverse order of removal, remembering to reconnect the earth lead to one of the fixing studs.

NUMBER PLATE LIGHTS..............[4]

Bulb Replacement (Fig. O:9)

Two single bulb light units, located in the rear bumper, are used to illuminate the rear number plate. The light assembly must be removed from the bumper to replace the bulb. The light is secured in position in the bumper by two spring clips which must be pressed inwards from the rear of the bumper to release the lamp.

Once removed, detach the lens cover and lens from the light body by lifting the tab on the cover clear of the two retaining lugs on the body and swinging it clear of the body. The bulb is of the bayonet type and is removed by gently depressing and turning it anti-clockwise.

When reassembling the light unit, ensure that the lens cover is located onto the rim on the top edge of the lamp body before pressing it into position over the retaining lugs.

IGNITION SWITCH ....[5]

The ignition switch is incorporated in the steering lock, but can be replaced separately without the need to remove the complete lock assembly. However, if the ignition switch/steering lock key is lost and the number is not known, it will be necessary to replace the complete steering lock and ignition switch assembly. Details of the lock replacement are included in the STEERING section.

To replace the ignition switch, first disconnect the battery, and detach the steering column upper and lower shrouds. Then disconnect the loom multi-plug connector at the side of the steering column. Remove the two screws securing the switch to the steering lock housing and detach the switch. Assemble the new switch to the lock in the reverse sequence of removal, and reconnect the loom plug (Fig. O:10)

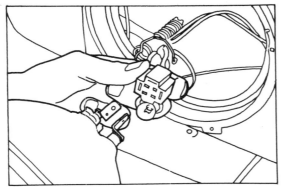

Fig. O:1 Removing the wiring connector from the rear of a sealed-beam headlamp

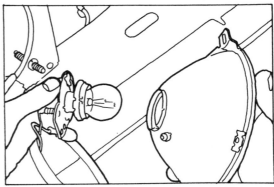

Fig. O:2 Detaching the bulb assembly from the headlight reflector - semi-sealed headlights

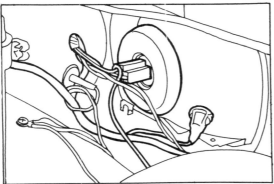

Fig. O:3 Access to the bulbs on rectangular type headlights is from the engine compartment

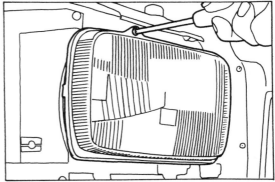

Fig. O:4 To remove a rectangular type headlight, undo the single screw as shown

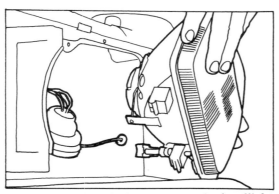

Fig. O:5 When replacing a rectangular headlight make sure tangs (arrowed) are engaged

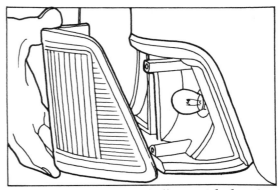

Fig. O:6 Detaching front indicator light lens to replace the bulb

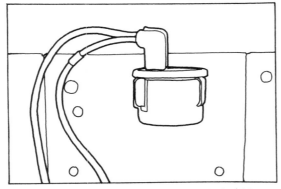

Fig. O:7 The indicator flasher unit is held by a clip adjacent to the bonnet release handle

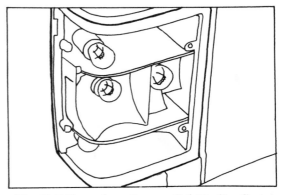

Fig. O:8 To replace the rear light bulbs, first detach the lens cover. Estate car type shown

INTERIOR LIGHT . . . . [6]

Bulb Replacement

Carefully prise out the light assembly from its location in the roof headlining (Fig. O:11).

Two types of bulb may be fitted, either a thin festoon type bulb or a round bulb with a bayonet fitting. Remove the bulb from the fitting.

Before fitting the new bulb, check that the interior of the light lens is clean and that all the wires are properly connected to the terminals.

Position the bulb in the terminal fitting and make sure that it is making proper contact, then install the unit in the roof panel.

STEERING COLUMN SWITCHES . . . . [7]

Replacement - Early Type (Up to October 1973)

The stalk switch for the indicators and lighting mainbeam can be easily replaced once the steering column shroud has been removed.

If a manual choke control is fitted, pull off the choke control knob and detach the plastic ring attaching the two parts of the column shroud at the upper end, adjacent to the steering wheel.

Undo the screws attaching the shroud to the steering column and detach the shroud halves.

Disconnect the wiring connector from the underside of the switch, then undo the two screws attaching the switch to the column bracket and detach the switch.

Refit the switch in the reverse order of removal, making sure that both halves of the column shroud are properly engaged with each other before tightening the securing screws (Fig. O:12).

Replacement, Later Type (October 1973 onwards)

Later models have stalk-type switches for the lighting and wipers mounted on the steering column in addition to the direction indicator switch. Both are easily replaced once the column shroud has been removed (Fig. O:13).

The lighting and wiper switches are incorporated in one unit and are mounted on the right-hand side of the column. The indicator/dip switch is at the left side of the column. The replacement procedure is similar for both switches (Fig. O:14).

First unclip the steering column upper shroud, then remove the three retaining screws and detach the lower shroud.

Remove the two bolts securing the relevant switch to the bracket on the steering column. Note that the lower bolt on the right-hand switch also secures the wiper switch earth lead. Detach the switch from the column and, disconnect the multi-plug connectors from the rear face of the relevant switch and remove the switch from the car.

Fit the new switch in the reverse sequence, not for-

getting the earth lead at the wiper switch. When installation is complete, check the function of the switch(es).

INSTRUMENT PANEL SWITCHES . . . . [8]

Removal/Installation - Pre October 1973

Lighting Switch

Pull the lighting switch knob from the stalk, then undo the switch ring nut using a suitable spanner, taking care not to damage the panel paintwork.

Position one hand up behind the instrument panel and detach the wiring loom from its retaining clips adjacent to the rear of the lighting switch.

Pull the lighting switch from its location and withdraw it from behind the instrument panel. Disconnect the wiring plug from the rear of the switch.

To install the switch, connect up the wiring plug and check the operation of the switch before refitting it in the reverse order of removal.

Windscreen Wiper Switch

Pull off the heater control knobs from their respective levers, noting that it will be necessary to lever out the locating dowel from the lower knob.

Lever off the heater control bezel - taking care to avoid damaging the paintwork on the panel. Pull the wiper switch knob from the stalk and unscrew the switch ring nut using a suitable spanner.

Working through the heater control aperture, disconnect the wiper switch wiring plug from the rear of the switch then withdraw the switch from behind the instrument panel.

The switch is installed in the reverse order of removal.

Heated Rear Window Switch

This switch is removed and installed following the same procedure as detailed for the Lighting Switch earlier.

Removal/Installation - October 1973 on

Three switches are located on the actual instrument panel assembly; the heated rear window and hazard flasher switches are located directly below the cigar lighter, and the panel light dimmer (Rheostat) switch is located at the drivers end of the panel below the fresh air vent. The two centre switches can be easily removed from the panel while it is in position, but the panel assembly must be removed to allow access to the panel light switch which is mounted on the fixed fascia panel behind the instrument panel.

Heated Rear Window Switch

Using a soft cloth or wad of paper to protect the surface of the instrument cluster bezel, as shown in Fig O:15, carefully prise the switch out of its location with a small electrical screwdriver. Disconnect the multi-plug connec-

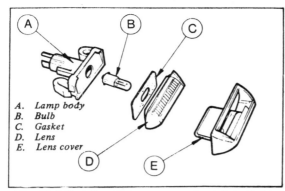

A. Lamp body
B. Bulb
C. Gasket
D. Lens
E. Lens cover

Fig. O:9 Details of the rear number plate light assembly. Estate car type shown

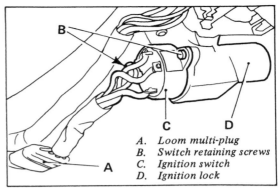

A. Loom multi-plug
B. Switch retaining screws
C. Ignition switch
D. Ignition lock

Fig. O:10 Ignition switch can be replaced without removing steering column lock

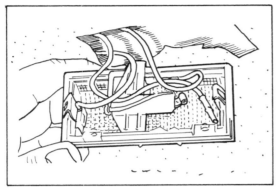

Fig. O:11 Removing the interior light assembly from the roof headlining

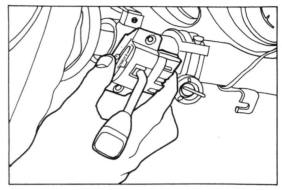

Fig. O:12 Removing the indicator switch from the steering column on early models

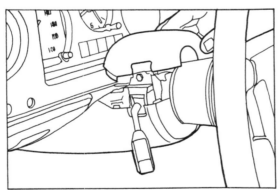

Fig. O:13 Removing the steering column upper and lower shrouds

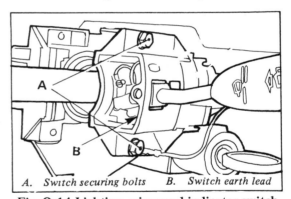

A. Switch securing bolts   B. Switch earth lead

Fig. O:14 Lighting, wiper and indicator switch installation on later models

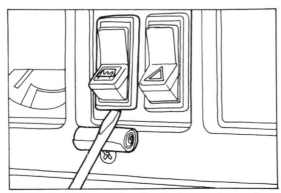

Fig. O:15 Removing the instrument panel switches on later models

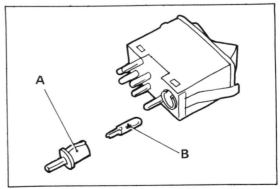

Fig. O:16 The hazard warning light switch has a bulb (B) inside the holder (A)

tor and withdraw the bulb holder from the rear of the switch.

To replace the bulb which is of the glass socket type, merely pull the bulb from the holder. Do not twist the bulb to remove it. Push the new bulb into position in the holder.

Hazard Warning Light Switch (if fitted)

The hazard warning light switch is removed in the same way as the heated rear window switch above. However, in this case the bulb holder is incorporated in the switch, and only the multi-plug connector need be disconnected.

To replace the bulb, carefully prise the bulb holder from the rear of the switch, then pull the bulb out of the holder (Fig. O:16). Push the new bulb into the holder and refit the holder in the switch body.

Instrument Illumination Switch (Rheostat)

The instrument panel assembly must be removed to gain access to the panel light switch. Pull the loom connections off the switch from the rear. Pull off the switch knob and unscrew the ring nut securing the switch body to the fascia panel then withdraw the switch from the rear. Refit switch in reverse order of removing (Fig. O:17).

Rear Wash/Wipe Switches

The switches are located on the lower part of the fascia panel to the right of the steering column on some Estate car variants (Fig. O:18).

To replace the switches, use a suitable size screwdriver to prise each switch from its location - taking great care to avoid damaging the panel paintwork in the process.

Withdraw the switch from its housing and disconnect the wiring connector from the rear. Installation is a reversal of the removal procedure.

GLOVE BOX LIGHT . . . . [9]

Bulb Replacement

Using a suitable tool or screwdriver, carefully prise the lens cover from its location. Pull the light assembly out and disconnect the earth wire terminal from the side of the light unit.

Pull the bulb holder from the lens and detach the bulb from the holder. Fit the new bulb in the reverse order of removal, reconnect the earth wire and press the light fully home to secure it.

INSTRUMENT PANEL ASSEMBLY . . . . . . [10]

Removal/Installation - Pre October 1973

Disconnect the battery, then, if a manual choke is fit-

ted, pull off the choke control knob and detach the plastic ring securing the two parts of the column shroud at the upper end adjacent to the steering wheel.

Undo the screws attaching the shroud to the steering column and detach the shroud halves - levering them apart with a thin knife blade if necessary.

Remove the screws attaching the fascia panel to the instrument cluster and detach the panel (Fig. O:19)

Undo and remove the screws securing the instrument cluster, then pull the cluster out sufficiently to gain access to the rear of the instruments.

Disconnect the wiring multi-pin connector and the speedo drive cable by depressing the cable connector to release it. Remove the instrument cluster.

Installation is a reversal of the removal procedure.

Instrument Panel Bulbs & Voltage Regulator

Remove the instrument cluster as described previously, then detach the relevant warning light or illumination bulb from the rear of the unit by pulling out the plastic plug from its location in the printed circuit (Fig. O:20).

The instrument voltage regulator is secured by a single crosshead screw to the rear of the instrument cluster. Undo the screw and replace the unit on the printed circuit board.

Removal - October 1973 onwards

1. Unclip and remove the upper shroud from the steering column. Remove the three crosshead screws and detach the column lower shroud.
2. Remove the crosshead screw and allow the fascia lower insulation panel to rest clear of the steering column.
3. Slacken off, but do not remove, the three bolts securing the steering column to the fascia rail and pedal bracket. This will allow the column to drop approximately 1/4 in (6 mm), giving the necessary clearance for the instrument panel to be removed (Fig. O:21).
4. Pull off the instrument panel light switch knob. Where a radio is fitted, also pull off the radio control knobs. Remove the two nuts located behind the radio knobs and lift off the radio surround panel.
5. Remove the six countersunk screws securing the instrument cluster and surrounding bezel to the fascia panel (Fig. O:22).
6. Pull the instrument assembly outwards to allow access to the electrical connections behind the panel. The multi-plug connectors are secured in position by retaining tabs at each side of the socket and these must be released by squeezing them together before the connectors can be removed (Fig. O:23).

Disconnect the two main loom connectors from the back of the instruments, then disconnect the two wires and the illumination bulb holder from the cigar lighter. Also disconnect the multi-plug connectors from the hazard flasher switch and heated rear window switch, if fitted.
7. Disconnect the speedometer cable from the rear of the speedometer.
8. Guide the instrument panel assembly clear of the fascia panel, keeping it square with the dash panel. If the

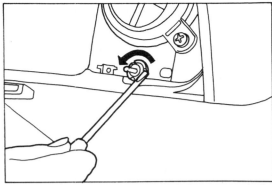

Fig. O:17 Removing the panel rheostat switch
from the instrument panel

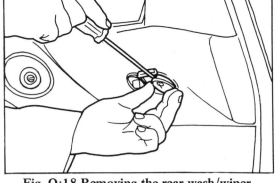

Fig. O:18 Removing the rear wash/wiper
switches on later models

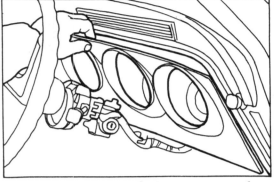

Fig. O:19 Removing the instrument panel
assembly on early models

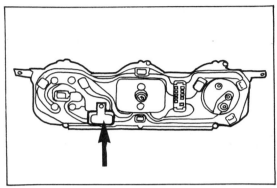

Fig. O:20 The location of early type panel
illumination bulbs

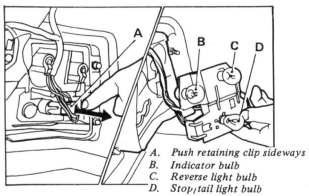

A. Push retaining clip sideways
B. Indicator bulb
C. Reverse light bulb
D. Stop/tail light bulb

Fig. O:21 Removing a panel illumination bulb
or warning lamp

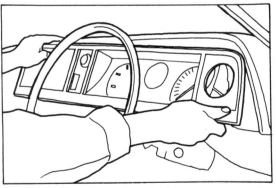

Fig. O:22 Withdrawing the instrument panel
clear of the steering column and fascia

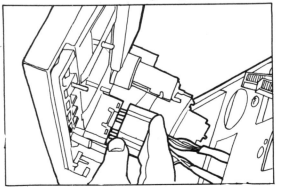

Fig. O:23 The multi-plug connectors can be
disconnected by squeezing together side latches

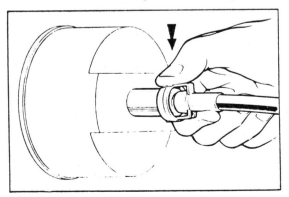

Fig. O:24 Disconnecting the speedo cable from
the rear of the speedometer

panel is allowed to tilt, the bezel will not clear the steering column switch bracket.

Installation

Installation is simply a reversal of the removal procedure, but special attention should be paid to the following points:

a) The two main loom multi-plug connectors for the instrument cluster are of different sizes so that they cannot be wrongly connected.

b) When installation is complete, check the function of all switches, instruments and warning lights.

Instrument Panel Bulbs & Voltage Regulator

Once the instrument panel assembly is removed from the fascia panel, the instrument illumination and warning light bulbs are easily replaced. The bulb holders are a twist-fit in the rear of the instrument assembly, and in some cases have a wiring connection which forms part of the wiring loom. The bulbs in each case are of the glass socket type and are a push fit into the holder.

Base, L, XL and 2000E models have five warning lights at the bottom centre of the instrument panel. GT and GXL models have four. GT and 2000E models have seven instrument panel illumination bulbs. Base, L and XL models have four.

Undo the single crosshead screw and remove the instrument voltage regulator if required.

Installation is a reversal of the removal procedure.

SPEEDOMETER CABLE . . . . [11]

Replacement

1. Remove the instrument panel assembly from the fascia panel as detailed in the relevant section previously, and disconnect the speedometer cable from the rear of the speedometer as shown in Fig. O:24.
2. Working from underneath the car, disconnect the speedo cable from the transmission extension housing. On manual models the cable is secured in the housing by a circlip which should be removed using circlip pliers. On automatic models, remove the bolt and spring washer securing the retaining clamp to the gearbox, detach the clamp and withdraw the speedo cable.
3. Disconnect the cable from the body clips. Pull the cable through the bulkhead panel and remove it from the engine compartment.
4. Insert the new cable through the bulkhead aperture and fit the grommet into its location in the dash panel. Feed the cable through the dash panel aperture until the colour band on the cable coincides with the grommet.
5. Check that the two clips and one tunnel bracket are in place. Route the cable along the side-member and across the bulkhead panel. The cable must pass under the side-member bracket. Check that the second colour band coincides with the first side-member clip and the third colour band aligns with the side-member bracket.
6. Connect the cable to the transmission extension hous-

ing and secure with the circlip or retainer clamp and bolt.
7. Connect the upper end of the cable to the speedometer, then refit the instrument panel assembly as detailed previously.

STOP LIGHT SWITCH . . . . [12]

The stop light switch is of the mechanical type and is located at the pedal bracket (Fig. O:25). To remove the switch, disconnect the loom wiring, release the locknut and unscrew the switch from its location.

When refitting the switch, adjust its position so that when the brake pedal is in the rest position, the switch plunger is depressed half its total travel. Secure the switch in position with the locknut and reconnect the wiring loom. Check the operation of the switch.

REVERSE LIGHT SWITCH . . . . [13]

Manual Transmission Only

The reverse light switch is located at the rear of the transmission gearshift housing at the base of the gear lever. To remove the switch, disconnect the wiring loom and unscrew the switch from the housing.

Screw the new switch into position and reconnect the wiring loom. Ensure that the loom is well clear of the exhaust and does not foul the transmission. Finally, check the operation of the switch.

FUEL GAUGE TANK UNIT . . . . [14]

The fuel gauge sender unit is located in the front face of the petrol tank and is a screw fit in the tank aperture.

Disconnect the battery before starting any work on the fuel tank - this is most important.

Syphon as much petrol as possible from the tank into a suitable metal sealed container.

Working from underneath the car at the rear, disconnect the wiring loom from the sender unit terminals. Disconnect the fuel supply pipe (also the fuel return pipe on later 'Emission' models) from the connections at the sender unit (Fig. O:26).

There is a special tool designed for unscrewing the sender unit, but if some care is taken the unit can also be unscrewed either using a bar located in the cut-outs around the edge of the unit, or by tapping it round with a blunt chisel. The unit is unscrewed anti-clockwise from the tank.

Always use a new seal when refitting the sender unit to the tank, as a used seal usually distorts on removal making it liable to leak and difficult to refit. Screw unit in clockwise until it is a tight fit.

Reconnect the fuel pipe(s), ensuring they are connected the correct way round if a return pipe is also fitted, and secure with clips. Reconnect the wiring loom.

Refill the tank with clean petrol. Reconnect the battery and check the function of the gauge.

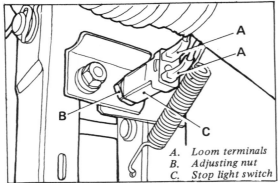

A. *Loom terminals*
B. *Adjusting nut*
C. *Stop light switch*

Fig. O:25 Stop light switch is screwed to pedal
bracket and secured by a locknut

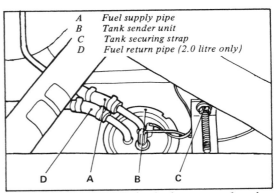

A   *Fuel supply pipe*
B   *Tank sender unit*
C   *Tank securing strap*
D   *Fuel return pipe (2.0 litre only)*

Fig. O:26 Details of the fuel gauge tank unit
installation

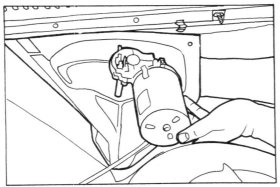

Fig. O:27 Withdraw wiper motor, complete
with mounting bracket, from its location

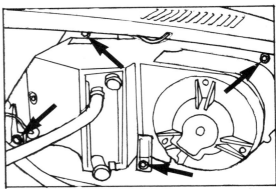

Fig. O:28 Slacken heater assembly bolts and
pull forwards to remove blower motor

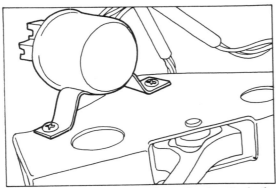

Fig. O:29 The hazard flasher relay is attached
to the bonnet release handle bracket

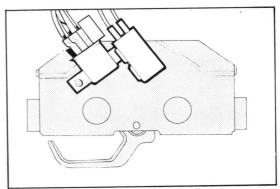

Fig. O:30 The heated rear window relay is
attached to bonnet release handle bracket

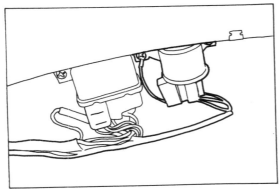

Fig. O:31 The headlamp and horn relays are
mounted on the inner wing panel

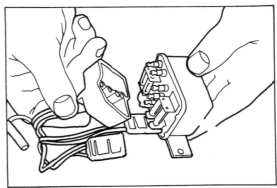

Fig. O:32 Headlamp relay fuses are mounted at
the rear of the relay unit

HORN . . . . [15]

The horn(s) are located on the front panel next to the radiator, and the radiator grille must be removed to gain access. The grille is secured in position by five cross-head screws.

Where twin horns are fitted, the feed wire connects to a wire junction which connects to both horns.

When refitting the horn(s), ensure the horn bracket is correctly positioned over the locating lug before tightening the securing bolt. Check the operation of the horns, after reconnecting the battery.

WINDSCREEN WIPER MOTOR . . . . [16]

Removal/Installation

The windscreen wiper motor is located on the engine compartment bulkhead and is accessible from the engine compartment.

To remove the motor, first disconnect the windscreen washer pipes from the nozzles, unclip the pipes and move them clear of the work area. Detach the cowling plate from over the wiper motor; this is secured by a single cross-head screw. Remove the five bolts securing the wiper linkage cover plate and detach the plate. Note that one of the bolts also secures the wiper motor earth lead for refitting later (Fig. O:27).

Disconnect the wiper motor wiring at the multi-plugs. Remove the two remaining bolts securing the wiper motor bracket to the vehicle body. Disconnect the wiper linkage from the operating arm at the motor; the connection is a tight 'push' fit and will have to be prised out with a screwdriver.

Slacken off, but do not remove, the four bolts securing the heater assembly. Pull the heater assembly forwards slightly, then guide the wiper motor and mounting bracket clear.

If required, the motor can be detached from the mounting plate by removing the three attaching bolts.

Installation is a simple reversal of the removal procedure. Do not tighten the motor bracket securing bolts until after the linkage cover plate has been fitted. Ensure that the motor earth lead is located at one of the plate securing bolts.

When installation is complete, test the operation of the wiper motor.

Foot Operated Washer Switch (if fitted)

Disconnect the battery, then remove the carpet from around the switch unit.

Disconnect the wiring connector and the water pipes from the switch. Undo the two securing screws and detach the switch from the floorpan.

Installation is a reversal of the removal procedure.

REAR WINDOW WIPER/WASH SYSTEM . . [17]

On estate cars equipped with a rear window wash/ wipe system, the wiper motor is located in the tailgate, and the washer reservoir is located behind the trim panel in the luggage compartment.

Wiper Motor

To remove the wiper motor, first prise off the trim panel from the inside of the tailgate.

On the outside of the tailgate, remove the wiper arm and the spindle nut, together with its washer and seal, from the wiper spindle.

Remove the three bolts securing the wiper motor assembly bracket inside the tailgate. Remove the screw securing the motor earth lead. Disconnect the multi-plug connector and withdraw the motor and linkage assembly from the tailgate.

To separate the motor from its mounting bracket, carefully prise the linkage rod off the motor operating arm, then remove the three bolts securing the motor to the bracket and detach the motor.

Reassemble the motor to the bracket and linkage and install in the tailgate in the reverse order of removing. Check the operation of the motor and the wipe action of the blade before refitting the tailgate trim panel.

Washer Pump

The rear screen washer pump is attached to the washer reservoir which must be removed before the pump can be detached.

The reservoir is located behind the trim panel on the left-hand side of the luggage compartment. To gain access to the reservoir, turn the two knobs retaining the cover panel so that the slots are vertical, then pull the top of the panel outwards and lift the panel upwards to disengage the lower retaining clips. Unhook the rubber retaining strap and carefully lift the reservoir from its retaining bracket.

Disconnect the multi-plug connector and the washer tube from the washer pump. Empty out the water from the reservoir. Carefully prise the pump out of its location in the side of the reservoir.

To refit the pump, locate it in position on the reservoir and gently press it into place. Refill the reservoir and install it in the reverse order of removing. Check the pump for correct functioning when installation is complete.

INTERIOR HEATER . . . . [18]

The heater motor and heater matrix are both easily removed from inside the engine compartment. The matrix removal is described in the COOLING SYSTEM section.

Heater Motor

Disconnect the multi-plug from the blower motor on the heater housing. Remove the three bolts securing the blower retaining plate to the heater housing and withdraw the blower assembly (Fig. O:28).

If required, the motor and fan can be detached from the retaining plate after disconnecting the cable plug connections and removing the centre-bolt on the outside of the retaining plate.

Ensure the cable plug connections are reconnected in

their correct positions when reassembling the motor to the retaining plate. Install the blower assembly in the reverse order of removing.

RELAYS.........................[19]

Relays are incorporated in several of the electrical circuits, and their function varies dependent on application. The various uses and locations of the relays are given below:

Indicator & Hazard Warning Relay

The relay in this case 'makes and breaks' the circuit at a predetermined frequency, thus causing the indicators lamps to flash.

The relay unit is located at the bonnet release lever bracket under the fascia and is retained by a spring clip. The heated rear window relay is also attached to this bracket. The dash panel lower insulation panel must be detached to allow access to the relay (Fig. O:29)

Heated Rear Window Relay

The heated rear window relay allows full power to be fed directly to the heater element and is actuated by the operation of the control switch. This avoids high current passing through the switch contacts.

As stated above, the relay is located at the bonnet release lever bracket beside the indicator flasher unit. In this case the relay is attached to the bracket by two crosshead screws (Fig. O:30).

Inhibitor Switch Relay

This relay is fitted only to models with automatic transmission, and inhibits the operation of the starter motor when the selector lever is in any position other than 'P' or 'N'.

The switch relay is located on the right-hand inner wing panel, next to the battery, and is secured in position by two crosshead screws.

Headlamp Relay

This relay isolates the lighting switch from the full current passing through the headlamp main and dipped beams, and is activated by the lighting main beam switch.

The relay is mounted on the inner wing panel adjacent to the rear of the headlights (Fig. O:31).

Technical Data

BULB USAGE CHART

	Quantity	Wattage
Headlamps, Tungsten (semi-sealed beam)	2	45/40
Headlamps, Halogen	2	60/55
Driving lamps, Halogen	2	55
Side lights	2	4
Indicators, front/ rear	4	21
Stop/tail lights	2	21/5
Number plate lights	2	4
Reversing lights	2	21
Interior light(s)	1 (or 2)	6
Glove compartment light	1	2
Auto. trans. selector quadrant light	1	1.4
Cigar lighter illumination light	1	1.4
Clock illumination light	2	1.4
Rear number plate	1/ 2	4 cp
Interior light	1/ 2	6 watt
Instrument panel warning lights		
Base, L, XL and 2000E	5	1 cp
Cortina GT and GXL	4	1 cp
Instrument panel illumination		
Base, L and XL	3	3 watt
Base, L and XL	1	1 cp
2000E, GT and GXL	7	1 cp
Warning lamp switches:		
Heated rear window	1	1.3
Hazard flashers	1	1.3

Wiring Diagram

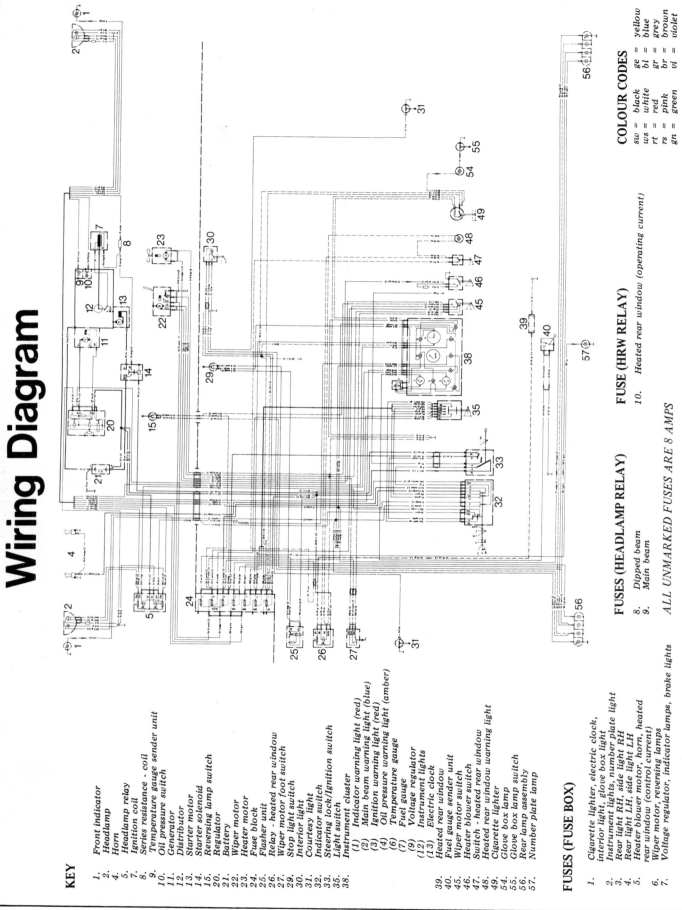

KEY

1. Front indicator
2. Headlamp
4. Horn
5. Headlamp relay
7. Ignition coil
8. Series resistance - coil
9. Temperature gauge sender unit
10. Oil pressure switch
11. Generator
12. Distributor
13. Starter motor
14. Starter solenoid
15. Reversing lamp switch
20. Regulator
21. Battery
22. Wiper motor
23. Heater motor
24. Fuse block
25. Flasher unit
26. Relay - heated rear window
27. Wiper motor foot switch
29. Stop light switch
30. Interior light
31. Courtesy light
32. Indicator switch
33. Steering lock/Ignition switch
35. Light switch
38. Instrument cluster
   (1) Indicator warning light (red)
   (2) Main beam warning light (blue)
   (3) Ignition warning light (red)
   (4) Oil pressure warning light (amber)
   (6) Temperature gauge
   (7) Fuel gauge
   (9) Voltage regulator
   (12) Instrument lights
   (13) Electric clock
39. Heated rear window
40. Fuel gauge sender unit
45. Wiper motor switch
46. Heater blower switch
47. Switch - heated rear window
48. Heated rear window warning light
49. Cigarette lighter
54. Glove box lamp
55. Glove box lamp switch
56. Rear lamp assembly
57. Number plate lamp

FUSES (FUSE BOX)

1. Cigarette lighter, electric clock, interior light, glove box light
2. Instrument lights, number plate light
3. Rear light RH, side light RH
4. Rear light LH, side light LH
5. Heater blower motor, horn, heated rear window (control current)
6. Wiper motor, reversing lamps
7. Voltage regulator, indicator lamps, brake lights

FUSES (HEADLAMP RELAY)

8. Dipped beam
9. Main beam

ALL UNMARKED FUSES ARE 8 AMPS

FUSE (HRW RELAY)

10. Heated rear window (operating current)

COLOUR CODES

sw =	black	ge =	yellow
ws =	white	bl =	blue
rt =	red	gr =	grey
rs =	pink	br =	brown
gn =	green	vi =	violet

CORTINA BASE AND 'L' MODELS TO OCT 73

Wiring Diagram

KEY

1. Front indicator
2. Headlamp
4. Horn
5. Headlamp relay
7. Ignition coil
8. Series resistance - coil
9. Temperature gauge sender unit
12. Distributor
13. Starter motor
15. Reversing lamp switch
19. Alternator with regulator
20. Battery sensing wire
21. Battery
22. Wiper motor
23. Heater motor
24. Fuse block
25. Flasher unit
26. Relay - heated rear window
27. Wiper motor foot switch
29. Stop light switch
30. Interior light
31. Courtesy light switch
32. Indicator warning light
33. Steering lock/ignition switch
35. Light switch
38. Instrument cluster
   (1) Indicator warning light (red)
   (2) Main beam warning light (blue)
   (3) Ignition warning light (red)
   (9) Voltage regulator
  (11) Tachometer
  (12) Instrument lights
  (13) Electric clock
39. Heated rear window
40. Fuel gauge sender unit
43. Console
   (5) Oil pressure gauge
   (6) Temperature gauge
   (7) Fuel gauge
  (10) Ammeter
  (12) Instrument lights
45. Wiper motor switch
46. Heater blower switch
47. Heated rear window switch
48. Heated rear window warning light
49. Cigarette lighter
54. Glove box lamp
55. Glove box lamp switch
56. Rear lamp assembly
57. Number plate lamp

ALL UNMARKED FUSES ARE 3 AMPS

FUSES (FUSE BOX)

1. Cigarette lighter, electric clock, interior light
2. Instrument lights, number plate light
3. Rear light RH, side light RH
4. Rear light LH, side light LH
5. Heater blower motor, horn, heater blower motor (control current)
6. Wiper motor, reversing lamps
7. Voltage regulator, indicator lamps, brake lights

FUSES (HEADLAMP RELAY)

8. Dipped beam
9. Main beam
10. Heated rear window (operating current)

COLOUR CODES

sw	=	black	ge =	yellow
ws	=	white	bl =	blue
rt	=	red	gr =	grey
rs	=	pink	br =	brown
gn	=	green	vi =	violet

CORTINA GT AND GXL MODELS TO OCT 73

Wiring Diagram

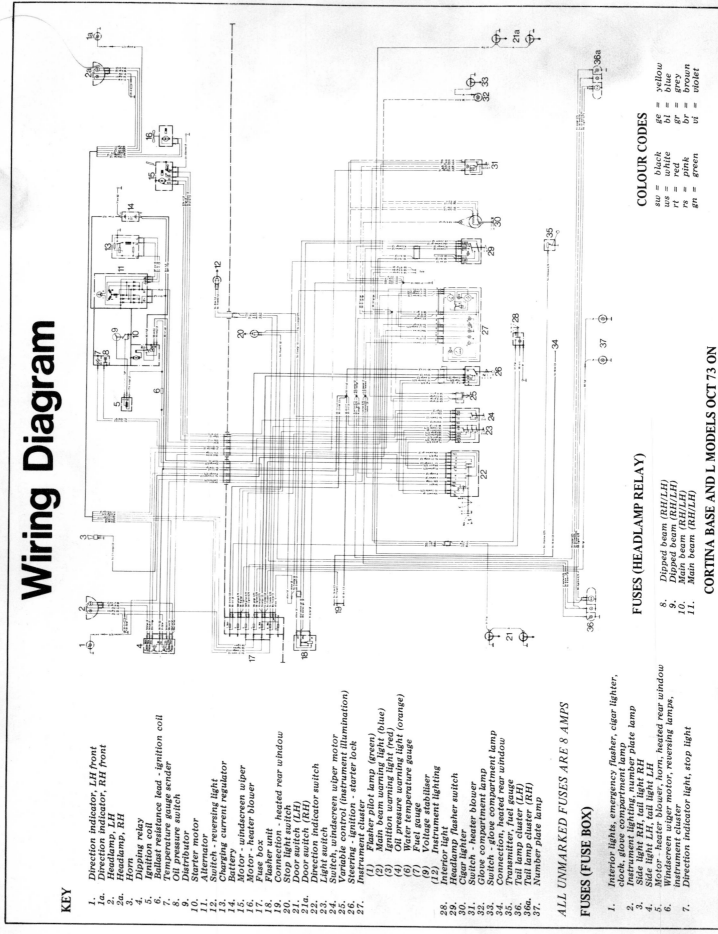

KEY

1. Direction indicator, LH front
1a. Direction indicator, RH front
2. Headlamp, LH
2a. Headlamp, RH
3. Horn
4. Dipping relay
5. Ignition coil
6. Ballast resistance lead - ignition coil
7. Temperature gauge sender
8. Oil pressure switch
9. Distributor
10. Starter motor
11. Alternator
12. Switch - reversing light
13. Charging current regulator
14. Battery
15. Motor - windscreen wiper
16. Motor - heater blower
17. Fuse box
18. Flasher unit
19. Connection - heated rear window
20. Stop light switch
21. Door switch (LH)
21a. Door switch (RH)
22. Direction indicator switch
23. Light switch
24. Switch, windscreen wiper motor
25. Variable control (instrument illumination)
26. Steering - ignition - starter lock
27. Instrument cluster
   (1) Flasher pilot lamp (green)
   (2) Main beam warning light (blue)
   (3) Ignition warning light (red)
   (4) Oil pressure warning light (orange)
   (6) Water temperature gauge
   (7) Fuel gauge
   (9) Voltage stabiliser
   (12) Instrument lighting
28. Interior light
29. Headlamp flasher switch
30. Cigar lighter
31. Switch - heater blower
32. Glove compartment lamp
33. Switch - glove compartment lamp
34. Connection, heated rear window
35. Transmitter, fuel gauge
36. Tail lamp cluster (LH)
36a. Tail lamp cluster (RH)
37. Number plate lamp

ALL UNMARKED FUSES ARE 8 AMPS

FUSES (FUSE BOX)

1. Interior lights, emergency flasher, cigar lighter, clock, glove compartment lamp
2. Instrument lighting, number plate lamp
3. Side light RH, tail light RH
4. Side light LH, tail light LH
5. Motor - heater blower, horn, heated rear window
6. Windscreen wiper motor, reversing lamps, instrument cluster
7. Direction indicator light, stop light

COLOUR CODES

sw =	black	ge =	yellow
ws =	white	bl =	blue
rt =	red	gr =	grey
rs =	pink	br =	brown
gn =	green	vi =	violet

FUSES (HEADLAMP RELAY)

8. Dipped beam (RH/LH)
9. Dipped beam (RH/LH)
10. Main beam (RH/LH)
11. Main beam (RH/LH)

CORTINA BASE AND L MODELS OCT 73 ON

Wiring Diagram

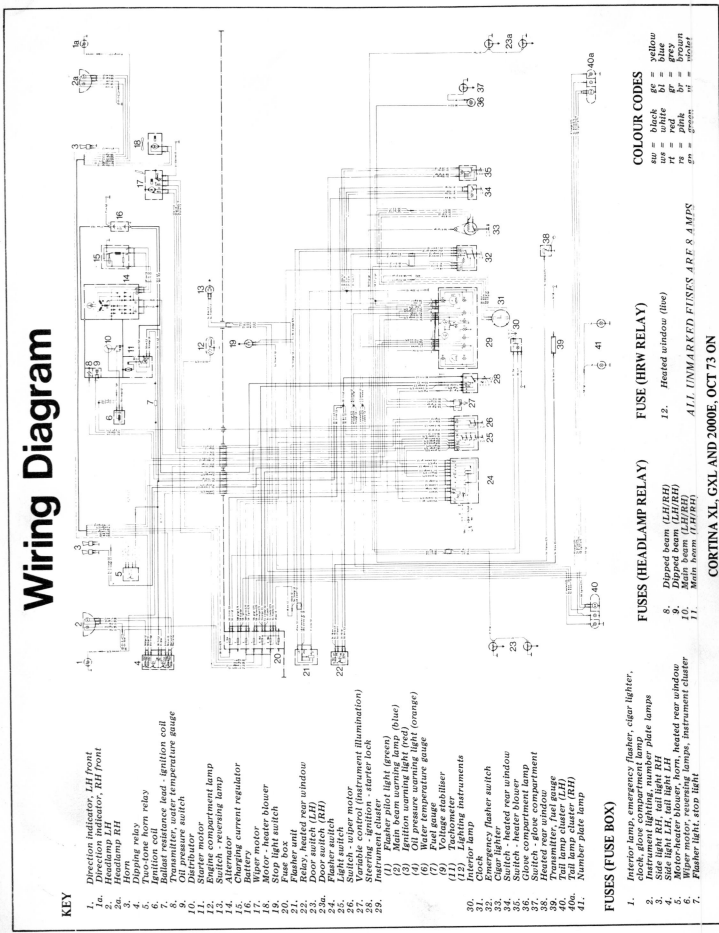

COLOUR CODES

sw	=	black	ge =	yellow
ws	=	white	bl =	blue
rt	=	red	gr =	grey
rs	=	pink	br =	brown
		green	ni =	violet

FUSE (HRW RELAY)

12. Heated window (live)

ALL UNMARKED FUSES ARE 8 AMPS

FUSES (HEADLAMP RELAY)

8. Dipped beam (LH/RH)
9. Dipped beam (LH/RH)
10. Main beam (LH/RH)
11. Main beam (LH/RH)

CORTINA XL, GXL AND 2000E, OCT 73 ON

KEY

1. Direction indicator, LH front
1a. Direction indicator, RH front
2. Headlamp LH
2a. Headlamp RH
3. Horn
4. Dipping relay
5. Two-tone horn relay
6. Ignition coil
7. Ballast resistance lead - ignition coil
8. Transmitter, water temperature gauge
9. Oil pressure switch
10. Distributor
11. Starter motor
12. Engine compartment lamp
13. Switch - reversing lamp
14. Alternator
15. Charging current regulator
16. Battery
17. Wiper motor
18. Motor - heater blower
19. Stop light switch
20. Fuse box
21. Flasher unit
22. Relay, heated rear window
23. Door switch (LH)
23a. Door switch (RH)
24. Flasher switch
25. Light switch
26. Switch - wiper motor
27. Variable control (instrument illumination)
28. Steering - ignition - starter lock
29. Instrument cluster
   (1) Flasher pilot light (green)
   (2) Main beam warning lamp (blue)
   (3) Ignition warning light (red)
   (4) Oil pressure warning light (orange)
   (6) Fuel gauge
   (7) Water temperature gauge
   (9) Voltage stabiliser
   (11) Tachometer
   (12) Lighting instruments
30. Interior lamp
31. Clock
32. Emergency flasher switch
33. Cigar lighter
34. Switch - heated rear window
35. Switch - heater blower
36. Glove compartment lamp
37. Switch - glove compartment
38. Heated rear window
39. Transmitter, fuel gauge
40. Tail lamp cluster (LH)
40a. Tail lamp cluster (RH)
41. Number plate lamp

FUSES (FUSE BOX)

1. Interior lamp, emergency flasher, cigar lighter, clock, glove compartment lamp
2. Instrument lighting, number plate lamps
3. Side light RH, tail light RH
4. Side light LH, tail light LH
5. Motor-heater blower, horn, heated rear window
6. Wiper motor, reversing lamps, instrument cluster
7. Flasher light, stop light

ELECTRICAL
Trouble Shooter

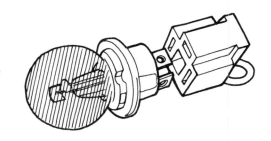

FAULT	CAUSE	CURE
STARTER		
Starter doesn't turn (lights dim)	1. Battery flat or worn. 2. Bad connection in battery circuit	1. Charge or fit new battery. 2. Check all feed and earth connections.
Starter doesn't turn (lights stay bright)	1. Faulty ignition switch 2. Broken starter circuit	1. Check switch. 2. Check starter circuit.
Solenoid switch chatters	1. Flat battery	1. Charge or replace battery.
Starter just spins	1. Bendix gear sticking	1. Remove starter and clean or replace Bendix gear.
CHARGING CIRCUIT		
Low or no charge rate	1. Broken or slipping drive belt 2. Poor connections on or faulty alternator	1. Fit new belt. 2. Check and replace alternator.
LIGHTING CIRCUIT		
No lights (or very dim)	1. Flat or faulty battery, bad battery connections	1. Check battery and connection.
Side and rear lights inoperative although stoplights and flashers work	1. Fuse blown	1. Fit correct value fuse.
One lamp fails	1. Blown bulb 2. Poor bulb contact 3. Bad earth connection. 4. Broken feed	1. Fit new bulb. 2/3. Check connections. 4. Check feed.
Flasher warning bulb stays on or flashers twice as fast	1. Faulty bulb or connection on front or rear of offending side	1. Fit new bulb, make good connection.
Lights dim when idling or at low speed	1. Loose drive belt 2. Flat battery 3. Faulty charging circuit	1. Tighten belt. 2/3. Check charge output and battery.
One dim light	1. Blackened bulb 2. Bad earth 3. Tarnished reflector	1/3. Fit new bulb or sealed-beam. 2. Check earth connections.
WINDSCREEN WIPERS		
Wipers do not work	1. Blown fuse 2. Poor connection 3. Faulty switch 4. Faulty motor	1. Fit fuse. 2. Check connections. 3. Check switch. 4. Remove and examine motor.
Motor operates slowly	1. Excessive resistance in circuit or wiper drive 2. Worn brushes	1. Check wiper circuit. 2. Remove motor and check brushes.

Body Fittings

RADIATOR GRILLE . . . . [1]

The radiator grille is screwed in position on the front panel. Open the bonnet to gain access to the grille upper retaining screws. Remove the upper and lower screws on later models and detach the radiator grille.

Before refitting the grille in position ensure that the plastic screw retainers or lower slot sleeves, depending on the model, are correctly assembled in their locations in the front upper and lower panels. Align the screw holes in the grille with the retainers and secure the grill in position.

FRONT BUMPER . . . . [2]

Removal and Installation

The front bumper is secured to the body front chassis extension bar member by two bolts, and to the front wing panels by a bolts at each end of the bumper (Fig. P:1).

The bolts at the chassis extension are accessible through the radiator grille aperture, after removing the grille (Fig. P:2).

The bolts at the ends of the bumper are accessible from under the wheel arch.

Withdraw the bumper and retaining brackets from the side-members to remove. Install in the reverse order, remembering to refit the plastic insulating pads between the bumper end mounting and the body.

Rubber Moulding

If damaged, the rubber moulding inset into the bumper is easily replaced. The moulding is secured by nuts and retaining tangs, accessible from the rear of the bumper.

Straighten the moulding tangs to release them from the bumper. After fitting the new moulding, twist the tangs with pliers to secure.

Underriders

The underriders are clamped by the chassis extension brackets to the bumper at the upper end and bolted to the body panel at the lower end. Access to the lower bolts is from under the front panel.

To remove the underriders the bumper must be removed first.

REAR BUMPER . . . . [3]

Removal and Installation (Fig. P:3)

Remove the licence plate lamps from the bumper by undoing the screws on saloon models or pressing together the two spring clips on the lamp body from behind the bumper on Estate models.

Inside the luggage compartment on saloon models, pull back the floor covering and remove the two bolts at each side securing the bumper brackets to the floor. Withdraw the bumper and bracket from the rear of the car.

On estate cars, undo the four bolts attaching the bumper to the chassis extension brackets. Install the bumper in the reverse order of removing.

DOOR STRIKER PLATE . . . . [4]

Adjust

If problems are experienced with door closure, the striker plate adjustment should be checked as follows:

Close the door to the first of the two locking positions, then visually check the relative positions of the lock support plate and the striker plate. The two edges should be parallel (Fig. P:4).

This is best checked by shining a torch through the door gap in the vicinity of the striker plate and viewing by looking upwards from the bottom of the door, or downwards from the top.

Check the distance the rear edge of the door stands proud of the adjacent panel. This should be 1/4 in (6 mm).

Adjust the horizontal position of the striker plate as necessary to fulfill these conditions. The striker plate is secured by four crosshead screws.

With the lock in the 'open' position, check the clearance between the lock claw and the striker at the position shown in Fig. P:5. This should be 0.08 in (2 mm).

This can be measured by sticking a ball of Plasticine on the striker post and checking the height of the Plasticine after gently closing the door.

If necessary, adjust the vertical position of the striker plate to obtain the correct clearance, but take care not to disturb the horizontal setting obtained above.

DOOR TRIM PANEL . . . .[5]

Removal (Fig. F:6)

1. Unscrew the private lock button from the lock rod at the top of the trim panel.

2. Carefully prise the window winder handle insert out of its location at the centre of the handle, slide it away from the handle button and disengage it from the two 'keyhole' slots in the handle. Remove the crosshead retaining screw now exposed and detach the handle and bezel from the shaft (Fig. P:7).

3. Remove the two crosshead screws from the underside of the armrest and detach the armrest from the door panel (Fig. P: 8). Where the arm rest is also secured by a locating peg, turn the armrest through 90° and withdraw the peg shaft from its location in the door panel.

Undo the two crosshead screws and remove the door pull handle on certain models.

4. Depress the trim panel around the door lock remote control handle bezel and slide the bezel forwards to disengage the retaining lugs (Fig. P: 9). Detach the bezel from the door panel.

5. Using a suitable flat tool, carefully prise the trim panel clips out of their locations in the inner door panel (Fig. P:10). The position of the clips can be located by feeling the trim panel surface around the outside of the panel. When all the clips have been disengaged, lift the trim panel clear of the door. Where fitted, remove the door pocket.

Extreme care must be taken when removing a trim panel which incorporates a map pocket as the trim panel board on this type of panel is split to accommodate the trim fastening and indiscriminate pulling on the lower edge of the board could result in the panel trim tearing.

6. If work is to be carried out on the door internal mechanism, carefully peel off the PCV sheet sealing the inner door panel outer edge. Take care not to tear the sheet.

Installation

7. If the plastic sealing sheet is torn or badly distorted, it should be replaced. A new sheet should be made using the trim panel as a template, cutting 0.2 in (5 mm) inside the edge of the trim panel.

8. To fit the sheet to the door panel, apply double-sided adhesive tape, 1/4 in (6 mm) from the edge of the door panel so that the fixing clip holes are covered. Any joints in the tape should overlap to provide a continuous seal. Apply the sheet to the door top edge and the sides, push the lower edge into the slot at the base of the door, then press the side into position, working upwards from the bottom edge. Cover the slot and lower edge of the sheet with tape.

9. If any of the trim panel retaining clips are damaged, they should be replaced. Insert the new clip into the larger diameter part of the 'keyhole' slot, then slide it into the smaller diameter part.

10. Locate the trim panel on the door with the private lock rod and remote handle assembly correctly located in their respective cut-outs in the panel. Push the retaining clips into their respective holes to secure the panel.

11. Press the remote control bezel into the trim pad so that the hooks engage on the housing lugs, then push the bezel rearwards until the holes are fully engaged.

12. Locate the armrest and door pull handle-ignition on the trim panel and secure with the crosshead screws. It may be necessary to align the clips in the door panel with a screwdriver before fitting the screws. If a clip is broken, fit a new clip by pushing the clip upwards as far as possible in the cut-out in the door panel and then pulling it into position.

13. Fit the window winder handle and bezel with the window in the closed position. Align the handle on the shaft in the appropriate position and secure with the crosshead screw. Locate the pegs on the plastic insert into the large ends of the channel keyhole cut-out and slide the insert towards the handle button to secure.

14. Screw the private lock button onto the lock rod at the top of the trim panel.

WINDOW WINDER MECHANISM . . . .[6]

Replacement

Remove the door trim panel and peel off the plastic sealing sheet as detailed previously.

Raise the window to the fully closed position. Remove the two screws securing the window glass to the winder mechanism bracket (Fig. P:11), and lower the glass to the bottom of the door shell.

Remove the two pairs of screws, shown in Figs. P:12 and P:13, securing the winder mechanism to the door shell. Disengage the winder tube from the clip at the front of the door (Fig. P:14) and remove the winder mechanism through the rear cut-out in the door shell (Fig. P:15).

Install the winder mechanism in the reverse order of removing. Do not fully tighten the two pairs of securing screws until installation is complete, and the action of the mechanism has been checked.

FRONT DOOR HANDLE. . . . .[7]

Replacement

Remove the door trim panel and peel the PVC sheet clear of the door inner panel apertures, as detailed previously.

Prise off the retaining clips and disengage the two control rods from the door lock assembly. Remove the two bolts attaching the handle to the door outer panel and withdraw the handle and rods from the door shell (Fig. P:16).

Install the handle in the reverse order of removal.

Remote Control - Removal & Installation

Remove the trim panel from the door as detailed previously. Slide the handle housing forwards in its aperture

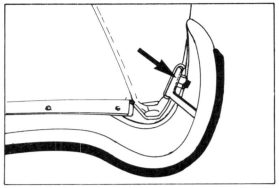

Fig. P:1 The bolts retaining the front bumper ends are accessible from under the wing

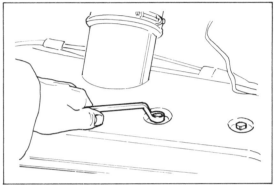

Fig. P:3 The rear bumper attachment bolts are under the boot floor covering on saloon models

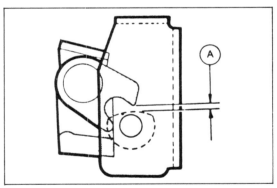

Fig. P:5 With lock in 'open' position, claw to striker clearance 'A' should be 0.008 in (2 mm)

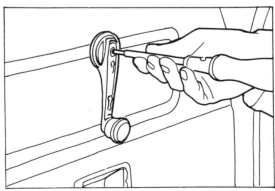

Fig. P:7 Carefully slide the plastic insert towards the centre to expose the handle retaining screw

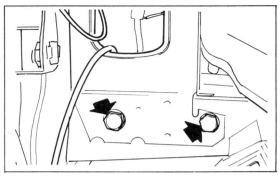

Fig. P:2 The front bumper bracket bolts are accessible with the radiator grill removed

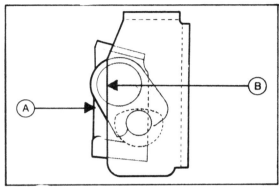

Fig. P:4 Striker plate edges (A) and (B) should be parallel with door in 'first' locking position

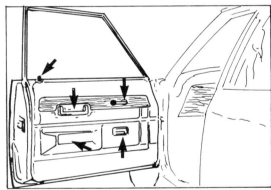

Fig. P:6 The items arrowed must be removed before the door trim panel can be detached

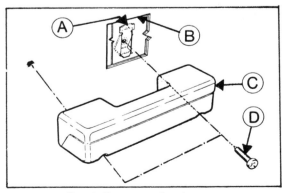

A. Speed clip   C. Armrest
B. Door inner panel   D. Retaining screw

Fig. P:8 To remove the armrest (excluding GXL models) unscrew the two screws to release it from the door inner panel (Fig. P:17). Un-hook the control rod from the lever at the rear of the housing and remove the remote control housing (Fig. P:18).

Install the assembly in the reverse order of removal.

REAR DOOR HANDLE . . . . [8]

Removal

Remove the trim panel from the rear door, as detailed previously. Pull down the plastic sheeting at the exterior handle location.

Prise the retaining clips off the exterior handle control rods and disengage the rods from the lock assembly lever. Remove the two bolts attaching the exterior handle to the door outer panel and withdraw the handle and rods from the door shell.

Installation

Insert the control rods on the handle through the aperture in the door shell. Position the handle on the door and secure it with the two retaining bolts. Refit the control rods in the lock assembly lever and secure with retaining clips.

Refit the plastic sealing sheet and door trim panel as detailed previously.

FRONT DOOR LOCK ASSEMBLY . . . . [9]

Removal

Remove the door trim panel, PVC sheet and door lock remote control handle from the front door as detailed previously.

Unclip the two control rods connecting the lock to the exterior handle and the lock barrel. Remove the three crosshead screws securing the lock to the rear edge of the door panel. Turn the lock rotor to the locked position ('U' of lock claw facing downwards), push the lock into the door shell and lower it sufficiently to allow the private lock rod to clear its housing at the top of the door shell. Disengage the remote control rod from the lock and withdraw the lock assembly through the lower rear aperture in the door panel (Fig. P:19).

Installation

Insert the lock assembly through the lower door aperture and engage the remote control rod on the lock lever. Lift the lock up into place so that the private lock rod engages in its housing at the top of the door shell. Secure the lock in position with the three retaining screws, then reconnect the exterior handle and lock barrel connecting rods.

Finally, refit the lock remote control handle and door trim panel.

REAR DOOR LOCK ASSEMBLY . . . . [10]

Removal

Remove the rear door trim panel and peel off the PVC sealing sheet. Drift out the pin securing the private lock lever crank to the door inner panel and detach the crank assembly.

Disengage the rod from the clip on the inner panel. Prise off the clip retaining the rods to the lock lever and manoeuvre it out of the lock lever bush. Disconnect the exterior handle rod from the lock lever, after prising the retaining clip clear of the rod.

Remove the three crosshead screws securing the lock to the rear edge of the door, and push the lock assembly into the door shell. Slide the remote control handle assembly forward to disengage the handle housing from the door inner panel, detach the control rod from the clip on the inner panel and turn the rod as necessary to disengage it from the lock lever bush. Remove the lock assembly from the door shell.

Installation

Insert the lock assembly into the door shell and connect the remote control handle rod to the appropriate lever on the lock.

Position the lock on the rear edge of the door panel and secure with the three retaining screws and shakeproof washers. Fit the remote control handle housing in the cut-out in the door panel and engage the remote control rod in the anti-rattle clip.

Reconnect the exterior handle rod to the lock and secure with the retaining clip. Engage the private lock rod in the appropriate lock lever bush and secure with the rod clip. Ensure the private lock rod is correctly engaged in its housing at the top of the door shell, then insert the square end of the bellcrank assembly in the hole in the door shell. Press the retaining pin into the bellcrank lever to secure. Finally, engage the rod in the anti-rattle clip.

Refit the plastic sheet on the door panel and install the trim panel as detailed previously.

BONNET RELEASE CABLE . . . . [11]

Adjustment

If difficulty is encountered in getting the bonnet release lever to open the bonnet properly, the release cable should be adjusted as follows. Ensure the cable is adequately lubricated and free from kinks before starting adjustment.

Open the bonnet and slacken the release cable clamp bolt at the front panel top crossmember (Fig. P:20). Slide the cable through the clamp until the bonnet release spring lever is positioned as shown in Fig. P:21. It may be necessary to detach the cable clips from their locations on the inner wing panel to achieve this condition. Hold the cable in the correct position and retighten the clamp bolt.

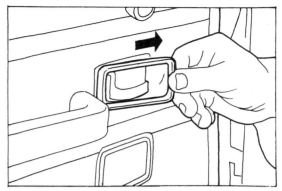

Fig. P:9 Slide the remote handle bezel forwards to disengage the retaining hooks behind

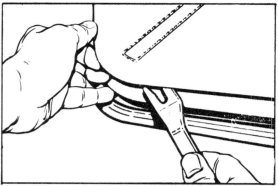

Fig. P:10 Lift the trim panel with a flat tool to disengage the trim clips from the door frame

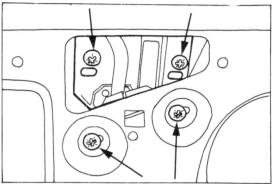

Fig. P:11 The door glass is secured to the lifter mechanism (A) and lifter bracket to door (B)

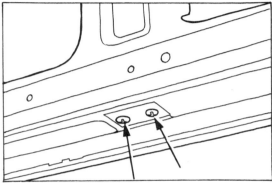

Fig. P:12 The window lifter bracket is secured at the bottom of the door by two screws

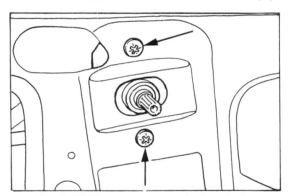

Fig. P:13 Two screws attach the winder mechanism bracket to the door panel

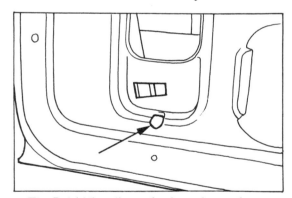

Fig. P:14 The clip at the front lower door aperture secures the winder tube lower end

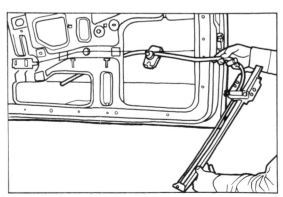

Fig. P:15 The window winder mechanism is removed through the rear aperture

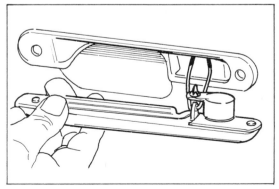

Fig. P:16 Undo the two bolts attaching the door handle and withdraw the handle

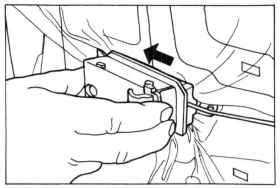

Fig. P:17 Slide the remote handle housing forwards to disengage it from the door

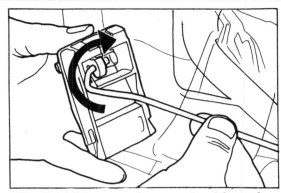

Fig. P:18 Disengage the control rod from the handle to remove the handle housing

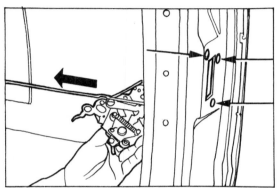

Fig. P:19 Withdraw the door lock mechanism after first undoing the three retaining screws

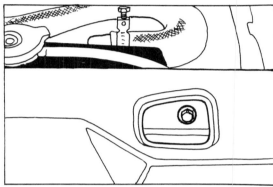

Fig. P:20 The bonnet release cable clamp bolt is accessible through the front panel aperture

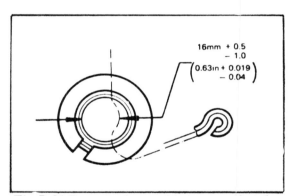

Fig. P:21 Bonnet release cable is set so that the release lever is positioned as shown

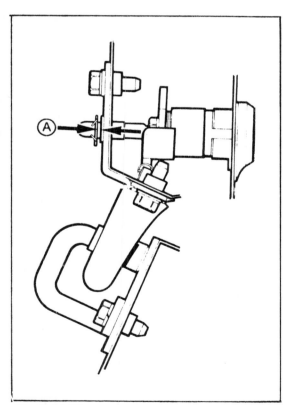

Fig. P:22 When refitting the boot lock, ensure clearance 'A' is between spindle clip and lid

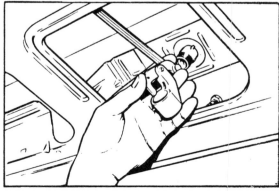

Fig. P:23 Remove the large retaining nut from the tailgate handle to detach the lock linkage

Close and release the bonnet to check the operation of the lock. The bonnet should 'pop-up' freely.

If, even after adjusting the cable, the bonnet still does not open freely this may be due to incorrect alignment of the striker post on the bonnet. Adjust the striker if necessary by slackening off the striker post locknut, aligning the striker post centrally with the sleeve in the front panel crossmember and retightening the locknut.

Cable Replacement

Remove the lower insulation panel from beneath the instrument panel. Detach the indicator flasher unit and heated rear window relay from their locations on the bonnet release lever bracket beneath the fascia panel.

Through the two access hoses in the lever bracket, slacken the two screws retaining the bracket to the cowl side panel and unhook the bracket from the screws. Disengage the release cable from the bracket by prising the retaining clip off the edge of the bracket. Prise the circlip off the lever pivot pin and remove the pin. Push the cable retaining pin out of its location in the lever and disconnect the cable from the lever.

Remove the radiator grille. Slacken the release cable clamp bolt on the front panel crossmember (Fig. P:20) and unhook the release cable from the bonnet lock spring. Unclip the cable from its retaining clips around the engine compartment, then, from inside the passenger compartment, pull the cable and grommet through the bulkhead into the passenger compartment.

Feed the new cable through the bulkhead into the engine compartment. Locate the grommet in the bulkhead aperture, ensuring that it is correctly located. Route the cable around the engage compartment and clip it into position. Connect the cable to the bonnet lock spring and secure with the clamp plate at the crossmember.

Attach the cable to the release lever with the retaining pin. Position the lever in its bracket, ensuring that the lever is the correct way round, then secure with the pivot pin and circlip. Locate the cable on the bracket and secure in position with the retaining clip. Hook the lever bracket onto the two retaining screws and tighten the screws. Refit the heated rear window relay and the flasher unit on the lever bracket, and replace the lower insulation panel.

Check the release cable adjustment at the bonnet release lock spring as detailed previously. Finally, refit the radiator grille.

BONNET PANEL . . . . [12]

Removal and Installation

Removal is simply a matter of removing the two bolts securing each hinge to the bonnet panel and lifting off the bonnet. Two people should be employed in lifting off the bonnet to avoid damaging the paintwork. It will facilitate alignment of the bonnet on installation if the positions of the hinges are marked by scribing around them prior to removal.

When fitting the bonnet, fit the hinge bolts loosely at first. Align the hinges with the lines previously marked, then tighten the securing bolts.

BOOT TAILGATE LOCK . . . . [13]

Boot Lock Replacement

On the underside of the boot lid, remove the spring clip from the end of the lock spindle. Remove the three retaining bolts and detach the lock.

Prise the clip from around the lock barrel cylinder and withdraw the lock barrel from the boot lid. Slacken the locknut, unscrew the lock spindle, then withdraw the cam, spacer and return spring.

Assemble and install the lock in the reverse order of removing. When fitting the spring clip on the end of the lock spindle, ensure that there is clearance between the clip and the lid inner panel (Fig. P:22).

Tailgate Lock Replacement

The lock assembly is easily removed after first removing the tailgate trim panel. Unscrew the large nut which secures the actuating linkage to the lock handle and disconnect the linkage (Fig. P:23).

Remove the three bolts securing the lock assembly and withdraw the lock together with the linkage from the tailgate panel.

Install the lock in the reverse order of removal.

Lock Barrel

The lock barrel is incorporated in the exterior handle casting, which must be removed from the tailgate first to allow the barrel to be removed.

Disconnect the lock actuating linkage from the handle as detailed earlier. Remove the two retaining nuts and detach the handle casing from the tailgate panel. Note the gasket fitted between the handle and the tailgate body panel.

To remove the lock barrel from the handle, extract the circlip from end of the handle casting and withdraw the spring and lock barrel.

Insert the new barrel together with the spring and secure with the circlip.

Assemble the gasket and handle casting on the tailgate and secure with the retaining nuts. Reconnect the linkage rod, aligning the cut-outs in the linkage with the lugs on the handle spigot, and secure with the large nut.

CENTRE CONSOLE . . . . [14]

Removal

1. On manual gearbox cars only, unscrew the gear lever knob and locking ring from the lever.
2. Carefully remove the clock from the console by levering it out of the surround with a screwdriver. Disconnect the clock and illumination bulb wires at the connectors.
3. Undo the two front console mounting screws, accessible through the clock aperture.
4. Undo the two rear console mounting screws at the sides. Lift the console assembly off the mounting brackets and clear of the gear lever.

Installation

Installation is a reversal of the removal procedure.

Accessories

RADIO & SPEAKER . . . . [1]

Installation

The following instructions describe the installation of a radio and loudspeaker into the fascia. The instructions are based on information received from Radiomobile Ltd, leading radio and tape player manufacturers.

A retractable aerial must be mounted in the appropriate position in the nearside front wing (see AERIAL later).

Components are provided in the Radiomobile installation kit for suppressing interference from the coil and alternator and details on their fitting is given in the SUPPRESSION section.

Pre-October 1973 Models

1. Disconnect the battery, then pull off the heater control knobs from their respective levers - note that it will be necessary to lever out the locating dowel from the lower knob.
2. Lever off the heater control bezel. Undo five screws and detach the radio/heater control panel from the fascia. Detach the radio aperture cover plate from the fascia panel.
3. Assemble the speaker to its mounting board using the parts supplied in the kit, connect the leads to the speaker terminals.
4. Pass the speaker through the fascia aperture and attach it to the mounting fixture.
5. Remove the control knobs, spindle nuts, dial and trim plates from the radio.
6. Fit the support bracket to the mounting place on the radio using the parts supplied in the fitting kit.
7. Connect the power, aerial and speaker leads also a temporary earth wire to the radio and reconnect the battery.
8. Refer to the operating instructions to determine the position of the aerial trimmer, and with the aerial fully extended, switch on the radio and tune to a weak station between 200 and 250 metres MW. Adjust the trimmer until full volume is achieved.
9. Disconnect the temporary earth lead and fit the radio mounting bracket to the fascia - take care not to disconnect the heater blower wire from the control switch when fitting the radio.
10. Replace the fascia cover panel and fit the trim plates and knobs to the radio. Refit the heater control bezel and the control lever knobs.

Post - October 1973 Models

1. Disconnect the battery.
2. Remove the seven screws securing the glove pocket on the passenger side of the car.
3. Assemble the speaker to its mounting board, using the screws, plain and shakeproof washers and nuts supplied in the kit.
4. Connect the speaker lead to the speaker.
5. Fit the clip nuts provided in the kit to the centre side fixing holes in the speaker mounting board and then pass the speaker assembly through the glove box aperture and into position beneath the fascia top roll where a mounting place has been provided.
6. Fix the speaker assembly in place using two self tapping screws provided. Take care not to damage the speaker during this operation.
7. Connect the radio power supply lead to the yellow fly lead located adjacent to the loom at the rear of the ignition switch.
8. Remove the control knobs, spindle nut escutcheons, spindle nuts, trim plates and dial mask from the radio.
9. Fit the support bracket to the mounting place on the underside of the radio using the parts supplied in the kit.
10. Connect the power, aerial and speaker leads to the radio and temporarily reconnect the battery. Refer to the operating instructions to determine the position of the aerial trimmer and with the aerial fully extended switch on the set and tune to a weak station between 200 and 250 metres MW. Adjust the trimmer until full volume is achieved.
11. Pass the radio unit through the glovebox aperture and locate it in position at the rear of the radio aperture in the fascia. Depending on the radio model, it may be necessary to open out the spindle hole centres in the metal panel at the rear of the radio aperture.
12. Attach the radio rear support bracket to the bracket attached to the body of the car and secure the front of the radio to the fascia using the new faceplate supplied in the kit and the spindle nuts previously removed. Replace the remaining spindle components and control knobs.
13. Replace the glove pocket and reconnect the battery.

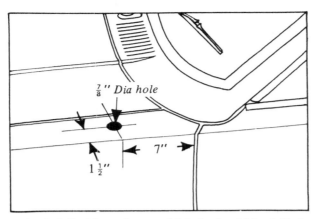

Fig. Q:1 Position where aerial hole should be drilled

$\frac{7}{8}''$ *Dia hole*

7"

$1\frac{1}{2}''$

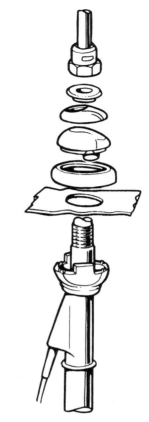

Fig. Q:2 Aerial assembly to wing panel

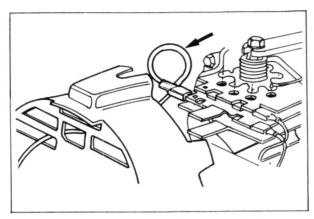

Fig. Q:3 Connecting 1 mfd capacitor lead to alternator terminal

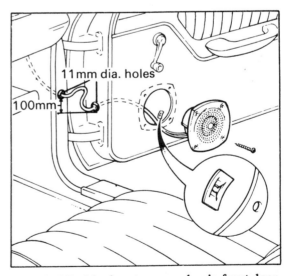

11mm dia. holes

100mm

Fig. Q:4 Positioning stereo speaker in front door

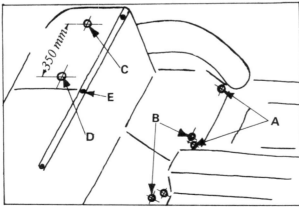

350 mm

C

E

D

B

A

Fig. Q:5 Existing anchorage points under rear seat and position of anchorage points on rear parcel shelf

A & B = Existing points
C = Existing anchorage
D = Hole to be drilled
E = Parcel shelf retaining screws

AERIAL . . . . [2]

Installation (Fig. Q:1)

1.   Mark and drill a 0.875 in (22 mm) diameter hole in the nearside front wing in the position shown in Fig. Q:0.
2.   Assemble the aerial to the wing as detailed in the instructions provided with the aerial.
3.   Mark and drill a 0.875 in (22 mm) diameter hole in the kick panel. Route the aerial lead through this hole in the kick panel using the rubber grommet supplied in the kit (Fig. Q:2).

SUPPRESSION . . . . [3]

NOTE: It is essential that paint is scraped away to expose bare metal at all points where an earth connection is to be made.
1.   Disconnect the battery.
2.   Connect a 1 mfd capacitor to the ignition coil (switch terminal) by removing the supply lead to coil, placing the crimped loop over the threaded stud on the coil and then replacing the supply lead by firmly pushing it home. Earth the capacitor and one end of the long flexible bonding strap supplied in the kit under the coil mounting bracket. Connect the other end of the strap under a suitable bolt on the engine block.
3.   Pull off the plug connector on the alternator back plate, withdraw the two screws securing the moulded end cover and remove the cover.
4.   Route the fly lead of a 1 mfd capacitor through one of the slots in the cover and connect it to the spare 0.19 in (4.8 mm) terminal blade attached to the main battery lead terminal on the alternator. See Fig. Q:3.
5.   Secure the capacitor mounting clip under the alternator rear fixing bolt and then replace the moulded cover.
6.   Fix the short bonding strap supplied in the kit between the plate welded to the engine sump and the adjacent crossmember. There is an existing suitable nut and bolt on the sump plate, but it will be necessary to drill a small fixing hole in the crossmember. When doing this, be careful not to damage the adjacent brake pipe.
7.   Reconnect the battery supply.

STEREO SPEAKERS . . . . [4]

Door Mounting (General)

1.   Remove the interior trim panel from the door after removing the door handle window winder, etc.
2.   Choose a speaker position so that the sound waves are not obstructed by the front seats and so that the speaker magnet is clear of the window winder mechanism. Where possible choose a position on the trim panel that coincides with an existing hole in the inner door panel. Make sure the speaker grille is clear of the window winder and door handle (Fig. Q:4).
3.   Using templates, cut a 5.2 in (132 mm) diameter hole in the panel and drill four 6 mm speaker mounting holes.
4.   When there is a clearance hole in the metal panel

behind the fixing holes, secure the speaker to the trim panel using clip nuts and screws. Make sure the curved side of each nut is on the inside of the door panel.
5.   If any of the fixing holes are backed by metal, drill a 2 mm hole and secure the screw directly to the metal.
6.   Before securing the speaker, drill a 11 mm diameter hole in the leading edge of the door and a corresponding hole in the door pillar. The second hole should be in the same vertical line as the first hole, but displaced about 10 cm from it (Fig. Q:4).
7.   Fit the grommets supplied to these holes and then route the speaker leads from the radio or tape player position through these grommets to the speaker position.
8.   Attach the leads to the speaker and secure the speaker, door trim, etc, ensuring that the speaker lead is clear of the window winding mechanism. Also make sure that the water shields are at the top.

BABY SEAT/CHILD HARNESS. . . . . [5]

Baby seats are normally suitable for children from the age of 6 to 9 months up to about 5 years, and child harness for children aged about 4 to 12 years. Safety seats or harnesses can be fitted 2 or 3 abreast, if required, doubling up the anchor plates at the anchorage points where necessary.

Most cars have 2 or 3 built-in anchorage points for each seating position, and these are normally concealed beneath the seats or behind the trim panels and filled with a plug or grommet (see Figs. Q: 5 and Q: 6). Always use the existing anchorage points, even if it means doubling up with a belt already fitted. In this case an anchor plate, wave washer and shouldered spacer must be used on both fittings. If the existing fixing bolt is too short, use the longer bolt normally supplied with the kit.

The seat or harness should be fitted as follows:
1.   Remove the rear seat cushion. The cushion is secured in position by two screws located beneath the seat, one on each side of the transmission tunnel. Bend back the flaps in the carpet to gain access to the screws. Lift the cushion off the floor and remove it from the car.
2.   Remove the rear seat backrest. This is secured inside the car by three retaining tabs which will be exposed once the cushion is removed. Bend back the tabs to release them from the loops on the backrest. The two retaining nuts which also secure the backrest are accessible from inside the luggage compartment. These are located behind the two notches in the top of the front trim panel. Pull the back rest from its location and remove it from the car so that it is out of the way.
3.   On saloon models, an additional hole must be drilled in the parcel shelf at the location shown in Fig. Q: 5 . This hole should be 7/16 in (11.5 mm) in diameter. The three 'pop' rivets securing the front edge of the parcel shelf trim must be drilled out to allow the spacers to be fitted between the trim and the metal parcel shelf at each of the anchorage points. The trim can be refixed with new 'pop' rivets or screws.
4.   On estate car models, anchorage points will have to be drilled at different locations. Always check for possible obstructions, such as brake pipes, wiring loom or fuel

Fig. Q:6 Correct assembly of anchorage point

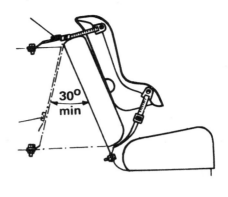

Fig. Q:7 How baby seat should be located (saloon and estate)

30° min

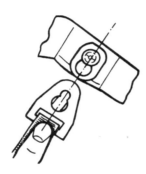

Fig. Q:8 Correct alignment of quick release buckle (KL)

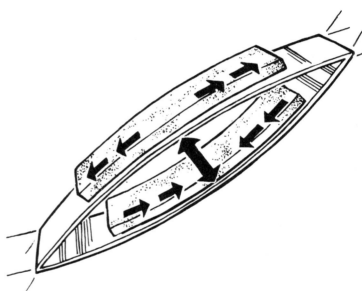

Fig. Q:9 Action of bitumen damping board

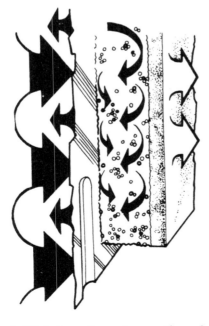

Fig. Q:10 Action of sound waves through Sound Barrier Mat

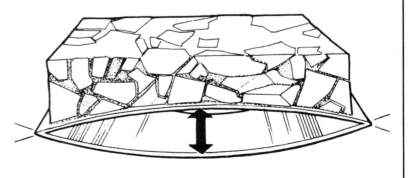

Fig. Q:11 Composite material, Acousticell, damps vibrations

tank, behind the panel before drilling the holes. It should be noted that the anchorage points must be in such a position that the harness straps will make an angle of at least 30° with the seat back once fitted (Fig. Q:7).

5. Fit the anchor plate, wave washer and shouldered spacer at each anchorage point, doubling up where an existing strap is already fitted, as noted previously (Fig. Q:6).

6. Refit the seat backrest and cushion in the reverse order of removing.

7. Adjust the seat straps to position the safety seat as high as possible.

8. Adjust the harness straps to fit as tightly as comfortable. The lap strap should rest over the bony part of the hip. Always ensure the crotch strap is used, where fitted.

SOUNDPROOFING . . . . [6]

In any car, a certain amount of noise is transmitted to the passenger compartment and, if of a high enough level, can not only be annoying, but also tiring on long journeys. Therefore, the elimination or reduction of this noise is desirable for more enjoyable and safer motoring.

The passengers in a car can be subjected to noise from various sources: the wind rushing round the body and blowing round badly sealed doors; mechanical noise from the engine, gearbox and back axle; the exhaust; tyres drumming on the road; and noise cause by the vibration of the car's sheet metal panels. By insulating the body of the car, it is possible to eliminate or considerably reduce a large proportion of this noise. Sound Service (Oxford) Ltd., of Witney, Oxon, are leading manufacturers of sound proofing materials, and their Autosound kit for the Cortina Mk. III contains a variety of these, each designed specifically to reduce or eliminate the various types of noise experienced in the car. The following is based on information supplied by the Company.

Before doing anything, the front seats should be removed as well as all the carpets and floor mats. Then the floor should be thoroughly cleaned.

With the floor/bulkhead area clear, check for any holes and seal them with the mastic sealing strip supplied in the Autosound kit. This should also be applied to all rubber grommets where cables and pipes pass through the bulkhead and to the area at the base of the steering column. The object is to obtain an air-tight seal between the engine and passenger compartments.

All the components of the kit are pre-cut to shape and numbers, and the next step should be to lay them out and identify them. Six rigid bitumen damper pads are included and these should be stuck in each footwell and in other areas of the floor where vibration is apparent. These can be found by gently tapping with a rubber hammer; if they emit a thumping sound, they should be treated. Each damper pad is self-adhesive on one side, allowing it to be stuck in place and it acts as a stiffener. As the panel vibrates, the board is alternately stretched and compressed and thus acts to slow down the vibration (see Fig. Q: 9), reducing the noise level.

The next job is to fit pre-cut pieces of Sound Barrier Mat to both sides of the bulkhead and to the gearbox hump. These are made from a grey foam material with a stiff rubber-like facing on one side. The material is glued in place on the panels, using the adhesive supplied in the kit, the foam being placed against the steel panel. In practice, this allows the sound waves to pass through the panel, into the foam where some of the energy of the vibrating air particles is dissipated as they pass through its tiny passages, and then bounce back from the stiff outer layer. In this way much of the sound is trapped between the two layers and gradually loses its energy as it bounces to and fro. Fig. Q:10 explains this more clearly.

For the under-bonnet area, the Autosound kit includes some items in Neoprene faced felt. These are glued in place in the same manner as the Sound Barrier Mat, the smooth surface outermost. Like the foam material, the felt has tiny passages between its fibres that help dissipate energy of the vibrating air particles. This material cuts down multiple reflections of sound within the engine compartment, preventing the build up of noise.

The remaining material in the kit is made from a composite material called Acousticell. This is made from a mixture of foam and waste fibre to form a heavy mat. It provides damping of vibrations from the floor panels in two ways: by friction when the fibrous parts move against each other and the vibrating air particles passing through the tiny passages in the foam, see Fig. Q:11.

One further item provided is a roll of Weatherseal tape for sealing doors, etc. Rather than placing this round the entire opening, it is often more effective simply to place it where the air is actually leaking though the seal, and to find this is a simple matter. It is necessary to drive the car with a passenger who should have a section of normal garden hose. By holding one end of the hose to his ear and the other to the door seal, he can determine exactly where the seal is deficient. By marking the extremities of the leak with chalk or some similar means, it is a simple matter to cut the Weatherseal tape to size and install it exactly where needed.

The final job is to replace the carpets and seats and check the operation of all instruments and lights, etc., in case any wires have been displaced during the operation.

Contents

The kit may contain some small, irregular shaped, un-numbered pieces of Acousticell material, these are off-cuts and are used as packing material to help prevent damage to the kit in transit.

The first thing to do is to identify the parts by the numbers written on them

a) Parts 1 to 4 are made of Neoprene Coated felt. Note that these parts are to be stuck with the black part on the outside.

b) Parts 5 and 6 are made from a special Sound Barrier Mat without the foam backing, to avoid the absorption of water.

c) Parts 7, 8 and 9 are made of Sound Barrier mat. This material has a heavy layer with a shiny black surface bonded to a layer of grey foam. (Always fit these parts with the shiny black surface on the outside).

d) Parts 9 to 17 are made from felt in De-Luxe kits and from Acousticell in Super kits.

e) In addition to the above parts you will find the

following items:-
One litre of adhesive,
2 rigid damper boards,
4 pliable damper pads,
Strips of sealing mastic on a paper backing

Fitting the Kit - Saloon Models Only

1. Remove the rear seat squab by undoing the crosshead screw on either side of the forward edge of the seat base and then lifting the seat out.
2. Remove the rear seat back, which is held in place by a clip either side at the base, and a stud either side at the top. Undo the top studs (these are accessible through the boot) by turning the slots in the screw heads to the vertical position. The seat back will now be free at the top which can then be pulled forward whilst at the same time pushing the whole seat unit back downwards in order to free it from the bottom clips. Be careful not to damage the headlining during this operation.
3. Unbolt the seat belt anchors from the rear floor pan, so that the rear carpet may be lifted to fit the insulation.
4. Free the carpet edges by removing the plastic trims which run down either side of the car under the door apertures. These are held in place by crosshead screws.
floor, bulkhead and rear seat pan for any holes which must be carefully sealed with the sealing mastic strip supplied, since any small hole lets in water as well as noise. The mastic should also be applied to all rubber grommets where cables or pipes pass through, to ensure that the bulkhead is sealed. Particular attention should be paid to where the steering column passes into the engine compartment.
6. The damper boards and damper pads are next stuck in place. The two rigid damper boards are placed in the centre of the front footwells. The pliable damper pads can become brittle in cold weather and may need to be kept in a warm room for a while. Two are placed over the transmission hump just in front of the rear seat and one is stuck in each half of the rear seat pan. The exact positioning is not important.
7. Parts 1 to 4 are now stuck in place. Before applying the adhesive, thoroughly clean the bonnet lid, using detergent to remove all grease and dirt. If the adhesive is applied to both surfaces and allowed to dry, an immediate bond will be obtained when they are pressed together. However, it is generally easier if adhesive is applied to one surface only and the part can then be positioned carefully before the adhesive sets for all other parts except part 18 which should be stuck by the former method in the following order:
Front underbonnet pad. (1).
Middle underbonnet pad (2) behind part 1.

3 and 4 side sections of the underbonnet pad.
This part is fitted in the engine compartment on the driver's side. It is placed on the horizontal shelf containing the fuse box, with its straight edge against the vertical upper bulkhead panel.
The hole is for the choke cable. The irregular edge flaps down and should be stuck to the vertical lower bulkhead panel which holds the brake master cylinder. A slit is provided for the throttle cable, the speedo cable and the wires from the fuse box. Take care not to stick down the part covering the fuse box, as it will need to be folded back to allow access to the fuses. The part need not be in close contact with the panel all over, and is designed to cover certain nuts and bolts in this area. Part No. 6 is stuck to the vertical upper bulkhead above part 5. The cut-out clears the wiper motor.
8. Parts 7 to 17 are fitted in the passenger compartment. Part No. 7 is stuck to the toeboard on the passenger's side, on top of the existing insulation material. The curved cut-out clears the gearbox hump.
Part No. 8 is stuck to the toeboard on driver's side, corresponding with part 7.
9. Parts 9, 12, 14 and 16 are not stuck down, but adhesive is used to secure parts 13 and 17.
Fit part 9 and 10 in the front footwells, either side of transmission tunnel, and 11 and 12 in the rear footwells.
Part 13 is stuck over the transmission hump in front of the rear seat. Ensure that it is placed far enough forward to allow the rear seat squab to bed down properly when it is replaced.
The carpets can now be folded back into place and the door trims replaced.
Fit parts 14 and 15 on the rear seat floorpan.
Part 16 is designed to go over parts 14 and 15. It is threaded into the rear seat squab over the two support bars and simply rests in place when the seat squab is replaced.
Part 17 must be stuck in place, behind the rear seat back, from the ledge upwards. This ledge is formed where the two pieces of metal which form the upper and lower bulkhead are joined.
Part 18 is made from Sound Barrier Mat and is stuck in the boot area on the underside of the rear parcel shelf with the shiny black surface facing downwards.
10. Replace the rear seat back by turning the screw clip slots back to the horizontal position, then engage the bottom clips and push the top of the seat back onto the top clips. Should difficulty be experienced in engaging the screw clips, these may need bending. Also a second person can be helpful in pushing the seat back into position. Replace the rear seat squab and the seat belt anchors.
11. Check that the lights, indicators, horn etc., are working, in case any wires have been dislodged during fitting of the kit.

Tightening Torques

ENGINE (OHV)

Cylinder Head

Cylinder head bolts:
    Stage 1 .5 lb ft (0.7 kg m)
    Stage 2 . . . . 25 lb ft (3.5 kg m)
    Stage 3 . . . . 55 lb ft (7.5 kg m)
    Stage 4, after 10-20 min.. . . . . . 70 lb ft (9.5 kg m)
    Stage 5, after 15 min. . . . . 70 lb ft (9.5 kg m)
Rocker shaft bolts. . . . . 28 lb ft (4.0 kg m)
Rocker cover . . . . .4 lb ft (0.5 kg m)
Thermostat housing. . . . . 14 lb ft (2.0 kg m)
Inlet manifold. . . . . 14 lb ft (2.0 kg m)
Exhaust manifold . . . . 17 lb ft (2.5 kg m)

Cylinder Block

Main bearing caps . . . . 57 lb ft (8.0 kg m)
Big end bearing caps. . . . . 33 lb ft (4.8 kg m)
Crankshaft pulley . . . . 26 lb ft (3.8 kg m)
Camshaft sprocket. . . . . 14 lb ft (2.0 kg m)
Timing chain tensioner. . . . . .6 lb ft (1.0 kg m)
Front cover . . . . .6 lb ft (1.0 kg m)
Rear oil seal carrier . . . . 14 lb ft (2.0 kg m)
Flywheel . . . . 53 lb ft (7.5 kg m)
Clutch assembly . . . . 14 lb ft (2.0 kg m)
Sump drain plug . . . . 23 lb ft (3.4 kg m)
Oil pump. . . . . 14 lb ft (2.0 kg m)
Oil pump pick-up pipe . . . . 14 lb ft (2.0 kg m)
Oil pump cover . . . . .6 lb ft (1.0 kg m)
Fuel pump. . . . . 14 lb ft (2.0 kg m)

ENGINE (OHC)

Cylinder head

Cylinder head bolts:
    Stage 1 . . . . 35 lb ft (5.0 kg m)
    Stage 2 . . . . 45 lb ft (6.0 kg m)
    Stage 3, after 10-20 min wait. . . . . 65 lb ft (9.0 kg m)
    Stage 4, after 15 min . . . . 75 lb ft (10.5 kg m)
Inlet manifold. . . . . 14 lb ft (2.0 kg m)
Exhaust manifold . . . . 17 lb ft (2.5 kg m)
Spark plugs . . . . 18 lb ft (2.8 kg m)

Cylinder Block

Main bearing caps . . . . 70 lb ft (9.5 kg m)
Big end bearing caps. . . . . 33 lb ft (4.8 kg m)
Crankshaft pulley . . . . 42 lb ft (6.0 kg m)
Camshaft sprocket. . . . . 35 lb ft (5.0 kg m)
Auxiliary shaft sprocket . . . . 35 lb ft (5.0 kg m)
Oil pump. . . . . 14 lb ft (2.0 kg m)
Oil pump cover. . . . . .8 lb ft (1.3 kg m)
Sump drain plug . . . . 18 lb ft (2.8 kg m)
Flywheel . . . . 50 lb ft (7.0 kg m)
Clutch assembly . . . . 14 lb ft (2.0 kg m)
Timing belt cover . . . . 11 lb ft (1.7 kg m)
Fuel pump. . . . . 14 lb ft (2.0 kg m)

CLUTCH & MANUAL GEARBOX

Clutch assy. to flywheel . . . . 15 lb ft (2.0 kg m)
Mounting to extension housing . . . . . 36 lb ft (5.5 kg m)
Mounting to floorpan. . . . . 14 lb ft (2.2 kg m)

AUTOMATIC TRANSMISSION

BW35 Type
Drive plate to converter . . . . 35 lb ft (4.8 kg m)
Converter housing to engine . . . . . . 25 lb ft (3.5 kg m)
Oil pan to trans casing . . . . 11 lb ft (1.5 kg m)
Ford C4 Type
Drive plate to converter . . . . 30 lb ft (4.1 kg m)
Converter housing to engine . . . . . . 25 lb ft (3.5 kg m)
Oil pan to trans casing . . . . 16 lb ft (2.3 kg m)
Ford C3 Type
Drive plate to converter . . . . 30 lb ft (4.1 kg m)
Converter housing to engine . . . . . . 25 lb ft (3.5 kg m)
Oil pan to trans casing . . . . 15 lb ft (2.2 kg m)

PROPSHAFT

Rear flange to axle pinion flange . . . . 45 lb ft (6.5 kg m)
Centre bearing to floor pan . . . . 15 lb ft (2.2 kg m)

REAR SUSPENSION & AXLE

Axle shaft retainer plate . . . . 22 lb ft (3.2 kg m)
Shock absorber to axle. . . . . 45 lb ft (6.5 kg m)
Shock absorber to body . . . . 32 lb ft (4.5 kg m)
Upper radius arm mountings . . . . . . 45 lb ft (6.5 kg m)
Lower radius arm mountings . . . . . . 45 lb ft (6.5 kg m)
Stabiliser bar to radius arm . . . . 33 lb ft (5.0 kg m)

FRONT SUSPENSION

Shock absorber lower mount nuts. . . . .7 lb ft (1.0 kg m)
Shock absorber top mount bolt . . . . . 35 lb ft (4.8 kg m)
Stabiliser bar to link bolt/nut. . . . . . . .9 lb ft (1.3 kg m)
Stabiliser bar clamp bolts . . . . 18 lb ft (2.4 kg m)
Stabiliser bracket to body . . . . 18 lb ft (2.4 kg m)
Tie bar to lower arm . . . . 50 lb ft (6.9 kg m)

STEERING

Track rod to steering arm . . . . 20 lb ft (2.8 kg m)
Rack mounting clamp bolts. . . . . . . 18 lb ft (2.4 kg m)
Steering column mounting bolts. . . . . 22 lb ft (3.0 kg m)
Steering shaft clamp plate bolts . . . . 15 lb ft (2.2 kg m)
Flexible coupling to pinion shaft . . . . 15 lb ft (2.2 kg m)
Steering wheel . . . . 25 lb ft (3.4 kg m)

BRAKES

Caliper mounting bolts . . . . 50 lb ft (7.0 kg m)
Brake disc to front hub. . . . . 32 lb ft (4.5 kg m)
Rear brake backplate to axle . . . . . . 18 lb ft (2.5 kg m)
Bleed valves (maximum) . . . . .8 lb ft (1.1 kg m)

Index

Brief History

OCTOBER 1970

Mk 3 Cortina introduced. Completely new restyled body, redesigned front and rear suspension, rack and pinion type steering. 1300 and 1600 models have OHV engine. New OHC 'Pinto' engine fitted to 2000 cc models. Alternator standard on all models except 1300.

MID 1972

Model rationalisation, 1300 engine option dropped on certain models, 2000 engine not available for Base and 2-door 'L' models. OHC, 1600 engine replaces OHV 1600 engine on GT models.

APRIL 1973

Model rationalisation, 1300 Estate version dropped, along with 1600 GT and GXL, and 2000 2-door XL models.

SEPTEMBER 1973

1600 OHC engine replaces OHV engine. 1300, OHV engine retained. New close ratio gearbox on 1300 and 1600 models. Anti-roll bars now fitted to front and rear on all models. Improved sound insulation. Redesigned instrument panel with illuminated heater controls and 'eyeball' air vents to improve ventilation. New luxury 2000 E model introduced with vinyl roof and cloth upholstery as standard.

SPRING 1974

New French built automatic transmission fitted, known as Ford C3 (Bordeaux) in place of original Borg Warner 35 type. Limited number of Cortinas had Ford type C4 transmission fitted at this time during changeover.

SEPTEMBER 1974

2000 E Estate car introduced.

DECEMBER 1974

Improved specifications for 2000 GT, 2 and 4 door models. Cloth seat trim, improved seats, twin Halogen driving lamps, sports wheels and new style GT badge. 'L' models have restyled 'L' badge.

OCTOBER 1975

All models now have carpets, cloth upholstery, servo brakes, heated rear window, hazard warning flashers and cigar lighter as standard. Base model has black painted sills and radiator grill. 1300 L and 1600 L models have rectangular headlamps and low-level coach lines. Estate models now have rear wipe/washer as standard - except Base Estate. 2000 XL, GT and 'E' models all have improved specification.

FEBRUARY 1976

1300 models now have revised engine with new Ford 'Sonic idle' carburettor to improve fuel consumption - known as Economy model.

JULY 1976

Production ceased.